A Clash of Ideologies

Princeton Theological Monograph Series

K. C. Hanson, Charles M. Collier, and D. Christopher Spinks,
Series Editors

Recent volumes in the series:

Linda Hogan
Religion and the Politics of Peace and Conflict

Chris Budden
Following Jesus in Invaded Space: Doing Theology on Aboriginal Land

Jeff B. Pool
*God's Wounds: Hermeneutic of the Christian Symbol of
Divine Suffering, Volume One: Divine Vulnerability and Creation*

Lisa E. Dahill
*Reading from the Underside of Selfhood:
Bonhoeffer and Spiritual Formation*

Samuel A. Paul
*The Ubuntu God: Deconstructing a South African Narrative
of Oppression*

Jeanne M. Hoeft
*Agency, Culture, and Human Personhood: Pastoral Thelogy
and Intimate Partner Violence*

Ryan A. Neal
*Theology as Hope: On the Ground and Implications
of Jürgen Moltmann's Doctrine of Hope*

Scott A. Ellington
Risking Truth: Reshaping the World through Prayers of Lament

A Clash of Ideologies
Marxism, Liberation Theology, and Apocalypticism in New Testament Studies

RANDALL W. REED

◥PICKWICK *Publications* • Eugene, Oregon

A CLASH OF IDEOLOGIES
Marxism, Liberation Theology, and Apocalypticism in New Testament Studies

Princeton Theological Monograph Series 136

Copyright © 2010 Randall W. Reed. All rights reserved. Except for brief quotations in critical publications or reviews, no part of this book may be reproduced in any manner without prior written permission from the publisher. Write: Permissions, Wipf and Stock Publishers, 199 W. 8th Ave., Suite 3, Eugene, OR 97401.

Pickwick Publications
A Division of Wipf and Stock Publishers
199 W. 8th Ave., Suite 3
Eugene, OR 97401

www.wipfandstock.com

ISBN 13: 978-1-55635-514-1

Scripture quotations in English contained herein are from the New Revised Standard Version Bible, copyright © 1989 by the Division of Christian Education of the National Council of Churches of Christ in the U.S.A, and are used by permission.

Cataloging-in-Publication data:

Reed, Randall W.

    A clash of ideologies : Marxism, apocalypticism, and liberation theology / Randall W. Reed.

    xvi + 178 p.; 23 cm. — Includes bibliographical references and indexes.

    Princeton Theological Monograph Series 136

    ISBN 13: 978-1-55635-514-1

    1. Bible. N.T.—Criticism, interpretation, etc. 2. Apocalyptic literature—History and criticism. 3. Liberation theology. 4. Philosophy, Marxist. 5. Horsley, Richard A. I. Title. II. Series.

BT303.2 R45 2010

Manufactured in the U.S.A.

Contents

Acknowledgements / vii

Introduction / ix

1. Religion and Marxism / 1
2. The Logic of Liberation Theology / 22
3. The Logic of Apocalypticism / 41
4. Marxist New Testament Interpreters / 60
5. Richard A. Horsley / 93
6. Ideological Criticism / 114
7. The Critique of Biblical Studies / 135

Bibliography / 171

Index /

Acknowledgements

THE CREATION OF A PROJECT LIKE THIS IS ULTIMATELY A GROUP EFFORT. My ability to advance it to completion has only come about because of the understanding, support, encouragement and criticism of many people in my life. I wish to thank Martin Riesebrodt who has worked with me tirelessly over the course of this project and always came through in the clinch. Jonathan Z. Smith whose tutorials and conversations shaped much of my own thinking. And most importantly, Burton Mack, who has and continues to act as mentor and discussion partner.

I cannot thank enough Karen Torjesen who took the time to read early drafts of the manuscript and helped me navigate through difficult waters. Susan Meyer, Mark Cronan, and Melody Mooney all provided comfort and support when it was needed most. I should not fail to mention my appreciation for my colleague Tom Ellis who provided helpful feedback, and my editor, K. C. Hanson, patiently answered questions and was always supportive.

Lastly, I can only express an eternal gratitude to Laura Ammon who is as important to me as the air that I breathe. She painstakingly read every word of this text in successive drafts with insight and encouragement that never failed. Were it not for her constant encouragement and help this project would failed long ago. My debt to her can never be paid, but I endeavor to try each day . . . happily so.

Introduction

IN THE WORLD OF BIBLICAL STUDIES A VARIETY OF METHODS HAVE been employed that stem from disciplines outside of the field. Today one can find instances of biblical scholars using approaches from literary studies, archaeology, psychology, and sociology. The use of these approaches represents attempts to do readings of the text in new and exciting ways. Sociology has, in fact, contributed several different methods. Biblical scholars have turned to functionalism, sociology of knowledge approaches, and Weberian approaches in an attempt to do these sorts of innovative readings. This book will focus on one other sociological approach that has generated a literature in the discipline: Marxism.

The use of Marxism to understand the New Testament is not new. Friedrich Engels, Marx's co-author, intellectual companion, and benefactor, several times attempted brief forays into biblical material, including a discussion of the Book of Revelation.[1] And as early as 1908, Karl Kautsky wrote a monograph called *The Foundation of Christianity*, which undertook to show the roots of communism in early apostolic Christianity.[2] Thus it should come as no surprise that there is an interest in approaching the New Testament from a Marxist perspective.

The use of Marxism in biblical studies, however, has not been "isolated." It has often been paired with a particular theological agenda—that of Liberation Theology. Additionally, it has often focused on a particular subject matter: texts that contain apocalypses. The question is whether such a three-way connection can, in fact, be sustained. Is it possible to simultaneously employ all three of these different perspectives (Liberation Theology, Marxism, and apocalyptic) without violating the integrity of one or more of them?

Sociologically, then, my approach is one of ideological analysis. My use of the term "ideological" should not be understood, as is often the

---

1. See Kautsky, *Foundation*; and Marx and Engels, *On Religion*.
2. Kautsky, *Foundation*.

case, in the Marxist tradition, which sees ideology as a way of masking reality, particularly the reality of the conflict between capital and labor.[3] Rather I employ a more general notion of ideology that is closer to the notion of "world view" or intellectual system. Each one of these different approaches—whether Liberation Theology, Apocalyptic, and Marxism—contains a discreet ideology in this sense. As a result, there is a system of logic that supports each ideology. There are presuppositions that form the foundation of that ideology. And there are certain intellectual strategies and moves that are employed within that ideology.

My work is deeply indebted to the theoretical apparatus of Pierre Bourdieu. Bourdieu introduces the idea of the "field" in his work. The notion of a "field" draws on the semantic implications of both its "work" and "play" meanings. The individual who chooses a career enters a field in the process. Likewise, games like football and soccer are also played on a field. These two examples have several things in common: a field is a defined area. Certainly this is true to a heightened degree with games but it is likewise the case with occupations; the field of medicine is distinct from that of finance. Thus a field is importantly bounded. Those boundaries may be more or less clear, yet they are acknowledged to exist by the participants and often constitute an area of contestation.[4] Yet even this contestation is dependent on the universal acknowledgment of the existence of the boundary.

A field likewise has implication for practices. Practices are of course the object of much of Bourdieu's work.[5] The field constrains practices, it consists of rules that explicitly and implicitly function to define which practices are acceptable and which are unacceptable. Thus in American football points are scored in significantly different ways than in soccer. How many people are on the field, how long the game lasts, how time is split up, and what constitutes permissible and impermissible play are all determined by these rules.

---

3. Eagleton, *Ideology*, 1–31.

4. Bourdieu and Wacquant, *Invitation*, 100. It is precisely this level of contestation and ambiguity that means as Bourdieu says, "The boundaries of the field can only be determined by an empirical investigation."

5. Two of Bourdieu's more famous monographs *Outline of a Theory of Practice* and *The Logic of Practice* both focus on the notions of practice. It is these two works, in which the concepts I use here are introduced.

The field also constrains strategy, and herein lies its more important and constructive aspects. For the field determines what strategies might be employed in a given situation; the kind of strategies are developed through innovative application of available tools created by the field. Running, jumping, throwing, and blocking are essential components of American football. The construction of a "play" is the integration of these components towards the furtherance of the goal and strategies. Some strategies may even be constructed over the long term integrating multiple plays in their execution. Thus the field limits the strategies that might be employed (placing a player in the stands or on the other team is not allowed) but also provides the raw material for creativity within the field.

The notion of the field is only part of Bourdieu's work that I want to employ here. These rules that I have spoken of, in so far as they are internalized and foundational, are called "doxa" by Bourdieu.[6] Doxa then acts definitionally and as a form of limitation. It determines what can be done and what cannot be done. These rules once learned are unthought and yet function to regulate the game. No one watching a game who sees a player run out of bounds questions where the boundary line is, wishing to move it inches or feet from its respective position; that line is set as though from heaven itself. This constitutes the doxa and is presuppositional at its core and is the unthought driver of actions and arguments.[7] Doxa then is related to field in that the doxa constitutes the structure that lies below the conscious surface of the field. Like the very position of the goal posts, or the number of minutes in a game it is uncontested and never really considered. Yet these doxic presuppositions actually are the building blocks upon which the field is constructed.

With these theoretical concepts at hand, my goal is to first follow Bourdieu's urging and work to define the field of the three areas I have highlighted: Marxism, Liberation Theology, and apocalpyticism. I understand these three fields as systems, each dependent upon a doxa that does ultimately have some cohesion. Here I am interested in explor-

---

6. Bourdieu, *Outline*, 164. My use here of doxa is an adaptation of the notion as it was first introduced. Bourdieu introduces it in *Outline* in reference to larger social systems with the emphasis on its unacknowledged nature, which contrasts with both orthodoxy and heterodoxy.

7. For academics, Bourdieu talks about *epistemic doxa* as the particular kind of doxa that shapes the intellectual class. Bourdieu, *Scholastic Point of View*, 129.

ing the practical logic on which these systems are dependent. My goal then will be to uncover the doxa, those presuppositions upon which the fields are built.[8]

What I will attempt to show is that these three systems have competing and ultimately incongruous presuppositions. They are built upon different doxic systems and thus as scholars attempt to integrate the three fields they encounter what we might call doxic conflict—presuppositional incompatibility.

I will argue in this project that the three ideologies of Liberation Theology, apocalyptic, and Marxist analysis in New Testament studies are ultimately incompatible with each other at a presuppositional level. I will show that the apocalyptic system is dependent upon an activist God as the source of change and as a means to administrate power that is rejected by Marxism and, to a degree, by Liberation Theology. Likewise, Marxism understands religion as a superstructural mechanism that is ultimately counter-revolutionary. It sees religion as trying to solve real problems with "imaginary" solutions. Such a diagnosis is therefore antithetical to both Liberation Theology and apocalyptic. Finally, Liberation Theology specifically rejects the atheism of Marxism and the apocalyptic notion of supernatural intervention in the political world. Liberation Theology is founded upon a central notion of God's (and the Church's) preferential option for the poor which dictates its understanding of tradition, biblical texts and philosophy. As a result, when we turn to examine the work of biblical scholars, we find problems generated precisely by conflicts and contradictions in trying to connect these ideologies to New Testament studies. Ultimately, some of these New Testament interpreters will engage in interesting yet incongruous readings of the biblical texts, misappropriations of the theories or will abandon one or more of these ideologies as a result.

To demonstrate this thesis, I will examine Marxism's relationship to religion in chapter 1. Marx's critique is well known, and there can be no doubt that he saw religion as part of the ideological superstructure

---

8. In some instances the presuppositions I look for are not necessarily obscure, they may in fact be acknowledged at some level. Bourdieu talks about these presuppositional positions that rise into the discourse as "orthodoxy" and "heterodoxy" depending upon the participants perspective. In some cases the presuppositions have risen above the doxa level into the level of orthodoxy. Nonetheless as my project seeks to find the outlines of the field in question rather than just the doxa, I will consider both levels as necessary.

of society. To this end, Marx can say that the criticism of religion is the precondition of all criticism. I will go further, however, and trace the outline of the Marxist field through the mainline of Marxist thought. I will focus on the question of how later Marxist thinkers understood religion. I will argue that while the later Marxist tradition took a more nuanced position vis-à-vis religion, nonetheless, the initial critical tone that Marx took towards religion in his work ultimately remains the standard Marxist position.

In chapter 2 I will next detail the logic of the Liberation Theology field, specifically paying attention to the key components that are relevant for this project: its understanding of Marxism, its larger understanding of the role of the Bible in Liberation Theology, and its use and understanding of apocalyptic texts. I will show that Liberation Theology doxa begins with an experiential focus, a centering on the experience of the oppressed in Latin America which then specifically determines its reading of the New Testament text. As a result, it actually eschews apocalyptic texts, preferring more (humanly) activist texts instead. When Liberation Theology does address some of these themes it is given to interpreting them spiritually as meditations on hope. Finally, while its attitude towards Marxism has changed over time, in the end it uses Marxism only insofar as such gives it purchase on a critical approach to society, yet specifically rejects the notion that religion is part of the ideological apparatus of oppression.

After this, in chapter 3, I will briefly explore the logic of early Jewish and Christian apocalyptic. Drawing on the work of biblical scholars who have attempted to explain apocalyptic, I will look at recent work on how the apocalyptic world works. Beginning with notions of proper genre and the social function of apocalpyticism, I will integrate J. Z. Smith's notion that apocalyptic indicates an incongruous situation where new ideas and categories are experimented with by scribal elites. Yet, taking a cue from scholars who have begun to work on the issue of power in apocalyptic, I will argue that apocalyptic is bent on exercising power to control the behaviors and beliefs of its audience. Yet, its structure also is predicated on a notion of the justice of God (rather than human justice) and likewise a necessity for God to avenge wrongs against him (or his people) personally. These two notions mandate certain behaviors with a threat of divine judgment. But such judgment can only be delayed for a while before the legitimacy of the message is questioned. In the end, then, apocalyptic depends on a short-term solution for enforcing behavioral norms and theological beliefs.

In chapter 4, with these understandings as a beginning, I will then look at Marxist approaches to the New Testament. I will begin with the pioneers of modern interpretations of the New Testament from a Marxist perspective. I will examine the work of Jose Porofino Miranda, Fernando Belo, Michel Clévenot, and Ched Meyers. These individuals are generally not biblical scholars by profession, but their work is frequently cited in texts of New Testament scholars and has been highly influential in New Testament scholars use of Marxism.

These individuals have several things in common with each other. They are all committed to an explicitly Marxist approach to the text. For the most part, they are also specifically committed to Liberation Theology. And, finally, they all use texts that contain apocalypticism (most often the gospel of Mark). As a result, they are an ideal testing ground for my thesis that the fields of the three ideologies of Marxism, Liberation Theology, and apocalypticism cannot effectively coexist together. I will show how each thinker must, through various means, find ways to violate the presuppositions of one or more of these ideological systems in order to make their case.

Next, in chapter 5, I will examine the work of Richard Horsley. Horsley has been on the forefront of the debate over the historical Jesus and over the proper reading of Q. Horsley also begins with the same triad as above and yet—ultimately because of the problems I have outlined—is unable to maintain their congruence. He first dispenses with apocalypticism, and then moves completely into the camp of Liberation Theology. I will then show how he exemplifies the logic of Liberation Theology that has provocative ramifications for his readings of the texts.

In chapter 6, I will look at the work of the ideological criticism movement and specifically the work of Tina Pippin. The ideological criticism movement shows progression in a different direction than Horsley. While Horsley abandoned apocalypticism and Marxism, ideological criticism has moved away from apocalypticism and, to some degree, Liberation Theology and more in the direction of Marxism.

Tina Pippin serves as a dramatic example of this. Pippin is particularly interesting in our study in that she is focused on apocalyptic, specifically doing a Marxist-feminist reading of the Book of Revelation.

Pippin, then, while professing to also be an adherent of Liberation Theology, draws ever closer to the Marxist view of religion, coming to see the text itself as a tool, not of liberation, but of the furtherance of oppression. The work of ideological criticism, and Tina Pippin in particular, shows the problem of conflating the fields of Marxism, Liberation Theology, and apocalypticism and prove once again that coherence is only gained by choosing one.

Thus, following the analyses of New Testament scholarship I will note the peculiar twists and turns that these scholars take that are unmerited by their method, their texts or their theology. These unusual turns in argumentation come about as a result of the merger of incompatible fields that are dependent upon conflicting doxa that then requires the "papering over" of presuppositional contradictions. I will show that the simultaneous commitment to these varying texts, methods, and theologies ultimately causes the logical lacunae that appear in their projects and require either inconsistency or the abandonment of the goal of conjoining them.

Finally, in chapter 7, I will move to the contemporary scene where this tradition of scholarship has flowered in a variety of ways. Postcolonialism, a new secularist current in biblical studies and the New Atheism movement outside of biblical studies have all picked up on some of the issues that I have noted in the preceding chapters. Such a historical confluence of movement offers an interesting cultural moment in the intellectual tradition of the U.S. New Testament studies. It may very well be that this intersection may lead to an exciting new visioning of the text and debates about its role in American culture.

In the concluding chapter I will look towards the way that social-scientific methods and particularly Marxism might continue to contribute to the work in New Testament studies apart from attempts to collate fields. I will return to the question of apocalyptic and using the work of a contemporary Marxist, Slavoj Žižek, make some initial forays into gaining an understanding of apocalyptic's social role.

My task here, then, is an analytical one, not necessarily a constructive one. While I see great promise in the use of social-scientific methods and theories, and particularly Marxist theory in the reading of New Testament texts, my task is not to add to that literature. Instead, my goal here is to engage in historical explanation, to understand a particular strain and tradition within biblical studies and determine its causes. My focus then is on analysis. In so far as I can make a contribution to the larger work of New Testament studies it is one of caution and promise. I believe an examination of the history of the use of Marxist theory within New Testament studies can lead to an understanding of the kinds of hermeneutic moves that have resulted and may act to heighten awareness of the costs and requirements of using social-scientific theory in general. Yet I might also hope that it may reveal the great potential that is possible for biblical studies with the application of social-scientific approaches like Marxism.

Religion and Marxism

THE UNDERSTANDING OF RELIGION WITHIN MARXISM MIGHT, AT first glance, appear to be self-evident. At least since the 1950s and McCarthyism, the cliché "godless communists" has been part of the national lexicon. Yet several theologians have recently tried to argue that Marxism is actually compatible with religion; certainly this has been an interesting trend in Liberation theology.[1] Thus the question: How does Marxism understand religion? In this section, I will explore this important question. I will do so by looking at the tradition of Marxism, starting with Marx and working through a number of important thinkers in the Marxist tradition. My sample will of course be selective. There undoubtedly will be those Marxist thinkers who could be included but are left out.[2] Still my goal here will be to try to determine a general trend or line of argument that we can see in the Marxist tradition vis-à-vis religion.

Marx

In beginning this type of survey, one must begin with the founder: the work of Marx himself. Marx's position on religion is best known in the famous "opiate of the people" quote. Like that quote, the majority of Marx's work on religion stems from a fairly early, but prodigious, period in his publishing: the 1840s. I will examine his argument about religion in some detail in this section. I will then turn to his references to reli-

---

1. See chap. 2 below.

2. In some ways my selection is determined by the currents in New Testament studies. The individuals that I have selected here are either cited by those employing Marxist analysis to read New Testament texts or seem implicitly to underlie or illuminate the discussion of New Testament-Marxist approaches.

gion in his later works. These comments are far less extensive but seem to presuppose the argument of his early works.

Even before the "opiate" statement, Marx had advocated the criticism of Religion earlier in an article on censorship in 1842 where he argues that religion functions to underpin the authority of the state. "Christianity does not decide whether the constitutions are *good*, for it knows no distinction between them. It teaches, as religion is bound to teach: submit to authority, for *all authority* is from God."[3] The position Marx takes here is interesting as it highlights the use of religion for the purposes of the state. Marx's larger point in this article is that the adherence to religion does not separate a good state from a bad state. A theocratic state can be bad (he suggests the Byzantine state as an example) regardless of its piety. The determination of a state as good or bad can only be determined by reason not by religious purity.[4] Thus he concludes, "you will have to admit that the state must be built on the basis of free reason, and not of religion."[5]

The relationship between the state and religion is in fact a major subject of consideration in Marx's early work. In "On the Jewish Question" (1843), Marx sees the Christian state's persecution of Jews as rooted in a problematic opposition of Christianity to Judaism. The solution? "By making it impossible. And how is *religious* opposition made impossible? By abolishing *religion*." But Marx goes on to make a comment which is very provocative, "As soon as Jew and Christian come to see in their respective religions nothing more than *stages in the development of the human mind*—snake skins which have been cast off by *history*, and *man* as the snake who clothed himself in them—they will no longer find themselves in religious opposition, but in a purely critical, *scientific* and human relationship."[6] The important point made here is that humanity has already passed the point where religion is an asset to society. Instead *science* has replaced religion as the way to understand and live in the world.

When Marx begins "Contribution to the Critique of Hegel's Philosophy of Right" (1844) with the sentence, "For Germany, the *criti-*

3. Marx, *Supplement*.
4. Ibid.
5. Ibid.
6. Marx, *On the Jewish Question*, 28.

cism of religion has largely been completed; and the criticism of religion is the premise of all criticism,"[7] we understand Marx as stating a *fait accompli*; religion's usefulness has ended; it has been dethroned by science. For Marx, Feuerbach's criticism which saw god as a projection has issued the final verdict. Thus Marx states, "The basis of irreligious criticism is this: *man makes religion; religion does not make man.*"[8] Marx's comments must be seen as a part of his teleological understanding of history; the intellectual basis of religion has already withered away. It may have had a place in the past, but now human development has advanced to the point where religion is irrelevant at best, or as "On the Jewish Question" showed, destructive at worst.

It is in "Contribution" that we find the "opiate" saying. The passage comes early in the work and begins with an analysis of religion as a "general theory of the world."[9] Thus Marx sets up religion initially as a system of thought, emphasizing the idealist characteristic of it. He then continues: "Religious suffering is at the same time an *expression* of real suffering and a *protest* against real suffering. Religion is the sigh of the oppressed creature, the sentiment of a heartless world, and the soul of soulless conditions. It is the *opium* of the people.

"The abolition of religion, as the *illusory* happiness of men, is a demand for their real happiness. The call to abandon their illusions about their condition is a call to *abandon a condition that requires illusions*. The criticism of religion, therefore, *the embryonic criticism of this vale of tears* of which religion is the *halo*."[10] Religion thus indicates the profound problems that the capitalist situation has produced. It is in effect the symptom of the disease (Marx: condition) of capitalism. The criticism of religion, then, is a salve on the symptom, but does not produce a cure.

Thus Marx does not spend much more time engaged in an analysis of religion. Having unmasked religion as a human production, the matter for him is settled. Religion has functioned as a "theory,"[11] as a way of justifying and offering solace in the face of the oppression of

7. Marx, *Critique*, 53.
8. Ibid.
9. Ibid.
10. Ibid., 54.
11. Ibid., 53.

the real world. The criticism of religion, then, is the starting point that, however initially important, must be dispensed with. This is because the criticism of religion is the criticism of something imaginary. There are real things in much more need of criticism. "Thus the criticism of heaven is transformed into the criticism of earth, the *criticism of religion* into the *criticism of law*, and the *criticism of theology* into the *criticism of politics*."[12]

The early Marx, then, saw religion as the illusory construct of the human mind. In "The German Ideology" Marx goes on to link the development of religion to the effect of material production: "Morality, religion, metaphysics, all the rest of ideology and their corresponding forms of consciousness, thus no longer retain the semblance of independence. They have no history, no development; but men, developing their material production and their material intercourse, alter, along with this their real existence, their thinking and the products of their thinking. Life is not determined by consciousness, but consciousness by life."[13] The ideological nature of religion means that real change cannot happen by making changes to the ideology. Religion is epiphenomenal to the mode of "material production" and "material intercourse."

This all becomes explicit in Marx's "A Contribution to the Critique of Political Economy" (1859) when Marx articulates his base/superstructure model.

> In the social production of their life, men enter into definite relations that are indispensable and independent of their will, relations of production which correspond to a definite stage of development of their material productive forces. The sum total of these relations of production constitutes the economic structure of society, the real foundation, on which rises a legal and political superstructure and to which correspond definite forms of social consciousness. The mode of production of material life conditions the social, political and intellectual life process in general. It is not the consciousness of men that determines their being, but, on the contrary, their social being that determines the consciousness.[14]

---

12. Ibid., 54.
13. Marx, *German Ideology*, 154–55.
14. Marx, *Contribution*, 4.

Note that here religion has become the implied subcategory of the "intellectual life process in general." Marx has, as promised, moved past religion into the criticism of "earth, law and politics."

Thus when we get to the Marx's later work, we see only the occasional reference to religion. The most important case is Marx's discussion of commodity fetishism. In his explanation of this concept, Marx brings up the issue of religion but only as a corresponding example to commodity fetishism. "In order, therefore to find an analogy, we must have recourse to the mist-enveloped regions of the religious world. In that world the productions of the human brain appear as independent beings endowed with life, and entering into relation both with one another and the human race. So it is in the world of commodities with the products of men's hands."[15] The basic outline that we have seen of Marx's view of religion is maintained here. The main point is that religion is a human creation and therefore only serves to cloud reality ("mist-enveloped") rather than clarify it. Commodity fetishism functions similarly in that another creation, this time the commodity, is not taken as the human product it is.

Marx's view on religion, then, is clear from his early work through *Capital*. Religion is a form of misidentification of reality. At best, it functions as a symptom of the human misery produced by capitalism. At worst, it functions to propagate the authority of that oppressive system. In every case however, religion is not to be redeemed; it is to be criticized and then one moves on to the criticism of more important social elements and ultimately to a materialist philosophy.

Engels

Friedrich Engels reflects the evolutionary approach to religion that we found in Marx. Religion, for Marx, can be dispensed with because science has superseded it; fiction has been replaced with fact. Engels carries forward this line of thinking and talks more specifically about the time frame. Starting with a theory of pre-history where religion is invented as a reflection of natural forces, he traces religion in a fairly typical western nineteenth-century evolutionary model, beginning with polytheism and moving to Jewish monotheism. With the development of bourgeois

15. Marx, *Capital*, 321.

economics, the focus of religion moves from reflecting natural forces to reflecting social forces. The vagaries and crises produced by capitalism are now what are reflected in religious notions.

> It is still true that man proposes and God (that is, the alien domination of the capitalist mode of production) disposes. Mere knowledge, even if it went much further and deeper than that of bourgeois economic science, is not enough to bring social forces under the domination of society. What is above all necessary for this is a social *act*. And when this act has been accomplished, when society, by taking possession of all means of production and using them on a planned basis, has freed itself and all its members from the bondage in which they are now held by these means of production which they themselves have produced but which confront them as an irresistible alien force, when therefore man no longer merely proposes, but also disposes—only then will the last alien force which is still reflected in religion vanish; and with it will also vanish the religious reflection itself, for the simple reason that then there will be nothing left to reflect.[16]

Note that here Engels veers from Marx's position. For Marx religious criticism was complete, and therefore he does not bother with some sort of detailed analysis. Engels, to the contrary, recognizes the last vestiges of religion will survive until the ultimate fall of capitalism and therefore sees it as fit ground for exploration.

The key term for Engels is "reflection." Religion is a reflection of alien forces of domination. In pre-history these forces are natural. In modernity these forces are social and economic. Yet as long as there are these uncontrolled forces that hold sway of human life, religion will persevere. It is only with the advent of socialism that religion will ultimately disappear because within socialism there will no longer be these unpredictable forces.

Engels and Marx, then, agree that religion is an indication of the problems of capitalism. Marx focuses on the criticism of religion and proclaims that process as complete and leaves the subject behind. Engels, on the other hand, spends a little more time thinking about what will precipitate the ultimate elimination of religion. For him as

---

16. Engels, *Anti-Duhring*, 301–2.

well though, religion is ultimately an empty solution that fails to control the real problems of the world.[17]

Of course, no discussion of Engels can be complete without including Engels letter to Bloch in which he explains the economic determination in the last instance. Here, Engels is trying to excise the notion that Marx held to a strict base/superstructure model, where the superstructure was irrelevant to the base. In fact Marx maintained that the base was only determinative in the "last instance,"[18] argues Engels and that "they all react upon one another and upon the economic base."[19] Engels reiterates this notion in his letter stressing, "If somebody twists this into saying that the economic element is the *only* determining one, he transforms that proposition into a meaningless, abstract, senseless phrase."[20]

Engels then tries to explain the notion of determination in the last instance. He states: "The economic situation is the basis, but the various elements of the superstructure; . . . also exercise their influence upon the course of the historical struggles and in many cases preponderate in determining their *form* . . . We make history ourselves, but, in the first place, under very definite assumptions and conditions. Among these the economic ones are ultimately decisive."[21] Engels, then, reasserts the primacy of the economic base. Yet, he also understands superstructural elements as being determinative of the "form" of the struggle. Hence in his history of religion, Engels is able to see changes in religion as a form of class struggle. Yet after the Reformation, Engels concludes that religion has ceased to be a meaningful way of creating real change.

Thus Engels, like Marx, saw religion as an impediment to revolution. Engels deals with religion in a more concrete and historical way than Marx. He is interested in seeing religion's role in history. Yet even still, Engels believes the time for religion's usefulness for humanity

---

17. Engels, in his chronology of the history of religion talks about Christianity entering into its "final phase," which continues Marx's notion that religion had outlived its usefulness and been replaced by science. Engels likewise makes much of the combination of scientific achievement that has changed the world particularly with the advent of cell biology, electricity, and Darwin. See Engels, *Ludwig Feuerbach*.

18. Marx, *Selected Works*, 304.

19. Ibid.

20. Engels, *Letter*, 760.

21. Ibid.

has passed. The focus today must be on concrete changes to the base. Religion is no longer a suitable vehicle for such change.

Lenin

If there is a trinity of classical Marxism, V. I. Lenin is its third member. Lenin's work has long been hailed as one of the classical masterpieces of early Marxism. A true revolutionary, Lenin is known for his leadership role in the Russian Revolution. The transition of Russia from an agricultural monarchy to a modern soviet socialist state consumed all of Lenin's time. Much of his work, then, is practical and in regards to religion, almost always so. At one point he explains that he has not been able to reflect on the experiences of the Russian revolution, noting, "It is more pleasant and more useful to live through the experience of a revolution than to write about it."[22]

Thus, when we look at Lenin's approach to religion we must ascertain his views based on what he says in the middle of a revolutionary struggle. There are two prongs to Lenin's position on religion. On the one hand Lenin espouses freedom of religion, though he limits this particularly to the state. "Religion must be of no concern to the state, and religious societies must have no connection with governmental authority. Everyone must be absolutely free to profess any religion he pleases, or no religion whatever, i.e., to be an atheist, which every socialist is, as a rule . . . Complete separation of Church and State is what the socialist proletariat demands of the modern state and the modern church."[23] This should be seen in the context of Lenin's environment. In pre-revolutionary Russia, the Orthodox Church held tremendous sway. Lenin's call for freedom of religion was an attempt to break some of the power of the Orthodox Church. Ultimately, disestablishment was designed to create a politically level playing field.

However, when it comes to religion within the party, Lenin's position is somewhat different. We note that in the above quote he states that generally every socialist *is* an atheist. The reason for this is, of course, that religion is a tool of the bourgeoisie to perpetuate class oppression. Thus Lenin proclaims: "Our Programme is based entirely on the scien-

---

22. Lenin, *State and Revolution*, 255.
23. Lenin, *Socialism and Religion*, 84.

tific, and moreover the materialist, world-outlook. An explanation of our Programme, therefore, necessarily includes an explanation of the true historical and economic roots of the religious fog. Our propaganda necessarily includes the propaganda of atheism; the publication of the appropriate scientific literature..."[24] To that end, there can be no doubt that Lenin opposes religion in the same way as Marx and Engels who saw it as an "illusion."

But for Lenin there are also practical considerations. While the program of the Bolsheviks is clearly atheist, Lenin does not see a need to be dogmatic about it. His vision is clear: a debate about religion would be a distraction from the real issue of economic exploitation. In the short run, differences between party members on religion can be tolerated as long as there is unity on fighting for economic freedom. Thus, as Lenin says, "Unity in this really revolutionary struggle of the oppressed class for the creation of a paradise on earth is more important to us than unity of proletarian opinion on paradise in heaven."[25]

Lenin's perspective, then, is based on the base/superstructure model that Marx laid out. "Real" change is thus based on change at the base. Arguments at the superstructural level are ultimately immaterial. What will happen to religion after the revolution is not clear. Certainly, Lenin does not postulate a "withering" of religion, but rather sees this as perhaps a future battle—one which will occur after the elimination of capitalism.[26] Still Lenin does not see any positive benefit to be gleaned from a more "progressive" form of religion. In the end religion functions only to support capitalism, and the materialist stance must attempt to clear this "fog" through a fight against religion's systemic economic benefactor.[27]

---

24. Ibid., 86.
25. Ibid., 87.
26. Lenin makes a point in an earlier article that this is not either a subordination of ideals to tactics or a wavering. Rather it is focusing on the "root" of religion, which is the economic system that props it up and is propped up by it. Lenin, *Attitude*, 406.
27. It should be noted that Lenin's attitude towards religion may have had some relation to his practical experience with the orthodox clergy. He had nothing but problems with the religious clergy after the 1905 revolution. He found them to be quite conservative and struggled continually with them in the Duma. Lenin, *Classes and Parties*, 414–23.

Gramsci

Antonio Gramsci provides us with a different perspective on religion. An Italian dissident during the time of Mussolini, Gramsci reflected on religion from a unique vantage point as a citizen of a country that was the center of Catholicism. His work is supremely influential, if sometimes fragmentary, as it consists of notebooks written from prison. Still, Gramsci's work continues to have great relevance for the modern Marxist tradition and his perspective on religion is illuminating.

Gramsci's position on religion is not as oppositional as we have seen from the founders of Marxism. It is almost as though that battle is over. Gramsci does not generally argue that religion is problematic from a Marxist perspective. Rather, much of his effort is spent in an attempt to glean lessons from examples of the spread and persistence of religion.

This point is made in Gramsci's reflection on Machiavelli's *The Prince* in his work "The Modern Prince." In that text, Gramsci argues that Machiavelli's prince is not solely a manipulator of the populace, but rather a mythic cypher that is "an organism, a complex element of society in which a collective will, which has already been recognized and has to some extent asserted itself in action, begins to take concrete form."[28] In modern times this organism can no longer be an individual ruler or king for Gramsci, but is now found in "the political party":[29] which is "the modern Prince."

It is at this point that Gramsci defines religion as being about "the question of intellectual and moral reform" and more broadly equates it to a "world-view."[30] With this definition in mind, then, Gramsci claims that the goal of the modern Prince is to replace the current religious system with a new one—the socialist worldview. "The modern Prince, as it develops, revolutionizes the whole system of intellectual and moral relations, in that its development means precisely that any given act is seen as useful or harmful, as virtuous or as wicked, only in so far as it has as its point of reference the modern Prince itself, and helps to strengthen it or oppose it. In men's consciences, the Prince takes the

---

28. Gramsci, *Modern Prince*, 129.
29. Ibid.
30. Ibid., 132; cf. Gramsci, *State and Civil Society*, 267, where he indicates a "historical process" of development from religion to state to party.

place of the divinity or the categorical imperative and becomes the basis for a modern laicism and for a complete laiciastion of all aspects of life and of all customary relationships."[31] Thus the party becomes the moral standard by which actions are to be judged. The intellectual/moral system of religion is therefore replaced by the party.

This equation between the party and religion allows Gramsci to take seriously the history of religion and learn organizational lessons from it. Concretely, one of the real lessons particularly learned from the history of Catholicism is the need to keep the intellectual stratum in touch with the common people. Gramsci argues that Catholicism "has always been the most vigorous in the struggle to prevent the 'official' formation of two religions, one for the 'intellectuals' and one for the 'simple souls.'"[32] Unfortunately, the way the church has accomplished this is through the suppression of intellectual experimentation by means of "an iron discipline on the intellectuals."[33]

Gramsci applauds the ends but not the means of Catholicism's quest for unity. From his perspective, then, the church has taken the wrong path; instead of forcing the intellectuals to adhere to the general beliefs of the laity, as the church did, the party should bring the laity along to the insights of the intellectuals.[34] To that end there are two other points Gramsci makes: The first is the necessity of constantly fostering intellectuals from the people. Gramsci envisions a circular process. As the intellectual stratum advances, it brings the masses up with them (though not exactly at the same level) and new intellectuals are fostered from the masses. By recruiting individuals from the masses the party remains in touch with its constituency.[35]

The second point Gramsci makes is to argue the inherent educability of the masses. Everyone is already a philosopher, Gramsci argues,

31. Gramsci, *Modern Prince*, 133.
32. Gramsci, *Study of Philosphy*, 328.
33. Ibid., 331.

34. Ibid., 332. "The philosophy of praxis does not tend to leave the 'simple' in their primitive philosophy of common sense, but rather to lead them to a higher conception of life. If it affirms the need for contact between intellectuals and simple it is not in order to restrict scientific activity and preserve unity at the low level of the masses, but precisely in order to construct an intellectual-moral bloc which can make politically possible the intellectual progress of the mass and not of small intellectual groups" (ibid.).

35. Ibid., 335.

in that they engage in language, common sense, and religion. Each one of these is a system that Gramsci calls a "spontaneous philosophy."[36] The system most people have, however, is "disjointed and episodic,"[37] and generally inherited from the environment. What the "philosophy of praxis" (i.e., Marxism) offers instead is "intellectual order," which cannot be provided either by common sense nor religion.[38] But the philosophy of "common sense" means that the populace is already predisposed to, and capable of, the kind of reflection that Marxism involves. Religion and common sense will both be replaced, then, by the philosophy of praxis.

Thus in the end, Gramsci is no more disposed towards adherence to religion than Marx, Engels, or Lenin. Gramsci can appreciate the role of religion in providing a worldview, but clearly sees the goal of Marxism as replacing the worldview of religion with its own worldview. To this end, because of the equivalence that Gramsci sees between religion and Marxism, he can learn from the mistakes that religion has made. Nonetheless, in the final analysis, Gramsci offers no quarter for religion's continuation after the light of Marxism has shown.

Althusser

When we come to Louis Althusser the discourse changes focus from a straightforward discussion of religion to an understanding of religion as a sub-category of ideology. Certainly such a move has been prefigured in the work of Gramsci and even Marx himself, but it is with Althusser that the issue of ideology takes center stage. Althusser, as the father of Marxist structuralism, is less interested in the way individual elements of ideology work than in developing a model of ideology as a process/structure. As a result, while Althusser uses religion as an example (a fairly important example as we shall see), his position on religion per se is not as clearly defined.

It is in his article "Marxism and Humanism" (1965) where Althusser gives the first hints of what will later become his theory of ideology. In this article, Althusser is concerned with humanist readings of Marx,

36. Ibid., 323.
37. Ibid.
38. Ibid., 325.

particularly the 1844 manuscripts. Althusser wants to vigorously argue that Marx is distinctly "anti-humanist" because Marx's theory is scientific and historical, unbound by such a problematic category as the "essence of man."[39] Althusser, therefore, sees Humanism as an "ideology."[40]

Althusser then undertakes a preliminary understanding of ideology. First, he notes that ideology has "a historical existence and role within a given society."[41] Next he makes a clear distinction between ideology and science since for ideology "the practico-social function is more important than the theoretical function (function as knowledge)."[42] But this is not to say that ideology is some superstructural effluvia that will evaporate after the revolution. Rather, ideology is necessary to every society. He emphasizes, "*Historical materialism cannot conceive that even a communist society could ever do without ideology*."[43]

But the notion of ideology is more complex than this, for Althusser goes on to talk about what ideology *is*. Althusser explains that ideology "is a matter of the *lived* relation between men and their world."[44] It is a structure that "is the expression of the relation between men and the 'world,' that is, the (overdetermined) unity of the real relation and the imaginary relation between them and their real conditions of existence. In ideology, the real relation is inevitably invested in the imaginary relation, a relation that *express a will* (conservative, conformist, reformist or revolutionary), a hope or a nostalgia, rather than describing reality."[45] Thus ideology is a form of connection between how things "really are" and our imaginary vision of how they are. But ideology is particularly *not* passive; it "expresses a will" that moves towards a particular perspective.

What is just as important for Althusser is the notion that ideology is also formative for individuals and classes. Ideology is not some scheming plot that is inflicted on the masses by those in power. Those in power actually believe in the ideology that serves them and it functions

---

39. Althusser, *Marxism and Humanism*, 228–29.
40. Ibid., 230.
41. Ibid., 231.
42. Ibid.
43. Ibid., 232; emphasis original.
44. Ibid., 233.
45. Ibid., 233–34; emphasis original.

"not only in its rule over the exploited class, but in its own constitution of itself as the ruling class..."[46] Ideology, then, serves to justify, as well as construct, the class system.

Ideology as understood by Althusser has an important role in every society. Looking forward to the future classless society of communism, ideology is necessary *"if men are to be formed, transformed and equipped to respond to the demands of their conditions of existence."*[47] Ideology will retain its formative use even after the revolution. In fact, ideology will be particularly important in helping individuals adjust to this new world. The difference is that "ideology is the relay whereby, and the element in which, the relation between men and their conditions of existence is lived to the profit of all men."[48] Notice here that what is gone is the language of "imagination" and instead the more straightforward term of "relay" is used. Clearly, then, a significant difference of ideology in the post-revolutionary world is that it no longer functions to cloud the way the world works, but acts to aid individuals in coping with "the real world."

In his article "Ideology and Ideological State Apparatuses," Althusser extends his understanding of ideology. In this article he introduces a new category for comprehending the role of ideology: interpellation. *"All ideology hails or interpellates concrete individuals as concrete subjects..."*[49] Althusser envisions that in the process of ideology constructing the subject, it calls out to the individual. If the individual responds to the call, identifies themselves as the one being called, they then essentially become the subject of the call. Thus Althusser says, "ideology 'acts' or 'functions' in such a way that it 'recruits' subjects among the individuals..."[50]

Althusser gives an extended example of this using the Christian religion. The Christian religious ideology calls to the individual and says, "that God exists and that you are answerable to Him. It adds: God addresses himself to you through my voice... It says: this is who you are: you are Peter! This is your origin, you were created by God for all

46. Ibid., 235.
47. Ibid.
48. Ibid., 236.
49. Althusser, *Ideological State Apparatuses*, 173.
50. Ibid., 174.

eternity, although you were born in the 1920th year of Our Lord! This is your place in the world! This what you must do! By these means, if you observe the 'law of love' you will be saved, you, Peter, and will become part of the Glorious Body of Christ! Etc. . . ."[51] If Peter recognizes himself in that call, sees himself as occupying the place designated for him in the call and behaves in the way mandated by the call, then the ideology has served to reproduce the "Christian religious subject." Althusser notes that this is all dependent upon the existence of another absolute Subject: God. The Subject (God) is constituted by its acceptance by individuals that is presupposed by the interpellation which constitutes the individuals as subjects. At the same time, the acceptance of the interpellation is also dependent on making oneself obedient ("subject") to this master Subject. The end result of this is that the subjects, both God and the individual, are constituted by ideology and are therefore guaranteed that "everything will be all right in the end."[52]

Thus, through ideology, the religious subject is produced. This production, then, is part of a vast network of similar "ideological state apparatuses" which work to position the individual within society. Individuals, through ideology, "are inserted into practices governed by the rituals of the ISAs. They 'recognize' the existing state of affairs (*das Bestehende*), that it 'really is true that it is so and not otherwise', and that they must be obedient to God, to their conscience, to the priest, to de Gaulle, to the boss, to the engineer, that thou shalt 'love thy neighbor as thyself', etc. Their concrete, material behavior is simply the inscription in life of the admirable words of the prayer: '*Amen—so be it.*'"[53] From this point the individual is self-sufficient as a functioning cog within the larger system. Ideology keeps the individual properly positioned for the maintenance and perpetuation of the social matrix.

Clearly then, the role of religion must be confronted with suspicion from the perspective of Althusser. As his paramount example of the function of ideology, Althusser clearly identifies religion as the most problematic ISA (Ideological State Apparatus) within the capitalist system. It is the model upon which all other ISA's are constructed. For Althusser, ISA's are part of the class oppression, the struggle of the

51. Ibid., 177.
52. Ibid., 181.
53. Ibid.

ruling class over the proletariat. "For if it is true that the ISAs represent the *form* in which the ideology of the ruling class must *necessarily* be realized, and the form in which the ideology of the ruled class must *necessarily* be measured and confronted, ideologies are not born in the ISAs, but from the social classes at grips in the class struggle..."[54] In the last instance, then, the ISA is a product of the class conflict inherent in the base. The solution, then, cannot be found from simply battling or attempting to reformulate an ISA, instead the real crux of change comes from the structure (and contradiction) of the base.[55]

But finally, it is important to bear in mind the distinction made earlier between Marxism and ideology. While a form of ideology may be around even after the revolution, for Althusser, one must never confuse Marxism with ideology. Althusser makes this point in a focused way in his discussion of Gramsci's work on religion in his text *Reading Capital*. From Althusser's perspective, Gramsci's flaw is that he too easily conflated religion as a world-view and Marxism as a world-view. Althusser protests that Gramsci's work is problematic for not "calling attention to the fact that what distinguishes Marxism from the ideological 'conceptions of the world' is less the (important) formal difference that *Marxism puts an end to any supraterrestrial 'beyond'* (emph. mine), than the distinctive *form* of this absolute immanence (its 'earthliness'): *the form of scientificity.* This 'break' between the old religions or ideologies, even the 'organic' ones, and Marxism, *which is a science,* and which must become the 'organic' ideology of human history by producing a *new* form of ideology in the masses (an ideology which will depend on a science this time—*which has never been the case before*)..."[56] Althusser makes two important points in this text. First, that supernatural ("superterrestrial") aspect of religion is intensely problematic and is terminated by the advent of Marxism. Second, any future post-revolutionary ideology will need to be based not on the religions or ideologies that presently exist, but on the science of Marxism. Thus, while Althusser has a more sophisticated understanding of ideology than we have seen before, in the end he returns to the position of classical Marxism as ultimately atheist.

54. Ibid., 185–56.
55. Althusser, *Contradiction and Overdetermination*, 100.
56. Althusser and Balibar, *Reading Capital*, 131.

The move from considering religion as a separate topic to including it under a general theory of ideology is significant. Althusser sets the standard for what will be the general approach to religion for most of post-Althusserian Marxism. The issue now becomes the role of ideology in society in general, and particularly as a means of domination. Religion, as a subset of ideology, is understood to function in the same way as other ideological apparatuses (i.e. family, law, culture, etc.) This now will become the standard Marxist approach to religion. For example, in Terry Eagleton's study *Ideology: An Introduction*, he references religion a total of seven times; almost all appear in his examination of Marx, Gramsci, and Freud, who themselves specifically deal with religion. Other than those few instances, it is assumed that religion is covered under the general rubric of "ideology" or "superstructure."

It would not be an exaggeration to say that the tradition of Marxism has largely been dominated by the two figures of Gramsci and Althusser since the 1970s. However several thinkers also require some reflection as we watch the evolution of the Marxist tradition in the post-Athusserian era.

The Birmingham School and Jean Comaroff

The advent of British Cultural Studies, or the Birmingham School (as it is also known), took up the wisdom of Gramsci and (to a lesser degree) Althusser. The key notion that Stuart Hall and his colleagues at the Birmingham Institute for Cultural Studies fastened upon was "hegemony." For the Birmingham School, hegemony was an important concept in understanding subcultures. Their notion was that subcultures enacted certain forms of resistance that challenged the dominate hegemony.[57] Hegemony is certainly linked to ideology, and, in the introduction to their ground breaking work *Resistance through Ritual,* Hall and his colleagues argued that to maintain their position the ruling

57. The notion of hegemony was used by Gramsci and its meaning is not always clear in his work. Hall understands "'hegemony' to refer to the moment when a ruling class is able, not only to *coerce* a subordinate class to conform to its interests, but to exert a 'hegemony' or 'total social authority' over subordinate classes. This involves the exercise of a special kind of power—the power to frame alternatives and contain opportunities, *to win and shape consent,* so that the granting of legitimacy to the dominant classes appears not only 'spontaneous' but natural and normal." Clark et al., *Subcultures, Cultures and Class*, 38.

classes must attain an "ascendancy of social authority, not only in the state but in civil society as well, in culture and ideology."[58] A crisis in the dominant hegemony can lead to structural changes in addition to superstructural changes through a sort of "domino effect": "These discrepancies (contradictions) in situation, values and action then provide the real material and historical basis—under the right conditions—for more developed class strategies of open resistance, struggle and for counter-hegemonic strategies of rupture and transformation."[59] The key qualifier is, of course, "under the right conditions." The ideal result, indeed the theoretical result, is radical social change. And yet Hall et al. admits this is not generally the case since acts of resistance are often "pitched largely at the symbolic level,"[60] and thus "the problematic of a subordinate class experience can be 'lived through', negotiated or resisted; but it cannot be *resolved* at that level or by those means."[61] The problem here is that the dominoes must fall exactly right. Subcultural actions must lead to theoretical reflection and then political action. Left at the level of mere acts of resistance there is no revolution. In this way, the acts of resistance that Hall and his colleagues categorize are much like how Marx described religion: "the sigh of the oppressed spirit."

Jean Comaroff exemplifies precisely this problem of the relation between resistance and change in her work *Body of Power, Spirit of Resistance*. In this work she looks specifically at the religious rituals of South African Zionism. In surveying the interesting combination (Comaroff: *bricolage*) of Protestant and native ideas and rituals, dress, and style, Comaroff charts a form of resistance to colonialist/capitalist incursion into South Africa. Hence, "these symbolic orders share an opposition to the categories of bourgeois liberal secularism; and all promise to subvert the divisive structures of colonial society . . ."[62] Yet, despite this "promise," there lies a problem: this response is ultimately ineffectual. "Of course, the form of such resistance is largely implicit. I have argued that, while the colonial encounter objectivized Tshidi perceptions of the dominant power-relations in the universe, this has not

---

58. Ibid., 39.
59. Ibid., 43.
60. Ibid., 47.
61. Ibid.
62. Comaroff, *Body of Power*, 254.

given rise to an explicit consciousness of class or to modes of strategic class action . . . Even while their practice stems from a felt desire to cast off the shackles of domination, their structural predicament condemns them to reproduce the material and symbolic form of the neocolonial system."[63] But Comaroff is not deterred by such a discouraging diagnosis; she returns to the domino theory arguing that "so-called utopian movements have frequently motivated violent clashes," which then may have "long-term implications."[64] In the end, however, Comaroff settles for religious discontent that may act as a "'cradle' of social links and moral dissent"[65] but concedes that the possibility of such acts leading to participation in revolutionary activity is unlikely.[66]

The problem is two-fold. To return to the Birmingham School, they note, following Gramsci, that there are two aspects to power of the state: hegemony and coercion. When hegemony fails, the state resorts to coercion. While Hall et al. see this as a form of victory that potentially sets the stage for revolutionary action,[67] another view might see this coercion as a stop-gap measure until ideological hegemony can be re-established.[68]

The second problem is also pointed out by Hall et al., which has particular relevance to Comaroff's situation. Hall et al. have an analogous example in the British skinhead subculture. This subculture, in the form of "of working-class dress, in the displaced focusing on the football match and the 'occupation' of the football 'ends' . . . reassert, but 'imaginarily,' the values of a class . . ."[69] It is at this point that Hall et al. reference Althusser's definition of ideology as an "imaginary, lived relation." Likewise, Comaroff's Zionists are also engaged in an "imaginary" solution. As we have seen in our analysis of Althusser, it is precisely the "imaginary" nature that ensures that ideology will ultimately work

---

63. Ibid., 261.
64. Ibid., 262.
65. Ibid.
66. Ibid.
67. Clark et al., *Subcultures, Cultures and Class*, 68.
68. This is why Gramsci himself connected the loss of hegemony (his "War of Position") with the real preparations of the party for revolution ("Underground Warfare") as the loss of consent is ultimately necessary but not sufficient (see below).
69. Clark et al., *Subcultures, Cultures and Class*, 48.

for the dominant class since in a classless society ideology will lose the element of imagination.

Religion, as the ultimate example of ideology then, functions in exactly this way for Marxism. It provides an imaginary solution to real structural problems. In the case of Comaroff the problems stem from the results of western colonialism. But regardless of the source of the problem, be it western imperialism or class oppression, the solution that ideology develops ultimately fails as it essentially "misrecognizes"[70] the true nature of the problem. In the case of religion, from a Marxist perspective, we see a whole imaginary world is created in an attempt to solve the problems generated by the basic contradictions of capital. The result is the "mist-enveloped" reality that Marx spoke of that contains imaginary solutions to real problems.

Conclusion

The survey of the Marxist view of religion that has been done in this chapter has shown a number of important aspects. Preeminently, Marxism has, from its very inception, included a deep suspicion of religion. Its founders proclaimed Marxism to be atheist in its orientation and method. Religion was understood as a destructive tool used by capitalism to forward (and mask) its agenda. While religion may have predated the advent of modern capitalism and may even have had an important role in class struggle at some point in the past, nonetheless the founders of Marxism saw it as something that today distracts from the main goal of revolutionary change.

As the tradition has continued, the approach to religion has become more nuanced and more complicated, but Marxism's general antipathy towards religion has not abated. As I have shown, more modern interpreters like Gramsci and Althusser all have maintained the same general perspective towards religion as did Marx, Engels, and Lenin. They have all held a critical perspective on religion and most have envisioned its ultimate demise for a more scientific approach to the world.

The real difference between the founders of Marxism and the more modern thinkers is the shift from religion as an independent topic of investigation to religion as an exemplum of ideology. Whereas

---

70. Althusser, *Ideological State Apparatuses*, 183.

Marx claimed that criticism of religion was the necessary precondition to all criticism, thinkers like Althusser and Eagleton have not focused on the distinctive nature of religion (when they have dealt with it at all), focusing instead on ideology as a system that encompasses religion perforce.

In the end, however, whether it has the more significant standing that Marx gave it, or the more short shrift that Althusser gives it, the position of Marxism toward religion has remained antagonistic. The logic of the Marxist system depends on the primacy of the economic system. As Marxism has progressed, religion (and ideology in general) has been seen to have a greater role in the reproduction and continuation of that economic system. The way religion functions to ensure the perpetuation of capitalism has been explored in a variety of ways. Still the general trend has been to see religion as a consistently negative pull against the goal of revolution.

The exception here may be the Birmingham school. Yet even there, the best that someone like Comaroff can hope for is resistance that "in the last instance" leads to political awakening, that leads to political action, that ultimately leads to revolutionary change. The notion is that religion at its best might be a link in the chain towards real social rupture. Yet even Comaroff must concede in the end that the resistance she studies falls in the category of an "imaginary" solution and shows no clear revolutionary prospects.

Thus in regards to religion, despite hopes to the contrary, the force of the Marxist tradition is to uphold the skepticism towards religion first articulated by its founder. In the end, the materialist position of Marxism argues against some idealist notion that change can come from a different set of religious beliefs. The focus of change continually must be the economic base. An understanding of the superstructural function of religion and modification of it may help in some ways to thwart the flawless reproduction of the system, but cannot by itself generate structural change. Moreover, the majority tradition also holds, as Lenin stressed, that the argument about religion and the attempt to properly reform it, is ultimately effort that should be otherwise spent on bringing forward the revolution.

2

The Logic of Liberation Theology

LIBERATION THEOLOGY HAS BEEN A PART OF THE THEOLOGICAL LANDscape since the 1960s. While the writers of Liberation Theology trace their lineage back to Las Casas in the sixteenth century, its origin can be found more recently, with the proclamation of the Second Vatican Council in *Gaudium Et Specs* calling for greater human equality, both social and economic. Vatican II, however, was only the beginning. While the Second Vatican Council called for the Church to engage in a renewed involvement in the world and attention to the dignity of all humans specifically in regards to their political and economic aspects, the Latin American Bishops went even further. At Medellin in 1968 the conference of bishops took specific aim at the system of capitalism arguing that it "militates against the dignity of the human person."[1] Pronouncements were made as well at Puebla Mexico in 1979. Yet it was the publication of Gustavo Gutierrez's *A Theology of Liberation* that marks the full expression of Liberation Theology. Gutierrez certainly has been and continues to be a leading figure in the Liberation Theology movement. Others, however, have also contributed to this endeavor. In this section I will examine the logic of Liberation Theology, providing at an overview of its basic ideological system. Within this exploration I will focus on three key issues that will later play into an examination of New Testament scholarship: 1) Liberation Theology's relationship to Marxism, 2) Liberation Theology's approach to the Bible, and 3) a specific examination of Liberation Theology's perspective on apocalyptic texts.

---

1. (CELAM), "Medellin Document on Peace."

The Logic of Liberation Theology

One of the most important points of an ideology is its starting point. Liberation Theology is no exception to this. Liberation Theology starts from an experiential perspective, more specifically it begins from the experience of Latin America. Hugo Assmann makes this perfectly clear, "Perhaps the greatest merit of the theology of liberation is its insistence on the starting-point of its reflections: the situation of 'dominated (Latin) America'... In this theology, to a far greater extent than in new European political theology, the underlying realities of life in Latin America are becoming intertwined with the basic sources of faith."[2]

Gutierrez is no less clear on this issue. A theory of Latin American liberation must come from Latin Americans themselves: "And this theory must be Latin American, not to satisfy a desire for originality, but for the sake of elementary historical realism."[3] The focus is then on a "bottom up" approach to theology. Theology is not done in the ivory towers of distant first world academies but rather by "'militant theologians' working with the pilgrim people of God engaged in their pastoral responsibilities."[4]

The clear message of the authors of liberation theology is that they will not succumb to an intellectual colonization. Liberation Theology must be "home grown" and thus theologies from Europe and America, however well intentioned, are not sufficient.[5] The starting point of Liberation Theology, then, is specifically the experience of Latin Americans in all their particularity. Gutierrez explains it clearly, "But in order for this liberation to be authentic and complete, it has to be undertaken by the oppressed people themselves and so must stem from the values proper to these people. Only in this context can a true cultural revolution come about."[6] Liberation Theology, then, does not need to be "outsourced;" its validity depends on the fact that it is the voice of the oppressed *in* Latin America.

---

2. Assmann, *Nomad Church*, 38.

3. Gutierrez, *Theology of Liberation*, 91.

4. Boff, *Introducing Liberation Theology*, 19.

5. Assmann spends a portion of his book showing precisely why non-Latin American theologies are insufficient to the problems of Latin America. Assmann, *Nomad Church*, 29–31.

6. Gutierrez, *Theology of Liberation*, 91.

This ties in to the diagnosis of the problem for Liberation Theology. Daniel M. Bell has written a historical outline of the development of Liberation Theology that is helpful in attempting to grasp its logic. Bell asserts that beginning in the 1920s the dominant model for understanding the relationship between church and state in Latin America was the "New Christendom" model. The New Christendom model took the church out of politics and refocused its power on social issues. The laity was charged with putting the values of the church into practice as citizens engaged in political life; however, the church itself remained outside the political domain.

Bell notes, "the cornerstone of this vision is what came to be known as the 'distinction of planes,' a distinction between the spiritual and temporal order of existence."[7] One might hear the dim echo of Augustine's two cities here. However, unlike Augustine, the two planes are not completely separated, only differentiated. There is still crossover between the two. This entails the influence of one on the other. The state must surely be influenced by the witness of the Church through its members who are charged to govern according to the precepts of the Gospel. Yet the state itself is separate from the Church and in itself has no spiritual side. As Bell puts it, "No prince of the nations of this world can know anything of the spiritual Kingdom of God. The temporal authorities are incompetent in spiritual matters."[8] Spiritual matters, then, are the realm of the Church, but the church thereby abandons the role it played during the time of Christendom in which it was an active player on the political stage. Indirect influence now replaces direct political action on the part of the Church.

With a shift in the economic world, the notion of New Christendom became problematic for Latin American theologians. The ideology of development went hand in hand with this theology of New Christendom. Development held that Latin America was in the process of becoming a full-fledged industrialized player in the modern world. It merely needed investment by the industrialized nations to propel it along on its journey. Foreign investment, then, was necessary for the continued economic growth of Latin America and for it to become an economic equal in the global economy. Continued development would

---

7. Bell, *Liberation Theology*, 46.
8. Ibid., 47

serve to "raise all boats" and eventually improve the lives of the poor in third world nations. The Church then could withdraw from the political realm and focus on social issues making up for the, albeit temporary, inequalities that development created.

For Liberation Theology, in contrast, development was seen as highly problematic. Gutierrez makes several critiques of the notion of development. It pits underdeveloped nations against each other to gain foreign investors. As a result, developing nations were disinclined to be critical of their benefactors. But more importantly, Gutierrez suggests that development as a notion constructed by governments who control the world economy actually did not have the best interests of their client states in mind. "The poor countries are becoming ever more clearly aware that their underdevelopment is only the by-product of the development of other countries, because the kind of relationship which exists between the rich and poor countries. Moreover they are realizing that their own development will come about only with a struggle to break the domination of the rich countries."[9] Liberation Theology replaces the idea of development with the concept of "dependence" as a better way of expressing the relationship between developed and underdeveloped countries.

The theory of dependence, then, sees the inequity between the developed and underdeveloped nations as intentional rather than as an historical accident. The developed countries require a system of imbalance both between countries and within dependent countries. Using the categories of the "center" and the "periphery," Gutierrez argues that the system of dependence generates "progress and growing wealth for the few and social imbalances, political tension and poverty for the many."[10] Thus dependence creates a socially unequal situation at both the international and the national level.

We are now in a position to appreciate the position of Liberation Theology in regards to its demand for internal theological development. Western theologians, as well intentioned as they may be, are themselves the product of a system of dependence that benefits from the perpetuation of an unjust system. We may certainly understand if liberation theologians are suspicious of thinkers produced by the very system they

9. Gutierrez, *Theology of Liberation*, 26.
10. Ibid., 84.

see as the root of their own oppression as a people. Likewise, the formulation of New Christendom (rejected by the theory of dependence) creates a level of insulation between the clergy and the political needs of the people. While it is an improvement over traditional Christendom by empowering the laity for change, it separates the church from its duty toward justice in the world.

If the diagnosis of the problem for Liberation Theology is the system of dependence created by the international capitalist system, then what is the prescription? Leonard and Clodovis Boff indicate that Liberation Theology has several themes that result from its reflection of the problems I have elucidated above:

1. solidarity with the poor
2. real faith requires liberating action
3. God sides with the oppressed
4. God is actively working to set up the Kingdom of God in history
5. Jesus attacked oppression and his gospel is one of freedom from oppression
6. God is found in the struggle of the oppressed
7. Mary is a "prophetic and liberating woman,"
8. God supports the rights of the poor
9. "Liberated human potential becomes liberative."[11]

A quick examination of these themes shows several commonalities. First, there is a focus on the poor and the oppressed. Second, there is a clear siding by the divinity with the oppressed and the poor; God, Jesus, and Mary are all invoked on the side of liberation. Finally, there is clearly a class emphasis at the root of Liberation Theology's analysis. While the Boffs's rebel against oppression of any kind, including sexism and racism,[12] at bottom it is class oppression that is paramount.

The issue of class analysis is likewise essential to most Liberation Theologians. The tone for this was set in the Medellin Document on Peace, specifically the section entitled, "Tensions between Classes and

11. Boff, *Introducing Liberation Theology*, 43–61.
12. Ibid., 29.

Internal Colonialism." There the bishops identify some of the problems as "Extreme inequality among social classes," "Forms of Oppression of dominant groups and Sectors," and "Power unjustly exercised by certain dominant sectors."[13] Likewise Gutierrez, in diagnosing the problem, states,"only a class analysis will enable us to see what is really involved in the opposition between oppressed countries and dominant peoples."[14]

Liberation Theology and Marxism

The focus on a class analysis leads to the issue of Liberation Theology's use of Marxism. Clearly a controversial element, several Liberation theologians have attempted to explain their use of Marx. In Gutierrez's *Liberation Theology* Marx appears quite often. A quick look at the index shows at least ten direct textual invocations of Marx (not including references in footnotes). But more than the quantitative aspects, one sees Marx showing up indirectly in a wide array of places. In his chapter on "The Church in The Process of Liberation," Gutierrez states, "difficulties in reconciling justice and private ownership have led many to the conviction that 'private ownership of capital leads to the dichotomy of capital and labor . . .'"[15] Earlier Gutierrez advocates socialism saying, "socialism, moreover, represents the most fruitful and far-reaching approach."[16]

While Gutierrez is cautious, often letting others speak for him in the text, at one point he sounds a little like Lenin when he says, "Only a sufficiently broad, rich and intense revolutionary praxis, with the participation of different viewpoints, can create the conditions for fruitful theory. These conditions are beginning to appear. Without any loss of militancy or radicalness in the theory, they will undoubtedly lead to greater modifications than envisioned by those who sought refuge in easy solutions of the excommunication of those who did not accept their pat answers, schematizations, and uncritical attitudes toward the historical expressions of socialism."[17] Thus, much like Lenin, Gutierrez

---

13. (CELAM),"Medellin Document on Peace," 4.
14. Gutierrez, *Theology of Liberation*, 87.
15. Ibid., 111.
16. Ibid., 90.
17. Ibid.

envisions the developing of theory using a "revolutionary praxis" that results in a drive towards socialism.

The use of Marxism in Gutierrez's work has not gone unnoticed, and while in *A Theology of Liberation* Gutierrez seems rather blithe in his appropriation of it, he defends and limits his application of Marxism in *The Truth Shall Make You Free*. Here he makes a sharp distinction between his use of Marxism and a Marxist theory of liberation saying, "neither the social sciences generally nor the Latin American contribution to them can be reduced to the Marxist version."[18] Gutierrez makes this even clearer further on when he argues that despite the frequent references to Marx and the use of Marxist categories and analyses, "these facts do not, by themselves, mean an acceptance of Marxism..."[19]

The alert reader may wonder at this protest, but in the next breath Gutierrez makes clear why this is the case by adding, "especially insofar as Marxism embodies an all-embracing view of life and thus excludes the Christian faith and its requirements." He further clarifies, "There is *no question at all* of a possible acceptance of an atheistic ideology."[20] This defensive posture continues as Gutierrez protests that it is really not Marxism he is using at all, "As I have reminded the reader, once the situation of poverty and marginalization comes to play a part in theological reflections, an analysis of that situation from the sociological viewpoint becomes important, and requires recourse to relevant disciplines. This means that if there is a meeting, it is between *theology and the social sciences,* and not between theology and Marxist analysis, except to the extent that elements of the latter are found in contemporary social sciences, especially as these are practiced in the Latin American world."[21] This is a significant backtrack from the position Gutierrez took in *Liberation Theology,* and he takes this position with good reason. For while he protests that a certain branch of the Marxist tradition can separate class analysis from what he calls "metaphysical materialism," the fact of Gutierrez's forceful retraction indicates that he has come to the conclusion that he cannot successfully defend a marriage between

---

18. Gutierrez, *Truth*, 61.
19. Ibid.
20. Ibid.; emphasis original.
21. Ibid., 63.

Marx and the Church. Ultimately, it would seem, that for him Marxism is an irredeemably "atheistic ideology."

Juan Luis Segundo takes a different approach in his *The Liberation of Theology*. Clearly Gutierrez has identified the problem: Marxism entails an atheistic perspective that is ultimately incompatible with a position of faith. The Liberation that Marx envisioned was hampered by religion not aided by it. Segundo takes two tacts in addressing this. On the one hand, Segundo argues that Marx stopped short in his analysis. Marx argued that religion functions as a protest against real suffering.[22] This being the case, continues Segundo, Marx's next move should have been to trace the relationship between religious protest and particular economic systems. One would expect to see religious variation dependent on differences in the infrastructure. But instead, Marx short-circuits all that with a call for the abolition of religion altogether. Segundo thinks this does not follow: "Instead of 'abolition' one would expect Marx to have talked about 'changing' religion so that it might accentuate and eventually correct the situation being protested against."[23] Thus Marx fails to completely realize his theoretical apparatus.

Segundo continues this line of attack a little later on. If religion is one more ideological aspect of culture, then why is it marked for termination when other cultural ideological structures like art, politics, philosophy and law are not? He states, "I confess that I find it difficult to comprehend, within the single framework of historical materialism itself, how there can be different fates for different forms of the ideological superstructure."[24] Thus Segundo argues that Marx is engaged in a form of negative exceptionalism, singling out religion for different treatment than the rest of the ideological superstructure.

The second tact that Segundo takes is related to the first. Here he argues that there is simply a logical inconsistency in the way Marx deals with religion. Taking the state as his example, Segundo shows that while Marx eventually envisions its destruction similar to the end of religion, it still has utility early on in the revolutionary process. In fact, it is a necessary component of the socialist transition to communism. From Segundo's perspective Marx should have treated religion the same way,

---

22. Marx, *Critique*, 16.
23. Segundo, *Liberation of Theology*, 17.
24. Ibid., 58.

but in fact, Marx sees religion as having no value for the revolution at all. Thus, instead of the gradual "withering away" of religion, "he makes its abolition a precondition for the revolution rather than an effect..."[25] Segundo notes the distinction for Marx is that "philosophy can *make* errors... but religion *is* an error..."[26]

This notion of religion as "error" troubles Segundo. He questions its origin: "In the context of historical materialism it is very difficult to explain how such an ideological and superstructural form could ever have arisen from the division of labor. For this particular form seems to be almost wholly independent. Unlike other superstructural forms, it does not possess the ambiguous two-sided characteristics that typify such forms and help to explain their useful functions."[27] Instead Segundo requires that the relative autonomy of the superstructure be taken seriously. To understand that "all the superstructures including religion, can play a determining role in furthering and retarding any possible social change within the existing economic framework."[28] The fact that Marxism as it has developed has failed to do this means that the marriage between Marxist thought and Liberation Theology is fraught at best. Segundo concludes, "My observations about Marxist sociology ... present liberation theology with a serious problem."[29]

The crux of the issue for Segundo seems to have to do with the difference between ideology and faith. In *The Liberation of Theology* Segundo tries to make a distinction between the two. For Segundo the dividing line lies in the fact that ideologies are historically conditioned. They are inspired by particular events and conditions that require a particular response. Ideologies, then, create a specific way of making sense and determining appropriate action in the face of a particular set of historical realities, what Segundo calls a "provisional but necessary system of means and ends..."[30] For Segundo, then, there is never a place outside of ideology. Ideology is key for living in the world.

---

25. Ibid., 59..

26. Ibid.

27. Ibid. Engel's theory of "reflection" actually tries to give precisely the sort of theory of generation that Segundo is asking for (see above).

28. Ibid., 60.

29. Ibid., 62.

30. Ibid., 116.

This being the case, what is faith? Here the issue becomes less clear. While Segundo makes the expected move of contrasting faith with ideology in that ideology is historically conditioned and faith is "permanent and unique;"[31] he does not want to suggest that faith and ideology are opposed. Rather, Segundo sees ideology as the incarnation of faith, the word become flesh. Thus Segundo can say "faith without ideologies: Dead faith."[32] Concluding, "Faith, then, is a liberative process. It is converted into freedom for history, which means freedom *for ideologies*."[33] Ideologies, then, are an instantiation of faith. Faith and ideology are not opposites, rather they are complementary with the former expressed in the latter.

But this does not answer the question of the nature of faith. Segundo is critical of seeing faith as static. "We are used to picturing our faith as a plane of eternal certitudes which are destined to be professed on the one hand and translated into action on the other."[34] Instead Segundo makes reference to communication theory and uses the language of "proto-learning" which he also calls "simple learning." He contrasts this with "deutro-learning" which he refers to as "learning to learn."[35] It is the second concept, "learning to learn," which characterizes faith. Both of these are differentiated from "eternal certitudes" in that they are ultimately not determinative of content but rather constitute a process. Segundo compares this to a child who learns mathematical procedures. The procedures do not determine either the numbers given in the problem, nor do they reflect the answer, rather they determine how the numbers are used to come up with an acceptable answer.[36] Following that model, faith, then, "is the total process to which man submits, a processing of learning in and through ideologies how to create the ideologies needed to handle new and unforeseen situations in history."[37] Faith is not ideological; it is the process of producing ideologies.

31. Ibid.
32. Ibid., 106.
33. Ibid., 110; emphasis original.
34. Ibid., 109.
35. Ibid., 118.
36. Ibid., 119.
37. Ibid., 120.

What we have seen, then, is a very careful argument. Segundo's initial attack on Marx does not dispute the integrity of his larger social analysis but merely quibbles with his reading of the role of religion in society (both capitalist and coming socialist). The way is provided, then, to alleviate the biggest problem of Marxist analysis that ultimately requires the abandonment of religion. Following this analysis, Segundo's careful distinction between faith and ideologies allows him to create a "big tent" that includes both Marx and faith. By historicizing ideology and subordinating ideology to faith Segundo can adopt some Marxism as is called for in analyzing the historical moment, and yet avoid the commitment to a radical critique of religion that Marx prescribes.

Liberation Theology and the Bible

The alert reader may find some of Segundo's explanations somewhat unsatisfying. The allusion to mathematics seems particularly problematic. If faith and ideology are like the creation of math problem with formulas, one may ask, is not historical reality much different than mathematics? Where do these "formulas" for creating ideologies come from? Are they to be derived from the Bible and, if so, what parts? Are they to be derived from Church tradition and, again, if so, what parts? Where do we find the principle of selection that allows us to accept the Jesus of "love thy enemy" over Joshua's genocidal crusades? Since Liberation Theologians have found themselves the subject of Vatican reprimands how do we make similar distinctions with regard to Church tradition? Thus we must now explore the relationship between Liberation Theology and the biblical text.

The issue of the Bible's position on violence encapsulates these issues. Segundo struggles with the problem of ideology versus faith in a study of violence in the text. The argument about the appropriate role for Christians and violence centers upon the sayings of Jesus such as "Love your enemies," and "Do not resist evil." Christian pacificism has made this argument using these passages particularly in the work of John Yoder.[38] Ultimately the pacifist argument is based on the concept of love. However, while acknowledging the importance of these sayings, Segundo takes a different approach, "Jesus *did not spell out* the exact

38. Yoder, *Politics of Jesus*.

kind of mutual love that his followers had to display. And he did not, precisely so that Christians would be left free to operate imaginatively and creatively, to figure out what would be the most effective and comprehensive sort of mutual love at a given moment in history."[39] What Segundo ultimately argues, then, is that Jesus's pacifistic approach is a historically appropriate ideology for *Jesus's time*, not necessarily our own. The Bible itself, then, is necessarily ideological; it is a historical product and therefore an ideological product. We cannot take its perspective as normative for our time, because by Segundo's definition of ideology it is always historically conditioned. There is for Segundo no such thing as a universal ideology. Ideologies are always local and particular.

So what, then, is the role of the Bible for faith? Here again, Segundo returns to the language of communication introduced above. The Bible functions as part of the "deutero-learning process." His language leaves the level of specificity and becomes far more process oriented. "If we learn how to learn in and through the Bible, then we must keep going back to this learning process and entrusting ourselves to it. We must keep in contact with this process which reconstructs the historical experiences of a people and a community."[40] Again what seems missing here is any notion of a principle of either selection or limitation. Yet moments later this problem of selection arises again, "An important consequence of all this is that faith, when properly understood, can never dissociate itself from the ideologies in which it is embodied—both in the Bible and in subsequent history. *It certainly can, and should, dissociate itself as much as possible from the 'ideological' tendencies that wrongly subordinate it to a specific brand of historical oppression.*"[41] One might quickly ask why it "can and should" do *anything*? Where is the controlling principle that demands such dissociation?

The answer is only given implicitly. Segundo wraps up his discussion of violence on the topics "ideology and relativity," opting for the latter. He states clearly, "We will never be able to reduce the faith to a specific book or page of the Bible, to a specific Creed or to a specific dogma."[42] But a more nuanced approach is found in Segundo's analysis of

---

39. Segundo, *Liberation of Theology*, 155; emphasis original.
40. Ibid., 181.
41. Ibid.; emphasis mine.
42. Ibid.

Jesus's parable of the Good Samaritan. Here the issue is who constitutes the neighbor?[43] Segundo's argument is that the category of neighbor is a subset of humanity; it necessarily includes some and excludes others. That exclusion Segundo names as a form of violence.[44] The point here then is that violence is a part of the Jesus tradition and can occur even if it is not in the usual forms. Segundo ties this to modern life by saying, "This means we must abandon the simplistic notion that prompts us to discover violence only when a revolutionary shoots a gun on the one hand, and to talk about nonviolence as if it were compatible with impersonal laws and their attendant coercive force on the other hand."[45] Thus the choice is not between violence and nonviolence, a choice between Malcolm and Martin; rather, there is no choice but violence.

That being the case, the question the believer must wrestle with is what sort of violence will be most effective in bringing about "the richest and most promising possibilities for love."[46] What is the dividing line? Again, we are returned to the issue of the historical moment. "Wherever the rules come from, in themselves they possess no morality apart from the broader context of human historical reality . . . The problem is no matter how much amplitude we give to the context, the latter will always be subject to a certain amount of relativism. However broad they may be, contexts change with history."[47] The end result of this line of argumentation is that the Bible can only be a form of "thought experiment;" it is a "teaching tool"[48] that cannot determine what is moral/immoral appropriate/inappropriate in the given historical moment. Rather what is ultimately the most important issue is the situation at present with which the individual is faced.

The answer, then, to the question of a principle of selection is to bring us back to the first point we noticed: Liberation starts from an

---

43. The question is perhaps more complicated than Segundo recognizes in that Luke switches the question midway. The first question is "who is my neighbor?" but the parable ends with Jesus asking "who proved more neighborly?" The two questions have different answers and affect the way the parable is understood (see Crossan, *In Parables*, 57ff.; Scott, *Hear Then the Parable*, 151ff.).

44. Segundo, *Liberation of Theology*, 159.

45. Ibid., 160.

46. Ibid., 172–73.

47. Ibid., 174.

48. It is perhaps not surprising in the end that a member of the "teaching order" should make faith equivalent to a form of education.

experiential place. The experience of oppression acts as the ultimate arbiter of what is accepted and rejected, be it from the Bible, Church doctrine or social theory. Thus while the Bible and tradition may inform and in some ways shape the response of Liberation Theology, Liberation Theology's primary foundation is the experience of oppression. Likewise with Marxism, Liberation Theology may find material helpful in Marxism; yet in the end, through a variety of different tactics, Liberation Theology distances itself from a thorough-going application of Marxist analysis.

The issue is not whether Liberation Theology accepts the Bible—as a branch of Catholic theology it of course does—rather the question is one of the hermeneutic employed. We have already addressed this in a partial way with the discussion of Segundo and his distinction between faith and ideology. Still a fuller exploration of the issue of the use of the Bible in Liberation Theology is called for.

What may surprise the reader of Liberation Theology is the dearth of biblical references that one finds in these writers' texts. Take Gutierrez's *A Theology of Liberation*, for example: the vast majority of his New Testament citations come in three of his thirteen chapters. Likewise, the Boff brothers' *Introducing Liberation Theology* contains the majority of its biblical citations in chapter 4. The rest of the chapters have less than five biblical citations each.

When one looks for sustained exegesis of particular passages, one is similarly disappointed. The closest thing one finds to an in-depth examination of the biblical text in Gutierrez's texts is his exploration of the notion of poverty in the Bible.[49] However, even here the student of biblical studies may not find satisfaction. In the nine pages that Gutierrez devotes to this topic, he covers the entirety of the biblical text. His analysis ranges from Genesis to the Gospels to James with lightening speed, never stopping in any one place very long. One might argue, of course, that Gutierrez never claims to be a biblical scholar, and he assumes the heavy lifting is accomplished by the scholars who populate his footnotes. However, as we have seen repeatedly, the presupposition of Liberation Theology is not predicated upon a discovery from the text. Rather, Liberation Theology starts from the position of the oppressed[50]

---

49. Gutierrez, *Theology of Liberation*, 291–99.

50. Not to belabor the point but Leonardo Boff emphasizes this when he says, "The theology of liberation, then begins with actual liberative practice. Its aim is liberative

and then appeals to the text for authority. Thus the Liberation Scholar will cite the biblical text when it suits his/her purpose, but the logic of the situation always trumps that of exegesis.

Liberation Theology and Apocalypticism

A particularly interesting example of this is the way Liberation Theology deals with apocalyptic literature. I should say at the outset that a clear elaboration of apocalyptic texts is missing from the main thinkers of Liberation Theology. What is talked about in the works of Liberation Theology is instead "eschatology." Gutierrez has a chapter in *A Theology of Liberation* entitled "Eschatology and Politics," and it is here that he comes closest to addressing the apocalyptic aspect of the biblical texts.

The word "apocalyptic" itself never appears. Instead Gutierrez uses the term "eschatology" and more often "utopia." In his chapter, however, Gutierrez seems to have more the gospel notion of the "Kingdom of God" in mind than the millennial aftermath of the New Jerusalem from Revelation. Gutierrez makes this clear when speaking of the message of Jesus, saying, "This message becomes present and active because of what Metz calls the *memoria Christi*: 'commemorating the advent of the Kingdom of God in the love of Jesus towards marginated men.' The proclamation of the saving message is translated into promises of freedom, justice and peace which make up the 'eschatological proviso' . . ."[51] Here the notion of Kingdom of God is clearly linked with ideas of "freedom, justice and peace" and targeted at the oppressed "marginated" individuals.

But of course even Jesus's notion of the Kingdom of God is problematic, particularly since Gutierrez relies on Cullmann's understanding of the concept. Cullmann, following to a large degree Bultmann's understanding of Jesus as an existential prophet, argues that he "was concerned *only* with the conversion of the individual and was not interested in a reform of social structures."[52] This was because, following the (former) consensus in New Testament studies stemming from

---

efficacy. It makes itself responsible for an analysis of social, conflictual reality, of course, and has it starting point in the outlook of the poor." Boff, *When Theology Listens*, 14.

51. Gutierrez, *Theology of Liberation*, 222–23.

52. Cullmann, *Jesus and the Revolutionaries*, 13; cited in Gutierrez, *Theology of Liberation*, 230.

Schweitzer, Jesus's apocalypticism was ultimately misguided. Such a quagmire offers little in the way of material for expropriation by Liberation Theology. Gutierrez attempts a criticism of such a position, opining, "This approach does not provide a sufficiently sound basis for an understanding of the attitude of Jesus regarding political life. The interpretation is based on Jesus's words but tends to diffuse or debilitate the tension between the present and the future which characterizes his preaching on the Kingdom."[53] It is noteworthy that Gutierrez does not attempt to marshal much textual evidence to support his contention; rather, he is content to cite the sayings "mercy not sacrifice" (Matt 12:7) and "contrite hearts not holocausts" (Psalm 51). Neither of these passages are explicated in any detail; instead, their meaning and validity are assumed.

Gutierrez has his own line to walk, however, and he does not want to be accused of a millennialist approach that brings about the Kingdom of God as a political entity in the here and now, which might be interpreted as a return to the old notions of Christendom. Likewise, he is opposed to identifying the Kingdom with either socialism or communism. Instead he postulates a more convoluted connection:

> The Kingdom must not be confused with the establishment of a just society. Nor does it mean that this just society constitutes a "necessary condition" for the arrival of the Kingdom nor that they are closely linked, nor that they converge. More profoundly, the announcement of the Kingdom reveals to society itself the aspiration for a just society and leads it to discover unsuspected dimensions and unexplored paths. The Kingdom is realized in a society of brotherhood and justice; and, in turn, this realization opens up the promise and hope of complete communion of all men with God. The political is grafted into the eternal.[54]

The Kingdom of God, then, is not *a* society, but any society or even group in which justice is realized.

Again, we should pause just a moment to reflect on the way this argument is constructed. We note that it is based less on hardnosed biblical exegesis and more on slogans and postulations. Wherein lies the authority then? It is not upon a greater understanding of the text, but a presupposition that supposes the text to be a priori in concert with

---

53. Gutierrez, *Theology of Liberation*, 230.
54. Ibid., 231–32.

the needs of the poor and the oppressed. The presumption is that the theology exists first, the interpretation of the text is just the application of that theology.[55]

The notion of "utopia" is also extremely important for Gutierrez. A large portion of his chapter is centered upon explicating this concept. A utopia is characterized for Gutierrez by three things: 1) "its relationship to present historical reality"; 2) "a denunciation of the existing order"; and 3) "an annunciation of what is not yet, but will be . . . a new society."[56] What is of particular importance is that this is not a passive message. This is not a prediction about forces that are beyond the control; rather, "it is a projection into the future, a dynamic and mobilizing force in history."[57] In this way it is really closer to a goal than a dream.

Utopian ideas may be thought of as out of step with reality whereas ideology offers a systemization of reality. But Gutierrez reverses such a notion. Contrasting utopia with the Marxist notion that ideology leads to false consciousness, Gutierrez argues, "Utopia, however, leads to an authentic and scientific knowledge of reality and to a praxis which transforms what exists."[58] Utopia, then, contains both diagnosis and prescription for that which ails society. Political liberation is thus aligned clearly with utopia while ideology is about reinforcing the status quo. Gutierrez links this not just to personal change but also to human transformation. "Political liberation appears as a path toward the utopia of a freer more human man, the protagonist of his own history."[59] Note the way that Gutierrez is able to combine Cullmann's more existential understanding of the transformed individual with the Liberation Theology goal of liberation from political/structural oppression.

Ultimately then, utopia becomes a form of hope. It presents both what is wrong with society and what can be changed. It is to this language of hope that Gutierrez finally resorts. "In this way hope makes

---

55. Perhaps I should point out that personally I have no dog in this fight. The analysis I am making here is not an attempt to "debunk" Liberation Theology as "unbiblical" as some fundamentalists have tried to do, nor to attack it as unscholarly; rather, my point is to stress the limits of the system based on the presuppositions that it is built upon.

56. Gutierrez, *Theology of Liberation*, 233.

57. Ibid.

58. Ibid., 235.

59. Ibid., 236.

us radically free to commit ourselves to social praxis, motivated by a liberating utopia and with the means which the scientific analysis of reality provides for us. And our hope not only frees us for this commitment; it simultaneously demands and judges it."[60] But Gutierrez does not endorse apocalyptic in this process even with its happy ending of justice for all. He states rather emphatically, "The Gospel does not provide a utopia for us, this is a human work."[61] The goal of utopia is not a direct representation of the text; rather, it is an indirect understanding of it. "For whoever lives by them, faith, charity and hope are a radical factor in spiritual freedom and historical creativity and initiative."[62] Thus, political action is the result of the faith of the Bible but not necessarily the message of the Bible. Therefore we can see why Gutierrez does not appeal to Mark 13, Daniel, or Revelation. Such overt utopian representations are problematic in two ways. First, they are dependent on divine action not human action. Secondly, they would appear to give us a utopia, and Gutierrez is convinced that such is the effect of the text but not given *in* the text.

Conclusion

The logic of Liberation Theology has been made manifest through our exploration. Liberation Theology is predicated upon a singular experiential premise: Latin American oppression. Those outside of that experiential continuum are in no position to be able to either contribute or critique the theology that arises from it. This is not constrained to individuals (like North American/European theologians and biblical scholars) but extends temporally as well. The Bible itself must be subject to same sort of critique. It is not to be accepted whole cloth, but must be viewed through the lens of that primary experience.

The result of this is a stinging critique of the exploitation of the southern hemisphere by the northern, and a prescription for significant change that is both economic and social; the difference being, of course, that this is not the result of simple philosophical reflection but is crowned as the "will of God." As we have seen, Liberation Theology

---

60. Ibid., 238.
61. Ibid.
62. Ibid.

is in some ways precariously balanced. It borrows from Marxism, the Bible and church doctrine and yet is skeptical of all of these. This is only appropriate because of its starting point. Each of these powerful intellectual/spiritual forces comes from outside of the Latin American context. The notion of Liberation itself then becomes the final arbiter of what is acceptable and the principle of interpretation.

Clearly if we dig deeper and ask the question, "How do we know God is on the side of the poor?" at the end of the day the Liberation theologians must concede that it is simply that they can conceive nothing else. Notions of corporate sin and salvation are employed; humanist conceptions of the intrinsic value of men and women are explicated, but in the end all of these rest upon philosophic and biblical foundations that are themselves not free from critique and exception. Instead, it is only this primary experiential foundation that is the bedrock upon which Liberation Theology is built, and, in the final analysis, all of Liberation Theology is founded upon the intuition that oppression could not possibly be God's will.

3

The Logic of Apocalypticism

THE WORLD OF APOCALYPTICISM IS EXCITING AND FRIGHTENING, filled with monsters and demons, battling angelic armies spilling rivers of blood. The logic of this world has been the subject of scholarly inquiry for most of the last 100 years with the most famous pronouncement given by prominent New Testament scholar Ernst Käsemann, "apocalyptic was the mother of all Christian theology."[1] While such a pronouncement is no longer universally accepted,[2] it is nevertheless a sure sign of the importance of apocalyptic within the understanding of early Christianity. But the question remains: What is apocalypticism, and what is the logic of the system that it employs?

In an attempt to answer that, I will begin with an examination of the scholarly discussion on the genre of apocalypticism which has seemed to consume much attention of scholars who are investigating this phenomenon. I will argue that the focus on the problem of genre has largely served to avoid a real historical understanding of the social impact of apocalyptic. This trend in the discipline ultimately broke down, but as it did so the focus became seeing apocalyptic as a psychological phenomenon rather than a social phenomenon. I will then look at the helpful work of noted historian of religion Jonathan Z. Smith and several others who have reframed the discussion in a different direction that emphasizes the social/political aspect of apocalyptic and particularly its use as an ideological tool of power. Finally, I will attempt to make some steps towards explicating a theory of apocalyptic.

---

1. Käsemann, "Beginnings," 40.
2. Borg, *Portraits of Jesus*.

The Genre of Apocalyptic

The issue of genre has dominated the scholarly discussion on apocalypticism. The focus of this discussion has been attempting to devise a definition of apocalyptic literature that successfully encapsulated its literary form. I will show in this section that this discussion avoided the important issue of the social function of apocalyptic at the outset. The other effect of this focus was to move the study of apocalyptic away from the mainstream of New Testament studies and the concomitant theological ramifications that it held. Ultimately, scholars came to realize that the question of function could not be separated from the question of content. Additionally, scholars rebelled against the exclusion of Paul and Jesus from this line of exploration. However, even after the original consensus broke down, there has still been a general move away from understanding apocalyptic as a social/political phenomenon.

The issue of the genre of apocalyptic was confronted head on in a seminal issue of the cutting edge biblical journal *Semeia*. Each *Semeia* issue is generally focused around a single issue, and issue 14 was on apocalypticism. The first point made in the *Semeia* issue is that the literature usually attributed to the category "apocalypses" is diverse. John J. Collins brings this point to the fore when he states that the goal of this *Semeia* issue is to "attain consistency and clarity in the use of the term [apocalypse] on the assumption that the single name "apocalypse" should refer to a single coherent and recognizable type of writing."[3] This is, of course, to say that such coherence was previously not self-evident. The problem in some ways lies with the fact that the term "apocalypse" is not solely a scholarly construction; the term existed in antiquity with its most well known use being the title of the last book of the New Testament.[4] Nonetheless, attempts at a clear definition of what constitutes an apocalypse only reached a level of consensus in *Semeia* 14 (1979). It was in his article introducing that volume where Collins articulates the dominant definition of the genre of apocalypse as, "revelatory literature with a narrative framework, in which revelation is mediated by an otherworldly being to a human recipient, disclosing a transcendent reality which is both temporal insofar as it envisages eschatological

---

3. Collins, *Morphology of a Genre*, 2–3.

4. Ibid. Though Collins cautions that even the word does not always indicate that a text is actually an apocalypse as the *Apocalypse of Moses* shows.

salvation, and spatial insofar as it involves another, supernatural world."[5] The genre, then, can account for two types of apocalypses: those that involve a tour of heaven and those that deal with the end of the world and the afterlife.[6]

In examining this definition one should pay attention to what is included and what is excluded. What is included is the requirement that there be an otherworldly being in charge of transmission of the message and a human being who is the recipient. Thus prophecy, which may involve the transmission of a message from a human agent, is thereby disqualified. Likewise, prophetic dreams also do not qualify as apocalypses because they do not involve a divine mediator.

On the other hand, what is clearly missing from such a definition is any identification of function or reason for the development of such literature.[7] In fact, the definition is remarkable in its lack of any sort of connection to history. The definition exists only as an ideal type to describe an assemblage of literature; it appears to float above the river of time.

It is interesting to see the ramifications of this position. The whole argument about apocalypses is, by virtue of this definition, removed from the center of Biblical Studies and relegated to its periphery with the study of apocryphal works. A good example of this is found in Adela Yarbro Collins's article on "Early Christian Apocalypses" (found in *Semeia* 14 as well). The majority of the works that Yarbro Collins surveys are noncanonical works, with the one exception being the biblical book of Revelation. It is intriguing to notice the way she deals with Mark 13 (certainly one of the most important apocalyptic texts). That text is relegated to the end of the article where it comes under the heading of "related types" and the sub-heading of "oracles." In just a few sentences she dismisses it as outside the arena of investigation. "Whether this text and its parallels fit our definition of apocalypse depends on whether Jesus is to be understood as an otherworldly mediator. The judgment one

---

5. Ibid., 9.

6. Revelation clearly encompasses both kinds in that its focus is the end of time, yet John is lifted up and shown heaven.

7. Adella Yarbro Collins concedes that this is a deficiency of the definition and proposes an addendum in *Semeia* 36 which will be discussed below Collins, *Introduction*, 6. It is interesting to note, however, the Yarbro Collins does not notice this deficiency in *Semeia* 14 in her contribution to the volume.

makes on this issue depends on one's understanding of the Christology of each Synoptic gospel. The decision not to include Mark 13 pars. with the apocalypses in this essay is based on the judgment that the Jesus of the synoptic gospels is not an otherworldly being in the same sense as the resurrected Christ and the angels are, who appear as mediators in the apocalypses."[8] Yarbro Collins has definitionally relegated Mark 13 outside the realm of investigation. Likewise, no discussion of Paul's apocalypticism is relevant for her survey. What is subject to investigation for Yarbro Collins is only the theologically safe arenas of extra-canonical literature and the ever-ignored book of Revelation.[9]

This conversation is continued in the impressive tome *Apocalypticism in the Mediterranean World and the Near East*, which came out of a conference on apocalypticism in Uppsala, Sweden, in 1979 (though the papers were not published until 1983). In this volume the approach to apocalypticism was not as constrained as in *Semeia* 14. While *Semeia* 14 was only concerned with issues of genre, Uppsala, while addressing the issue of genre first, also included a section on the "Sociology of Apocalypticism and the '*Sitz im Leben*' (situation in the life of the church) of Apocalypses" as well.

---

8. Collins, "The Early Christian Apocalypses," 97.

9. Linton, "Reading the Apocalypse," has recently touched upon similar themes. His article establishes quite clearly that the nature of genre definition in general is a peculiarly limiting interpretive move. "By constructing a generic category, interpreters place boundaries around a group of works to set them off from others. By including an individual work within one of these categories, they place boundaries around it to set it off from some works and alongside others" (16). In creating a genre and then defining a text as having a position within that genre, the critic makes an interpretive move that is often hidden from view. The inclusion of a text within a genre presages particular forms of interpretation and then excludes others. While Linton's diagnosis is correct, I believe his solution which is merely to muddy the waters with talk about "hybrid" genres is problematic and ultimately he calls for the abandonment of genre altogether (41). Yet the problem is not that of genre per se but one of the exclusion that takes place because of its rigid implementation. Genre should be treated more like the Weberian notion of "ideal type." The point however of the ideal type is that it is not in any sense real—it is by design an admitted scholarly construction, nor is unitary, there may always be variety of ideal types against which to compare a phenomenon against. Thus genre as a form of ideal type is certainly important and the creation of "apocalypse" as a genre is certainly permissible and helpful in looking at a text. Likewise, as Linton points out, the genre of "prophecy" also might help, as would a variety of others like "myth" or "martyrdom narratives" to name a few.

The conference at Uppsala in many ways opened new vistas in understanding apocalypticism. Wayne Meeks's article brought the issue of Paul and apocalypticism back into focus.[10] While Meeks is a self-described functionalist,[11] his real contribution is not so much his application of theory,[12] but rather his assertion that Paul should be included again in the study of apocalypse. To make this argument he stipulates four conditions that would constitute a text as appropriately labeled as apocalyptic. Chief among these conditions are "Time moves toward that climax, which separates 'this age' from 'the age to come'" and "central among the events to happen 'at the end of days' is *judgment*."[13] Interestingly enough, he does not deal with how the message is delivered (no mandatory otherworldly messenger) but only requires that it be delivered to "the author or prophet."[14] The definitional criteria that Meeks suggests serves to bring the discussion of apocalyptic back into the canon and put Paul (and Jesus, though this is not addressed in Meeks's article[15]) back into the conversation.

The other important point Meeks's article makes is to understand the function of apocalyptic sociologically, not as a form of resistance as some scholars who I will examine later have done, but rather as an exercise of power to quell resistance. He states, "[Paul] uses future eschatological language to *restrain* innovation and to counsel stability and order . . ."[16] For Meeks, Paul employs apocalyptic language consistently

10. Meeks, "Social Functions."

11. Ibid., 687.

12. Meeks use of theory is actually fairly thin here. His major sociological reference seems to Max Weber who was *not* a functionalist, the rest of his citations come from biblical scholars who have dabbled in sociology like Berger and Gager with some reference to the literature on millennial movements from individuals like Woolsey and Burridge.

13. Meeks, "Social Functions," 689; emphasis original.

14. Ibid. Interestingly, while Meeks is aware of the *Semeia* 14 volume, he does not bother to argue with it. In fact, the only reference he has to the article in which Collins outlines the definition of genre apocalypse is in the context of Meeks preamble about the difficulty of defining apocalyptic before proceeding to generate just such a definition.

15. Luise Schottroff in her article does address Mark 13 ("Die Gegenwart"). But she does not engage the issue of genre or the work of Collins. Her work focuses more on finding a traditional *Sitz im Leben* for the synoptic apocalypse in Mark, Matthew, and Luke.

16. Meeks, "Social Functions," 700; emphasis original.

to support "solidarity and stability" in the face of perceived threats to the community.[17]

The work of the Uppsala conference, then, moves apocalypticism away from the theologically safe-harbor of the noncanonical texts and back into the mainstream of New Testament studies.[18] The final section of the Uppsala conference proceedings refocuses the discussion back to a theory of apocalyptic that is grounded in its social function for its writers/hearers.

When Adela Yarbro Collins pens the introduction to *Semeia* 36 (the second *Semeia* issue devoted to apocalypticism), then, the connection between genre and social function is no longer an issue that can be ignored. And indeed fully half of the volume is devoted to the issue of the social function of apocalypses. However, in her introduction to the volume, Yarbro Collins, who also edits this volume, is still quite critical of such attempts to amend the *Semeia* 14 definition to include social function. The pivotal points of critique for her seem to revolve around the ideas that: 1) modifications to the definition make it less useful as they include other types of data that are not apocalypses (i.e., prophecy);[19] and 2) any definition proposed must be universal. For instance, she criticizes David Hellholm's proposal that the *Semeia* 14 definition be amended to include "intended for a group in crisis with the purpose of exhortation and/or consolation by means of divine authority"[20] as problematic since "what is a crisis from the perspective of the implied author may not be a crisis from the perspective of every hearer or reader of the text."[21]

Still, the winds had changed since *Semeia* 14. In *Semeia* 36, David Hellholm makes a sophisticated argument from semiotics arguing that function is one of the three necessary components of genre.[22] David

---

17. Ibid.

18. Adela Yarbro Collins contribution to this volume even attempts to do some sort of sociological work as well. However she does it very cautiously, objecting that "generalizations about the function of apocalypticism would be premature at this stage of the discussion. The most appropriate approach for the present seems to be the investigation of the function of particular apocalyptic writings in their historical settings," Collins, "Persecution and Vengeance," 729.

19. Collins, "Introduction," 1.

20. Hellholm, "Problem of Apocalyptic Genre," 27.

21. Collins, "Introduction," 6.

22. Hellholm, "Problem of Apocalyptic Genre," 17.

Aune, agreeing with Hellholm, suggests the functions of apocalypse are legitimation and cognitive/behavioral modification.[23]

In the end then, even Yarbro Collins must concede a need for some expansion of the definition in *Semeia* 14. In order to address the issue of function she adds to John Collins original definition that apocalypses are, "intended to interpret present, earthly circumstances in light of the supernatural world and of the future, and to influence both the understanding and the behavior of the audience by means of divine authority."[24] What is important here is that even the most stalwart of those who have dismissed an understanding of apocalypticism in terms of its social function ultimately have been forced to include it in their definition of the genre.

A review of the scholarship on apocalypses, then, has shown that any theory of apocalyptic must include a discussion of the function of apocalyptic. It is not enough to understand the "what" of apocalypses; an equally important question is found in the "why" of apocalypses.

The Social Function of Apocalypticism

Having achieved general acknowledgment of the importance of the social function of apocalypticism, the next question is, what is that function? The first significant attempt at understanding the social function of apocalypticism was John G. Gager's essay "The End Time and the Rise of Community" in his 1975 classic *Kingdom and Community*.[25] Gager's essay included a potpourri of sociological and anthropological theories, but it made clear the affinity previously hinted at by anthropologists that there was a similarity between early Christianity and millenarian movements.[26]

---

23. Aune, "Genre of Apocalypse," 88.

24. Collins, "Introduction," 7. One wonders whether such a definition could withstand Collins own withering critique, since it is unclear how prophecy does not function in the same way with its formula of "thus saith the Lord."

25. It should be noted that Gager's work predates *Semeia* 14 and the discussion that we have just surveyed. His work is unconcerned with the definition of the genre of apocalyptic. However his work has continued to be highly influential in the discussion of the social function of apocalyptic.

26. Gager cites both Worsley and Burridge in the first page of his essay in Gager, *Kingdom and Community*, 20. cf. Worsley, *The Trumpet Shall Sound*. and Burridge, *New Heaven, New Earth*.

In that discussion Gager presents several key notions which have come to be dominant in any discussion of the social function of apocalypticism. The first is the concept of "relative deprivation." The work of Burridge and Worsley relate the rise of millenarianism to class and root it in economic oppression.[27] Gager, however, does not understand early Christians as economically downtrodden and therefore modifies the notion of deprivation to *relative* deprivation. Now the issue is not how poor the individual is, but their own perception of their poverty or disadvantage in relation to their expectations.[28]

Gager also introduces the notion of cognitive dissonance derived from Sociologist Leon Festinger's study on failed prophecy. Festinger argued that when a millennialist expectation is disconfirmed the result is "cognitive dissonance." What happens afterward is not necessarily the dissolution of the movement but rather an increase in evangelization.[29] Gager uses Festinger's theory of cognitive dissonance to explain both the crucifixion and the millennialist expectations of the early Christians. The disappointment which followed both the death of Jesus and the continual delay of the *parousia* constitute an example of such dissonance.[30] He couples Festinger's notion of renewed push for conversion with a need for a revised ideological component. He suggests, "the total process of adjustment includes a social (proselytism) as well as an intellectual (rationalization) component."[31] Thus there is a moment of intellectual creativity in light of the failure of the millennium to arrive.

27. Worsley, *Trumpet Shall Sound*, 225.

28. It should be noted that Worsley lays some of the groundwork for this view in the introduction to his second edition when he responds to George Shepperson's work. He concedes that among the wealthy and middle classes there can be "'miseries of the rich' and particular categories of even the rich are likely to experience frustration..."(xi) though he ultimately dismisses these groups as "coteries, not movements."(xi)

29. Festinger's study examined a U.F.O. Cult during the 1950s. At that time the cult had messianic overtones and the believers held that the U.F.O.'s would one day come and take them to their home planet. The leader of the cult twice set a date as to when this would happen. After the first failure, the community, rather than disbanding, engaged in increased evangelization for the new date that the leader had set. In the end the second date came and went as well with the result that the group ultimately disbanded. Festinger's study has not come through the years unscathed. Attempts at replicating his results have had mixed results and generally have not validated his thesis. See the collection of essays in Stone, *Expecting Armageddon*.

30. Gager, *Kingdom and Community*, 37–48.

31. Ibid. 47

Perhaps the most important element that Gager added to the conversation, however, is his theory of apocalyptic as a form of mythical psychotherapy. He states clearly, "the relationship between myth and audience parallels the relationship between analyst and patient . . ."[32] For Gager the therapeutic experience is one of experiencing the past as present. Thus in the act of hearing/reading a myth, current reality is suspended and the reality of the writing takes precedence. The future becomes present in myth in the same way that the past becomes present in therapy.[33]

Gager's theory of apocalyptic has not been widely accepted. However, the direction he takes in understanding apocalyptic as a psychological response has, in fact, dominated the discussion. The majority of scholars who have written on apocalyptic have taken the same tact as Gager, seeing apocalyptic as having some effect on the psyche and looking for an explanation within the realm of the psychoanalytic.

An example of this can be found in John J. Collins work *The Apocalyptic Imagination*. As we noted before in our examination of *Semeia* 14, the issue of the social function of apocalyptic is not something that occupies Collins's attention. He is a "hard data" man, focusing on typologies and readings of the text, only cautiously inching into more speculative arenas like authorship and provenance. When it comes to a sociology of apocalypticism Collins is skeptical. "Older scholarship in this area has suffered from excessive hastiness because of the tendency to assume that the setting of one or two well-known apocalypses is representative of the whole genre. We will refrain deliberately from applying a sociological or anthropological model."[34] He therefore gives notions of relative deprivation (though not using that term) some credence but only "if we allow that the distresses may be of various kinds"[35]

Yet Collins cannot refrain completely from addressing the issue of "literary function" of the text, largely because of the pressure we have surveyed above culminating in *Semeia* 36. He suggests, then, that

---

32. Ibid., 51.
33. Ibid., 55.
34. Collins, *Apocalyptic Imagination*, 29.
35. Ibid.

apocalyptic "provides a resolution in the *imagination* . . ."[36] He returns to this language in his conclusion, "Most of all it entails an appreciation of the great resource that lies in the human imagination to construct a symbolic world where the integrity of values can be maintained in the face of social and political powerlessness and even the threat of death."[37] Note that even Collins ultimately resorts to a psychological explanation for understanding apocalyptic. Not quite ready to follow Gager in putting the apocalypticist on the couch, Collins moves more in the direction of symbolic interaction. Still at its root, for Collins, apocalypticism is about a way of addressing a psychological state of deprivation that ultimately provides some psychic resolution.

In *Semeia* 36, David Hellholm likewise uses psychological categories in his understanding of the function of apocalyptic. Hellholm's proposed addition to the *Semeia* 14 definition "intended for a group in crisis with the purpose of exhortation and/or consolation by means of divine authority"[38] indicates this perspective clearly. Here again the language of psychology dominates the discussion of the function of apocalyptic.

Two exceptions to this trend are found in *Semeia* 36, which warrant our attention. David Aune suggests a tripartite function that invites investigation. "Function: (a) to legitimate the transcendent authorization of the message, (b) by mediating a new actualization of the original revelatory experience through literary devices, structures and imagery, which function to "conceal" the message which the text "reveals" so that (c) the recipients of the message will be encouraged to modify their cognitive and behavioral stance in conformity with transcendent perspectives."[39] In his definition Aune indicates two interesting lines of discussion. On the one hand, there is self-legitimation of the message itself. On the other hand, there is an exercise of power designed to control the hearers and produce a particular form of behavior. Aune here appeals to Hans Dieter Betz's argument that Roman apocalypses function to "scare" people into correct behavior.[40] While Aune eschews

36. Ibid., 32. emphasis mine.
37. Ibid., 215.
38. Hellholm, "Problem of Apocalyptic Genre," 27.
39. Aune, "Genre of Apocalypse," 88.
40. Betz, "Problem of Apocalyptic Genre," 595; cited in Aune, "Genre of Apocalypse," 90.

the language of power for the more theologically acceptable *"parenesis,"* he makes an important advance in the discussion when he states "in this sense apocalypses are basically ideological . . ."[41]

Likewise Leonard Thompson challenges the psychological approach to apocalyptic, particularly in regard to Revelation. Thompson does this by attacking the "crisis theory" approach. In essence he does a critical reading of the Roman sources regarding Domitian's "reign of terror" to which Revelation is understood to be a response. Thompson finds no evidence that supports this understanding of Domitian. In fact, in regards to the conflict between the wealthy and the poor, "during the reign of Domitian the emperor sought to minimize these tensions."[42] In the end, Thompson concludes, "there is no indication that a social, political climate of persecution and oppression determined Christian opinion."[43]

The result of this, then, is that Thompson causes us to ask whether crisis theory can still work if there is no crisis. Certainly, as the move from a theory of deprivation to a theory of *relative* deprivation shows, there is increasingly little ground upon which to build this notion of crisis. In fact, as Thompson points out, "such a broadening reduces the explanatory power of 'deprivation,' for . . . any person or group at any time can be seen as deprived."[44]

Thompson then proposes a different model for understanding the apocalypticism of Revelation. Instead of the crisis model, which he claims is based on binary oppositions, Thompson proposes an approach that emphasizes "proportions and homologues."[45] He explains, "With regard to the Apocalypse of John, proportions and homologues in his literary production disclose the structure processes which guide John's unfolding of Christian existence. For example, tracing references through the book to proper sexual expression yields such proportions as fornication::non-fornication::outside New Jerusalem:inside Jerusalem::outside the Church:inside the Church:social accommodation::social isolation. Every dimension, every moment, and every object that can be encoun-

---

41. Aune, "Genre of Apocalypse," 90.
42. Thompson, *Sociological Analysis*, 160.
43. Ibid., 162.
44. Ibid., 167.
45. Ibid., 168.

tered in life gains meaning by taking its place as a proportion in the seer's world."[46] Thompson has been criticized for a lack of clarity in his term "homologues,"[47] and while he rebels against a materialist reading of the text, in the end he cannot escape from it.[48] What he attempts to avoid is a "vulgar" approach to social theorizing, but certainly it can be granted that ideology functions to construct a situation as well as interpret it (as the work of Althusser has shown above). Nonetheless apocalypses (contrary to the protestations of the apocalypticists) do not appear from heaven; ultimately we must seek some kind of historical/social circumstance that produces them.

While Thompson's own interpretation is less useful, his critique of crisis theory points out the problem of unlimited elasticity in regards to the terms crisis and relative deprivation. Thus Thompson, along with Aune, points us toward looking at different categories that are not as dependent on psychoanalytic principles.

In constructing a theory of the logic of apocalyptic apart from psychological explanations, Jonathan Z. Smith's work exemplifies a different approach. Coming at the issue from the perspective of History of Religion, Smith published two seminal articles that shed light on this issue. In his first article "Wisdom and Apocalyptic" (1975), Smith furthers our understanding of apocalyptic by asking the question, "Who are apocalypticists?" In a close reading of the Babylonian ritual of the humiliation of the king, Smith comes to an important conclusion. He states: "I would argue that wisdom and apocalyptic are related in that they are both essentially scribal phenomena. It is the paradigmatic thought of the scribe—a way of thinking that is both pragmatic and

---

46. Ibid.

47. Thompson tries to be more explicit in his book on Revelation in explaining his meaning of homologues. But ultimately his definition of "any correspondence of structure, position, or character in the different dimensions of John's world" is far too general to be particularly useful. Thompson, *Book of Revelation*, 78; cf. Yarbro Collins critique of this (Collins, *Revelation*, 749).

48. Thompson even seems to back down from his position that there was no crisis. He states: "At the same time Christianity is viewed clearly as a social ill to be dealt with, if Christians are brought before a tribunal; for in that case they would probably be killed if, after due opportunity was given them, they did not confess the religious dimension of the common, public Roman life" (*Sociological Analysis*, 170.) Even if there was not a Domitian persecution, certainly a position such as Thompson describes here could be reasonably understood as a crisis or at least a dangerous situation.

speculative—which has given rise to both."[49] Further on, after a comparison with the Egyptian "Potter's Oracle," Smith extends this suggestion by noting, "I am tempted to describe apocalypticism as *wisdom lacking a royal patron*."[50]

One of the important issues here, as Smith goes on to point out,[51] is that such a contention has significant ramifications in regard to function. The notion which is found in many studies of apocalypses, that apocalypses reflect some situation of crisis and often persecution is called into question as is the notion that the apocalypse offers some sort of therapeutic response. Smith likewise questions the class basis of apocalypticism. It is not the struggling under-classes who rebel against the imperial boot; rather, apocalypticism is an elite response to political displacement.

In the examples that Smith examines what has occurred in the apocalyptic situation is the end of native kingship. Conquering powers have now installed a new king and with it a concomitant shift in royal patronage has followed. The apocalypse, then, is the wringing cry of the elites in their new situation. What is important for Smith is precisely the fact that in times of transition moments of intellectual rethinking come. Both wisdom and apocalyptic "depend on . . . the problematics of applying these paradigms to new situations . . ."[52] As the world changes the intellectual stratum is required to rethink the situation. In that period they formulate a new application of existing categories as well as the invention of new ones. Apocalypticism represents an example of this kind of intellectual labor.

Smith expands his understanding of apocalypticism in an examination of the Babylonian Atiku festival text and the Hainuwele myth from New Guinea in an article called "A Pearl of Great Price and a Cargo of Yams" (1982). Here he makes explicit the circumstance of apocalypticism. "The situation of apocalypticism seems to me to be the cessation of native kingship; the *literature* of apocalypticism appears to me to be the expression of archaic, scribal wisdom as it comes to lack a royal patron. Indeed, I would suggest further that the perception of

---

49. Smith, "Wisdom and Apocalyptic," 74.
50. Ibid., 81; emphasis original.
51. Ibid.
52. Ibid., 85.

the meaning of the fact of the cessation of native kingship moves from the *apocalyptic pattern* that the wrong king is on the throne, that the cosmos will be thereby destroyed, and that the right god will either restore proper native kingship (his terrestrial counterpart) or will assume kingship himself . . ."[53] The hallmark of apocalypticism is the recognition that there is something wrong with the world—namely "the wrong king is on the throne." Smith's theory of apocalypticism is important in that it focuses on a problem that is not theological or psychological but political.[54] Of course the solution given is one that is theologically cast; the ending of the infidel kingship is initiated not by a popular uprising (from below) but by the action of the god(s) (from above).

What is most important, however, is that Smith understands the apocalyptic situation, not as one of persecution or oppression but rather as one of "incongruity."[55] When turning to the myth of Hainuwele, Smith sees something similar to apocalyptic. In the case of New Guinea, the advent of colonial contact has caused a breakdown in the indigenous system of exchange. The result is once again a situation of incongruity just as it is in the origin of apocalypses.

What the myth does, however, is also essential to Smith's theory of apocalyptic, because it "does not solve the problem, overcome the incongruity, or resolve the tension. Rather it results in thought. It is a testing of the adequacy and applicability of traditional patterns and categories to new situations and data in hopes of achieving rectification. It is an act of native exegetical ingenuity, a process of native work."[56] Smith's theory of apocalyptic is not that it engages some psychological need but rather produces an *intellectual* response to a situation of incongruity, a desire for, as Smith calls it, "intelligibility."[57]

Smith, then, aids our understanding of the logic of apocalyptic in two ways. First, by situating the class of the apocalypticists in the tradition of the learned scribes, we are forced to abandon notions of

---

53. Smith, "Pearl of Great Price," 94; emphasis original.

54. It should of course be acknowledged that the distinction between the political and the theological is a modern concept that is less applicable to antiquity. Nonetheless, moderns reading the texts often view the texts as expressions of spirituality. Smith refocuses our attention on the issues of class and power.

55. Smith, "Pearl of Great Price," 94.

56. Ibid., 100–101.

57. Ibid., 101.

apocalyptic as an expression of proletariat protest. While the apocalypticist may, in fact, now be poor and oppressed, their worldview, their *habitus* (to use Pierre Bourdieu's category)[58] is not of the lower classes. The second way Smith helps us is that he demonstrates the concern of the writer of apocalyptic is not one of psychological solace or militant action; it is rather a moment of creative intellectual problem-solving.

But there is another component to apocalyptic that corresponds to Smith's analysis. The logic of apocalyptic is also related to the issue of power. David Aune's and Wayne Meeks's work above gave us the first hint of this. Part of the apocalypse is a desire to exert pressure on the reader to produce a set of appropriate behaviors. John Collins also makes this point when he indicates, "Apocalypses surely were written to exhort and console. We should note, however, that exhortation and consolation are not the same thing, and that the nature of the exhortation is in no way implied in the apocalyptic form. Some of the apocalypses we have reviewed here were militant . . . Other apocalypses are quietistic . . . In some of these texts, the expectation of an 'end' seems to neutralize any urge toward militant action: God will act in the proper time; the pious person should wait patiently."[59] In either case, whether militant or quietistic, the apocalypse seeks to enforce a certain kind of behavior. The apocalypticist uses fear as a form of control of his/her audience.[60]

We can see this clearly in Revelation where the author is thundering against his opponent whom he calls "Balaam." His exhortation is "Repent then! If not, I will come to you soon and make war against them with the sword of my mouth (*romaphaia tou stomatos mou*)" (Rev 2:16). Of course, the sword immediately conjures up the vision which John has recounted in Rev 1:16, and will be brought back to mind in 19:15 in the final apocalyptic battle where Jesus is flanked by the armies of heaven and defeats the armies of the beast with the sword that comes out of his mouth (*romaphaia . . . te exelthouse ek tou stomatos autou*) (19:21). John threatens the followers of Balaam with the sword of Jesus if they do not correct their behavior and then shows quite graphically what that sword is capable of (namely the destruction of all the armies

---

58. Boudieu and Wacquant, *Invitation*.

59. Collins, "Prophecy to Apocalypticism," 159.

60. A point Hans Dieter Betz makes that is not relegated exclusively to Christian or Jewish apocalypses ("Problem of Apocalyptic Genre," 594–96).

of the world). The microcosm of behavioral demands in chapter 2, then, is reinforced in a macrocosmic way in chapter 19.

As important as the aspect of control is to the logic of apocalypticism, the basis of this control is ultimately rooted in a faith in divine action. At the bottom, the foundation of any attempt to compel a certain behavior is the promise that God will back the apocalypticist in the end, either though vengeance or reward in the afterlife/eschaton. John Collins puts this eloquently when he states, "The consolation of apocalyptic hope may have been considerable in the short term, but it was highly prone to disillusionment. It is the nature of apocalyptic eschatology that it cannot be fully realized in this life... Apocalyptic hope is invariably hope deferred."[61] The ultimate actor, then, in the apocalyptic drama is always the divinity. While the believers may be called to perform certain behaviors to ready themselves or even participate in the apocalypse, in the end it is the action of God that initiates and terminates the final battle, not the believers'.

Toward a Theory of Apocalypticism

If we take together the various thinkers we have surveyed, we come up with a whole picture of the logic of apocalypticism. Apocalyptic is a move of the powerful who have encountered a world which no longer works with the categories which have secured their power in the past. This incongruous situation calls for new experimentation with ideas and myths. The result of this, then, is that the forms of power and control that have previously been effective no longer can be counted on. Instead, there is the need for new categories, new mechanisms of control. The creation of apocalypses and apocalyptic myths is the result of this new creative moment. In the moment of change, there is an invention of new ways of understanding the world and of exercising control. Apocalyptic functions to try to enforce determined modes of behavior backed by threat and promise. Ultimately, however, apocalyptic must be thought of as a transitional form of control. Its dependence on divine action for fulfillment means that it has only short-term utility. Soon its power will wane.

---

61. Collins, "From Prophecy to Apocalypticism," 159.

By integrating the issue of power into our analysis, we solve part of the problem scholars have had understanding apocalyptic. As we have seen, the category of "crisis" and its counterpoint "relative deprivation" make sense only if we are to understand apocalyptic as the "cry of the oppressed masses." But if instead we follow the path of Smith and others who see this not as a bottom up movement, but as a top down phenomenon then the only "crisis" that must exist in the apocalyptic situation is a challenge to authority. This challenge to authority may have its roots in a historical situation like the destruction of Jerusalem or the fall of the temple (cf. Mark 13), but it may only be a struggle in the group as seen in the seven letters in Revelation. Couple this with the insights of Smith, who understands the creators of apocalyptic as the purveyors of wisdom doing their trade in another venue, and we may dispense with the necessity of a historically grounded crisis. A historical crisis *may* spark an apocalypse, but it is not required.

The goal of apocalyptic, then, in light of this new incongruous situation, is to build a new intellectual construct that makes the world intelligible. But likewise it also re-establishes the authority of those who must worry about becoming irrelevant in a new environment. The apocalyptic system, then, works to invoke a new (or revised) set of categories but does not simply do so for its own sake but for the sake of control and legitimacy. The ultimate guarantor here is the divine, and yet the danger is that apocalyptic involves betting the farm on a long-shot. Ultimately, the end will not arrive, and the promised divine action will not occur. The result of this "failed prophecy" is another problem, but one the writers of apocalyptic texts are willing to leave for the future.

The Logic of Three Systems—Conclusion

The three ideological systems that we have examined here all operate using a distinct set of presuppositions. They each have a logic and a worldview that is uniquely their own. They intersect in various ways particularly around the notions of action and religion. The answers they give, however, are very different.

We have seen that Marxism takes a dim view of religion. The tradition of Marxism has seen religion as an impediment to revolution. Religion, as a paradigmatic ideology, serves to prop up the capitalist establishment. Any attempt to create change, then, is only hampered by religion rather than aided by it.

To this end, an attempt to make a connection with Liberation Theology is entirely problematic. Liberation Theology relies on the use of Marxist analysis in an attempt to diagnosis the problems of Latin America. Its conclusion, that the class oppression of the third world by the industrialized world and the dependence that is fostered therein is a valid application of Marxist principals. Yet, as Liberation Theologians have seen themselves, the Marxist apparatus also entails precisely this negative evaluation of religion that we reviewed in a previous chapter. Liberation Theologians understand the implementation of Marxist analysis is at best problematic. This is why such luminaries of Liberation Theology like Gutierrez and Segundo have worked to intellectually mitigate their dependence on Marxism.

Likewise, Liberation Theology avoids apocalypticism. Our examination of the logic of apocalyptic has made clear why this is the case. Apocalyptic may at the outset appear to offer a critical take on an oppressive society, yet it does so at the cost of a complete reliance on the divinity for actual liberation. It is only God who initiates and finally enacts the revolution. Humans are merely spectators in this divine drama. This is not the sort of direct action that the adherents of Liberation Theology want. The Liberation Theologians want to empower individuals to rise up together and make real social change. They reject the notion that God will do it for them.

Additionally, the conclusion that apocalyptic functions more often for the exercise of power than for the freedom of the oppressed is contraindicative to the aims of Liberation Theologians. Nonetheless, such a reading would in fact validate the skeptical perspective of Liberation Theology towards apocalypticism.

Finally, Marxism itself is as critical of apocalypticism as Liberation Theology is and for some of the same reasons. The reliance on a mythical entity for change would be rejected wholeheartedly by the Marxists we have examined. Additionally, it is interesting to note that the Marxist thinkers whom we have examined do not engage in apocalyptic speculation themselves. The reason for this is that Marxism sees itself as a science not a mythology or religion. Its interest is generally in a critical examination of the world as it is, rather than utopian dreams of the "end of time."[62] In fact, one criticism that might be made of Marx is that he did entirely too little reflection on post-revolutionary life.

The analysis of the logic of apocalyptic that has been done here might likewise show a basic correlation with the Marxist appraisal of religion. The idea that apocalyptic might function as a way of re-instituting power ideologically in a changed social environment would find an appreciative audience in Marxism.[63] Marxism, then, must ultimately reject apocalypticism as one more "imaginary" solution to the problems of society.

Thus, we see that there are clear points of conflict between each of these ideologies. There are key presuppositions that cannot be ignored. It is these assumptions, and the logics that they thereby create that forms the outline of these ideologies. In each case, as we have seen, each ideology holds exclusive claims which reject and are rejected by the claims of the others.

This leads us then to the next section. Those who have attempted Marxist approaches to the New Testament, in fact, try to do what the authors of these ideologies themselves have not done. They have attempted to merge these three ideologies in a variety of ways. I will next closely examine precisely this sort of conjunction and look at the ways that scholars have addressed these issues.

---

62. Here I am speaking only of the authors I have surveyed. There certainly may be what might called "Marxist Fiction," a most interesting modern example is Ursula LeGuin's *The Dispossessed*. Perhaps the movie trilogy "The Matrix" might also fall into this category.

63. This may not be a particularly surprising result. Many of the thinkers who have been influential in following this line of reasoning in looking at the sources and effects of power (Weber, Bourdieu, Foucault, etc.) all have been influenced to a greater or lesser degree by Marxist thinkers.

4

Marxist New Testament Interpreters

MARXISM MADE ITSELF KNOWN IN BIBLICAL STUDIES THROUGH THE advent of Liberation Theology. New Testament interpreters were often attracted to Liberation Theology and sought to overcome the divide between Marxist analysis and Christianity by identifying the message of Christianity as sympathetic with Marxist goals: the liberation of the poor and oppressed.

These New Testament interpreters were aided to some degree by clues from the Liberation Theologians themselves. Gustavo Gutierrez whose *Theology of Liberation* is the classic text of the liberation theology movement provides an example,

> Contemporary man . . . has gradually abandoned a simple reformist attitude regarding the existing social order, for by its very shallowness this reformism perpetuates the existing system. The revolutionary situation which prevails today, especially in the third world is an expression of this growing radicalization. To support the social revolution means to abolish the present status quo and to attempt to replace it with a qualitatively different one; it means an attempt to put an end to the domination of some countries by others, of some social classes by others, of some people by others. The liberation of these countries, social classes and people undermines the very foundation of the present order.[1]

Certainly the language here is striking. Gutierrez rejects reformism explicitly and demands the elimination of "the present status quo" and "the present order." Such language is akin to the Biblical tradition of apocalypticism. Apocalypticism too envisions a complete change of the social order which it views as corrupt and oppressive. As we have seen in

1. Gutierrez, *Theology of Liberation*, 48.

our survey, there are significant problems in regards to the application of apocalypticism for Liberation Theology. Yet for individuals working with the concept of liberation in the New Testament, apocalypticism bridges both the Marxist critique of capitalism as well as the Biblical demand for justice.

In this chapter I will begin looking at Marxist approaches to the New Testament. I will specifically examine individuals coming out of the Marxist tradition who are reading the biblical text. I call these individuals "Marxist New Testament interpreters." While these individuals may have had formal training in Biblical Studies they are not considered New Testament Scholars *per se*. However, their work has been tremendously influential in the field of New Testament studies, particularly in attempts to apply Marxism to the text.

My argument will show a common set of problems for these interpreters. Individuals reading the text from a Marxist perspective are consistently drawn to the more apocalyptic texts that speak of a radical world-altering moment in which injustice and poverty are vanquished. These texts envision a social revolution that is appealing to Marxist scholars. And yet, the fly in the ointment in these texts is that the revolution they predict is not the rising up of the proletariat, but rather the supernatural intervention of a supreme being. Often, particularly in Christian apocalyptic texts, believers are bystanders in the final battle (at least believers who are still alive), the army which battles the forces of oppression is composed of angels and/or the souls of martyred believers not the (very human) vanguard party.

Apocalyptic, then, is a two-edged sword. On the one hand, it envisions a world free of oppression, where justice and right prevail, and it does so in a single radical transformative moment. On the other hand, it generally excludes any human source for this transformation, opting instead for divine power over people power. Our analysis of apocalypticism in the previous chapter shows why this is and how apocalypticism functions to sustain authority within the apocalyptic community. Thus, the Marxists who I will examine here must wrestle precisely with the contradictions that apocalyptic presents them. What we will see is an intricate dance which embraces part of the apocalyptic message while at the same time attempting to side-step the core of its logic, a dance that ultimately consists of a series of logical and textual pirouettes.

Jose Porofino Miranda: *Marx and the Bible*

Jose Porofino Miranda is a noted liberation theologian who takes the study of the Bible seriously.[2] His book *Marx and the Bible* is a manifesto of Christian theology from a Marxist perspective. He begins quite boldly by arguing that the Bible condemns private property. Indeed from Miranda's perspective it can do nothing else because private ownership requires exploitation which in turn requires violence.[3] In contrast Miranda notes that "almsgiving" is sometimes equated with "justice" in certain biblical texts. This, he suggests, is entirely comprehensible since almsgiving is in fact merely returning to the poor what was stolen from them. In this way, then, it is justice. Miranda cites the standard Biblical passages from Jesus and the Prophets and while he is willing to engage the issue of whether a particular saying is authentic[4] he takes the position (a theological one to be sure) that the Bible speaks with one voice and that the authors of the Biblical texts are in unity–especially on this issue of justice for the poor and condemnation of the system of private property.

Thus, Miranda is clearly not interested in specific exegetical problems like categorizing the authentic sayings of the historical Jesus; his sights are set on a much larger target. Miranda wants to give his readers a Marxist reading of the entire Bible. Flying from the Hebrew Bible to the New Testament and back again, comparing the prophets and Paul, Matthew and the epistles of John, Miranda argues that the Bible has a single unified message that is based on the nature of God. That message is that God cannot be known apart from justice. It is through justice that God is revealed.

One is immediately struck by the audacity of such a reading. To attempt a reading of the entire text is quite an undertaking. But Miranda knows his biblical scholarship and is quick to cite leaders in the field in his analysis of the various texts. However, he fails to take sufficient account of the historical, social, and political situations that generate these texts. In particular, Miranda employs prophetic texts from Jeremiah,

---

2. Gottwald and Horsley, *Bible in Latin American Theology*.

3. Miranda, *Marx and the Bible*, 23.

4. An example of this is Miranda's interesting argument for the authenticity of the "eye of needle" saying, suggesting that the idea of it being difficult for a rich person to enter heaven was so outrageous that it had to stem from Jesus (17).

Isaiah, Hosea, and others that are sometimes in conflict with one another on pivotal issues. However, since Miranda ultimately sees a unity of Scripture he feels free to employ texts without the necessary historical/social contextualization.

But a critique like the one I have just provided perhaps misses the point for Miranda, because he is not really interested in engaging biblical scholars or the historical issues surrounding the texts. What Miranda is doing is creating a theology. This theology has links to the existentialist theology of neo-orthodoxy that was prevalent during the 1960s when he was writing. One of the primary tenets of neo-orthodoxy was to dispute/abandon the idea of talking about God. The adherents of neo-orthodoxy held that God cannot be grasped by human comprehension. Such a God would be, to use the phrase cited so often from Rudolf Otto, "Wholly Other."[5] The founders of neo-orthodoxy called not for knowledge about God (which ultimately was impossible), but rather a response *to* God.

The God of liberation, on the other hand is cast as deliverer, as the one who intervenes into human history on the side of justice. Miranda, then, blends historical narrative with apocalyptic language; he is able to incorporate both the Exodus and the Kingdom of God language of Jesus. It is an earthly kingdom that Jesus has in mind, says Miranda, one that is just and not oppressive. That such a kingdom requires the entire reshaping of the current world does not trouble Miranda, for he knows our world needs just such a radical reshaping. This apocalyptic language is contrasted with heavenly language—it is on earth that this kingdom is to come, not in heaven, as some of the texts seem to contend.

The use of apocalyptic language is seen clearly in Miranda's chapter on Law. There he seems to be setting up what we will see done in a more sophisticated way in the work of Richard Horsley. First, he interprets the Greek word *krienen* to mean to "deal justly" or "to create justice." The bent here is obviously activist. Miranda goes even further and grounds his analysis in the Hebrew text where he interprets *mišpaṭ* as essentially the same thing as *krienen* and understands the "war of Yahweh" as a war

---

5. Otto, *Idea of the Holy*. The influence of this book on Rudolf Bultmann, one of the most notable neo-orthodox theologians, is seen throughout his writings. Most notably it can be seen in Bultmann's essay "What Does It Mean to Speak of God?" where he lays out a neo-orthodox theology of God that is founded on Otto's concept of "Wholly Other."

for justice. He then goes on to relate this to the last judgment, which is now no longer in the eschaton. He is very clear when he proclaims, "There is an *ultimum* in human history, and this *ultimum* is defined and characterized, as in Marx, by the complete realization of justice on earth."[6]

Miranda uses Jesus to support this notion of justice, and he invokes an understanding of Jesus quite common especially to neo-orthodox scholars. Here the idea of "realized eschatology" is key. The notion of realized eschatology is found in the New Testament (particularly in John) as an expression of the idea that the kingdom of God is at once both present and future. In John, one sees the expression "I tell you . . . is coming and is now here" (*lego humin erchetai hora kai nun estin*). The idea of "realized eschatology" plays with the eschatological notions of the future in an attempt to make them immediately present in Jesus. Miranda picks up this idea and connects it with his notion of justice from the Hebrew Bible. Jesus, then, is the imposition of God on earth. Through Jesus, God delivers an act of justice in the world. Jesus acts as deliverer and seeks to wipe out injustice. In these acts, Jesus manifests Yahweh to his contemporaries.

What we see here is the beginning of a Christology that Miranda will expand upon. It is thoroughly liberationist in that it focuses on justice, yet it also invokes apocalyptic motifs while at the same time subverting these same motifs. Jesus is God in the sense that God is known and is present through justice. Insofar as Jesus embodies justice, he too embodies God. The death of Jesus is the ultimate example of the injustice of civilization and the law. Thus this Christology is incarnational, but only insofar as Jesus incarnates justice over against an unjust world.

When it comes to the concept of faith, we once again see in Miranda the use of apocalyptic in service of the idea of justice. In fact, faith is faith in God who is expressed in justice. Miranda expresses this in a tripartite formulation: First, there is the identification of faith as hope. This is a hope that believes that there is hope for the world, that the world is not beyond salvation, that a just world is still a possibility. Second, faith is believing in God as the one who intervenes in history on behalf of justice. It is this God that is the rationale for hope. Third,

---

6. Miranda, *Marx and the Bible*, 137.

faith is the belief that this hope has taken on a tangible form in the historical event called Jesus Christ. In Jesus, the kingdom of God, which is justice, breaks into the world.

But here we begin to see the problem, for this is the kind of potent language which is tripped up by an unkind reality. The world is not just. Two thousand years after the momentous declaration by Jesus that the Kingdom is now here, we find in reality the kingdom is nowhere. The rich get richer, and the powerful exploit the powerless. The poor are still abundant, and the widow and orphan remain neglected. What then shall we make of the messy problem that Jesus (and Miranda eagerly links him to Paul, the Synoptics, and the Law and the Prophets of the Hebrew Bible) was clearly wrong? The apocalyptic language invoked by Miranda and the Bible leads one to anticipate strong divine action, yet one is left not with a divine bang but a very human whimper.

To Miranda's credit, he dismisses the attempts of the neo-orthodox thinkers to try to de-temporalize talk of the eschaton. Bultmann's solution was to personalize the apocalyptic through existential categories.[7] It is not the entire world that God will destroy and then rebuild, by *my personal* world that comes under the claim of God. Miranda will have none of this.

Miranda's solution is to transform the kingdom from object to imperative. Rather than understanding the Kingdom of God as a new order imposed by divine fiat that is irresistible and global in nature, Miranda understands the kingdom of God as a divine command for human action. He states, "The *proclamation* that the Kingdom is *arriving* has to *make* the Kingdom *arrive*."[8] This explains both the present and future references to the kingdom found in both John and Paul. And in fact, Miranda argues that the Kingdom has been kept from arriving precisely because believers fail to understand the human obligation to bring the Kingdom of Justice into being. "There is nothing that the west fears so much as our being convinced that the Kingdom of God has come. To the extent that we should realize that Jesus is the Messiah,

---

7. An illustration of this can be seen in Bultmann's sermon on Mark 13:31–33 where he expounds the verse "Heaven and earth will pass away" as "our lives will reach their term, when heaven and earth will in any case pass away for us, even though they continue to subsist for a time as afar as coming generations are concerned" (Bultmann, *World and the Beyond*).

8. Miranda, *Marx and the Bible*, 245.

the Kingdom of God would be achieved. The 'outcry' of the oppressed would cease forever, that 'outcry' which caused Yahweh to intervene in our history."[9] In the end, then, Miranda's solution is another strain of existential exegesis of apocalyptic along the same lines as Bultmann. But while Bultmann's work sent the entire apocalyptic discussion in to the personal sphere; Miranda, on the other hand, wants to maintain the vision of a new world ensconced in the apocalyptic while at the same time making it an historical, human event not a divine act. This is a fine line that Miranda attempts to walk.

Of course Miranda's solution comes at the price of sacrificing the clear message of many biblical texts. It is true that John and Paul often talk of the "already and not yet" as I have mentioned before. But the simple fact of the matter is that neither John nor Paul believed that the "not yet" would extend twenty centuries. Paul especially sees the *parousia* as an imminent event as Miranda himself admits.[10] While the later New Testament writers clearly struggle with the delay of the *parousia*, Revelation shows patently that such hope was not lost even at the end of the first century. There is often a human element involved in apocalyptic. Daniel speaks of "a little help" (Dan 11:34) and Mark states that, "the good news must first be proclaimed to all nations" (Mark 13:10). Yet Daniel, Mark and Revelation as well as 1 Thessalonians envision not the slowly growing bush of the mustard seed parable, but the invasion of the divine army wiping out the enemy and creating a new world.

To be fair, Miranda would reject this analysis. He would see it as an example of the ideology of the "eternal return" which is part and parcel of bourgeois western culture. It is precisely because we refuse to imagine a new world that we do not *have* a new world. Moreover, Miranda steadfastly holds, "It is not faithful to the Bible to attribute a really new *eschaton* exclusively to the fact that God intervenes from outside of history. This is not what the Bible teaches. According to Paul, the real concrete possibility of something truly new and unprecedented comes from the immanent development of history itself, directed, it is true, by God."[11]

---

9. Ibid., 249.
10. Ibid., 46.
11. Ibid., 279.

Miranda's final chapter shows perfectly his application of apocalyptic language. In this chapter, Miranda criticizes Marx himself for a failure of nerve. Marx does not envision a resurrection of the dead. Miranda demands that this is part and parcel of envisioning a new world free of injustice. Death, he argues, is in fact a result of the injustice in the world. He marshals Freud and Igor Caruso to back this point.[12] In the end, he states, the resurrection of the dead is the logical outcome of a thoroughgoing dialectics. "The negation of the resurrection of the dead is an ideology defensive of the status quo; it is the silencing of the sense of justice that history objectively stirs up; it is to kill the nerve of real hope of changing this world. The authentically dialectical Marxist and the Christian who remains faithful to the Bible are the last who will be able to renounce the resurrection of the dead."[13] This final move indicates the scope of Miranda's entire project. Miranda looks to create a biblically based liberation theology, one which is informed by biblical scholarship. And to this end, he employs great erudition in his philological discussions citing many of the most respected names of 1960's biblical scholarship. But in the final analysis he misses the trees for the forest. His desire to see a unified vision of the Bible as a single voice against oppression and injustice neglects the logic of the apocalyptic solutions that the Bible does in fact contain, as well as the injustices it perpetrates itself.

Miranda's work, then, attempts to draw a line encompassing both the Bible and Marxism. It is ultimately an argument that Christians are not in conflict with Marxism but rather that Christianity is a different expression of the same goals as Marxism. To do this, he creates a reading of the text which is vast and sweeping and which envisions the God of the Bible as the one who intervenes on the side of the poor and the oppressed in the name of Justice. This reading consistently employs apocalyptic tropes and texts in constructing this God. But ultimately Miranda must suppress the eschatological answer that many of the Biblical texts give to the problem of injustice.

From the study of the ideologies we have already done, Miranda has two problems. Certainly, as we have seen previously, the bright lights of Marxism would clearly disagree with an analysis which equates

12. Ibid., 281–84.
13. Ibid., 284–85.

Christianity and Marxism. His attempt to find revolutionary themes in the text is ultimately mitigated by the theological/mythical categories that he must use to express it. Ultimately Miranda stays at the "illusory" level; while calling for a revolution, he grounds that calling in a form that Marxists would see as contradictory to his goal.

Secondly, the appeal to apocalyptic fails as well. As has been made clear, Miranda must subvert the basic premise of apocalyptic which is founded on the response of the deity coming to set things right. The Kingdom of Justice is promised as the future act of God not the present acts of believers. Yet part of the reason apocalyptic cannot do what Miranda wants is that it is, as we have seen, set up intrinsically not to enforce justice but to sustain power. That Miranda works so hard to channel the impact of apocalyptic shows precisely the problematic nature of its logic.

Mark and Apocalypticism

The apocalyptic nature of Mark is a key point for several Marxist interpretations of Mark. It is also an important component of the argument presented here. As we will see Marxist approaches seem perennially drawn to the Gospel of Mark. Perhaps this is a result of the fallacy that sees Mark as closer to the historical point of origination and therefore a more reliable witness. However, it is my contention that like moths to the flame, Marxists are drawn to apocalyptic fantasies that have the audacity to envision bold new worlds. Yet, in this context such benefit comes at the price of the new world not arising from the masses throwing off their chains, but from the divine descending from on high.

It is therefore appropriate to lay out the argument for the apocalyptic nature of Mark. The history of this position is quite long and complicated. It is particularly problematized by the distinction made by neo-orthodox critics in the post-war era between "eschatological" and "apocalyptic." Eschatological texts are "world-shattering" (a term comfortable for existentialism) but did not necessarily deal with the end of time or the end of the physical world. Apocalyptic on the other hand is constituted by a hardnosed prophetic vision that sees the world is soon to end, often in fire and destruction.

Such a distinction can be seen in James M. Robinson's work *The Problem of History in Mark*. In dealing with the prologue of Mark and the exorcisms, Robinson shows that they are connected in envisioning a cosmic battle between Jesus and the forces of darkness. "The fact that the terms 'stronger,' 'Spirit,' and 'Satan' at the centre of the prologue form a coherent meaning of eschatological struggle has been confirmed by the exorcism debate, where all three elements recur."[14] Yet, lest we confuse such a conclusion with an instance of apocalyptic battle, Robinson clarifies his meaning by chastising Lightfoot who "erroneously sees in the temptation the whole of a preliminary struggle with evil which apocalypticism expected just before the end."[15]

For Robinson, then, in Mark there is a division between the "eschatological existence" of the believer into which the Christian is ushered into upon conversion and the apocalyptic "new Aeon" which is yet to come. This is part of the "already-not yet" conception that Cullmann popularized in his *Christ and Time*.[16] Such an approach is a deft theological move as it allows for the present time that has more theological importance than as just the hiatus before the end. The believer's "eschatological existence" is about living as if the Kingdom of God were here now, all the while allowing for its (infinite) deferral.

Yet the advantage of Robinson's analysis is that he recognizes the pieces of the argument that advance the thesis of Mark's apocalyptic nature. The understanding of miracles and exorcisms as battles in a cosmic conflict provides an important component.[17] Apocalyptic is often characterized by the battle between light and dark, the forces of good battling the forces of evil.[18] An interpretation of Mark that understands Jesus waging this war inevitably leads to an apocalyptic conclusion.

---

14. Robinson, *Problem of History*.

15. Ibid.

16. Cullmann, *Christ and Time*.

17. It is important to note that Robinson does not use the term "apocalyptic" in his description and rather is content referring to "cosmic conflict."

18. The inclusion of a cosmic battle in apocalyptic texts is by no means unique; it is seen clearly in Daniel, 1 Enoch and most importantly in the War Scroll from Qumran. The notion of apocalyptic is itself somewhat problematic as a wide variety of texts are labeled apocalypses by their authors, some with very little eschatological language (cf. Collins, *Morphology of a Genre*). However, it is clear that despite its problems it is the language used in New Testament studies as a synonym for "eschatological" (though sometimes freighted with theological baggage) and therefore the language I will employ here.

Norman Perrin's standard *The New Testament* argues that it is the structure of Mark that marks it as apocalyptic. In each of three parts there is a consistent pattern: Preaching and then the messenger is "delivered up." The Gospel of Mark begins this pattern with its introduction and the preaching of John the Baptist. Jesus continues this same sequence and then in Mark 13 predicts the same to happen to the church. At that moment then, the curtain is brought down at the end of the third act with the return of the Son of Man in the clouds.[19]

Adela Yarbro Collins makes a similar argument though based on genre.[20] She argues that Mark should be considered "an apocalyptic historical monograph."[21] What this means is that Mark is an innovative combination of an "apocalyptic view of history" which refers to the cosmic battles of Jesus and the moments of divine intervention in Mark's story (i.e. the baptism, transfiguration) and a "realistic historical narrative."[22] Yarbro Collins concludes that there are only vague similarities between Mark and other apocalypses, but what they do share is this "apocalyptic view of history" with its cosmic battles, the imposition of divine control on events and an interest in politics.

It is the work of Burton Mack which has most pointedly made the argument for the apocalyptic nature of Mark. Mack shows in his book *Myth of Innocence* that apocalyptic themes pervade the gospel of Mark. Building on the work of Norman Petersen, Mack specifically rejects the idea that Mark 13 (the so-called "little apocalypse") is an insertion of a pre-existing source by the author which is unrelated to the entirety of his text. Rather Mack argues in the strongest possible terms that Mark must be considered a holistic authorial work.[23] Mark was author, not editor, and Mark 13 "is critical, therefore, for the composition and intention of the gospel as a whole."[24]

19. Perrin, *New Testament*.
20. Collins, *Beginning of the Gospel.*.
21. Ibid., 27.
22. Ibid., 34.

23. This is not to suggest that Mack rejects the use of sources by Mark. In fact, an important aspect of his argument is precisely the use of a variety of sources that give us entrée into the different worlds of first century Christianity. But his argument hinges on the idea that even with the inclusion of external sources Mark's Gospel represents a single vision that receives its most complete expression in Mark 13.

24. Mack, *Myth*, 326. Correspondingly, even a conservative scholar like Beasley-Murray, after an exhaustive examination of the literature on the subject is forced to the

In the end, it is Mark's creativity that is primary for Mack, not his sources. This all ties into the discussion of the apocalyptic nature of the gospel of Mark. The apocalyptic orientation that is highlighted in Mark 13 is rampant throughout Mark's gospel.

If Mark's gospel is dependent upon apocalyptic thinking not just in Mark 13, but throughout the text, then an approach which attempts to separate the apocalyptic from the non-apocalyptic in Mark founders. The problem with apocalyptic in Mark is it is not just an ancillary redaction created to deal with a social problem that can be separated from the text. The apocalyptic mentality makes up the entirety of the text. Jesus, in Mark, is an apocalyptic warrior engaged in a battle with the powers of darkness from the moment he appears on the world stage. His crucifixion merely indicates a short delay of the apocalypse that, as events in Mark's time are making clear, is soon to be finished. Mark casts his lot completely with apocalypticism and it is the final guarantor of the kingdom for him. Attempts to neutralize this position ultimately must ignore the pervasiveness of this mindset in Mark or must explain it away. With this understanding of Mark at hand let us turn to some Marxists who have been drawn to this gospel.

Fernando Belo: *A Materialist Reading of the Gospel of Mark*

Fernando Belo's book, *A Materialist Reading of the Gospel of Mark* is generally considered one of the founding books of Marxist approaches to the New Testament. It is certainly the book which marks the entrance of Marxist approaches into the most recent discussion of New Testament scholarship and social science approaches. Belo's book is especially important, in my view, because it attempts in a systematic way to bridge the gap between New Testament Studies and Marxist praxis. And it is precisely that last part, the issue of praxis, which sets the tone for all Marxist analysis to come. For Belo and those who will follow him do not set upon the texts of the New Testament with a feigned disinter-

---

same conclusion: "it was difficult for me not to acknowledge Mark's hand throughout the length of the discourse. 'Conservative redactor' he may have been, but the whole discourse bears the imprint of his style." He goes on immediately to maintain the possibility of it being based on a source (Beasley-Murray, *Last Days*, 363).

est. Instead, there is a clear and present message contained in his study that identifies forthrightly with the movement of Liberation Theology.

The interest in Mark is itself a point for discussion. The gospel of Mark is marked by its apocalyptic tone. As I have just noted the message of Mark is one that is consistently future-oriented and finds its pinnacle in the little apocalypse of Mark 13.[25] There Mark makes clear, with his famous insertion "let the reader understand," that the apocalyptic discussion of Jesus is not idle soothsaying but of essential relevance for his readers. The past of Jesus's ministry and the present of Mark's community come together in this apocalyptic passage and reveal the message and the promise of the text.

That Marxist interpreters, then, should focus upon this text with its promise of divine intervention against the powers that oppress the people of its target community is both understandable and perplexing. It brings to the fore an issue that we have dealt with before: The ideological nature of apocalyptic notions. The key to deliverance in Mark is not found in the revolution of the Jesus movement but the coming of the Kingdom of God with power. This message of deliverance is a consistent deferral of present action to the future. Though it is expected to be imminent, it constitutes a denial of current personal/collective power in lieu of a coming supernatural power. Thus, for the Marxist interpreter one would expect that Mark offers on the one hand an acceptable diagnosis but on the other, as we have seen, an unacceptable prescription.

Belo's attempt to deal with the preceding is extremely instructive. Belo begins his particular reading of Mark with an appropriation of French Marxism, particularly the work of Althusser as well as a heavy dose of French literary structuralism, following Roland Barthes. His introductory "essay in formal theory" has given his readers headaches and is the cause for apologies both by the author and the publisher.[26] In some cases reviewers have encouraged reading the text in different order or skipping the first section altogether.

Yet it is worth noting several issues that Belo deals with in this first, theoretical section. First, regarding the concern which has previously beset the dialog between Christianity and Marxism—base/superstruc-

---

25. See discussion above.
26. Belo, *Materialist Reading*, xi, xiii.

ture—Belo quickly dispenses with this issue. He does this by creating three infrastructural categories: the infraeconomic, the infrapolitical or symbolic and the infraideological. Clearly, by making this move, Belo has moved ideology back into the infrastructure and thereby rendered the entire base/superstructure model superfluous. Thus, when he comes to defining superstructure, he states firmly that it "in every case already overdetermines the infrastructural"[27] which of course it must because it is now theoretically indistinguishable from the infrastructural. No longer epiphenomenal, Belo instead makes the superstructure the concrete instantiation of the infrastructure.[28]

Second, as will become clear, Belo is really not interested in moving behind the text to history. While he does spend some time discussing first century Palestine and Ancient Israel, his method is to "read" the various codes in the text following the work of French structuralists. So Belo uses some historical data to contextualize the text, but largely is interested in the text *qua* text.

Belo thus identifies four dominant codes in Mark. The first is the "mythological code" which includes miracles, apocalyptic sayings and the manifestations of the supernatural. The "actant code" is the acts of Jesus and the responses they provoke. The narrative is articulated in the "analytic code." Finally, there is the "social code." There are also a variety of other codes that Belo identifies, but they all play a largely subordinate role to the codes I have noted above. In the largest part of Belo's book, he goes through the text of Mark, pericope by pericope, drawing out the various strands of the codes that are contained in each one.

Several things result from this parsing. First, Belo finds that Jesus's strategy is opposed to the strategy of the zealots who are given voice by the crowd.[29] To that end, Belo argues that the "basilica" code in Mark (the code of the Kingdom of God) represents Jesus's alternative to the Zealots. The Zealots took an anti-Roman position that in Mark is

27. Ibid., 9.
28. Ibid.
29. The debate about Jesus's relation to the Zealots is a hotly contested issue (as we will discuss later). The argument that Jesus was himself influenced by the Zealots was made by S. G. F. Brandon, *Jesus and the Zealots*. While unwilling to characterize Jesus as a Zealot himself, Brandon suggests that Jesus was "pro-Zealot" based on characterizations of his disciples (at least one of whom is called a zealot) and the cleansing of the temple.

portrayed as the crowd looking for a Messiah to lead them against the Romans. But this movement is by no means progressive; rather, it is a reaffirmation of what Marx called the sub-Asiatic mode of production. The Zealots are not looking forward to a new world order, just the restoration of the old world order before Roman colonialism. If Jesus were to adopt such an approach, it "would reinscribe the hierarchy of the codes of the SOC [social codes] in the BAS [basilica code] circle and thereby do away with the difference which the practice of Jesus is delineating."[30] Notice that here Belo is particularly interested in the purity of the codes. The SOC code cannot pollute the BAS code. In fact, it is terribly important for Belo to keep such codes separated. Only by such separation can he construct a vision of Jesus's practice that can be distinguished from apocalyptic ideology and mythology.

This "different practice" to which Belo refers is his understanding of the analytic code. This code finds its telos in the idea of sharing as opposed to buying. The idea of circulation is then removed from the strictly economic realm where exchange values predominate and is repositioned into a new world that has a different method of exchange. "The movement of the messianic narrative at the economic level consists in the extension to the whole world of this *circle* as a *table* at which the poor are filled, a pooling and sharing of all one has . . ."[31]

Likewise, Belo focuses upon the issue of gentile inclusion. Belo argues that Jesus's unwillingness to fulfill the messianic ambitions is, in a certain sense, about gentile inclusion. To be king of the Jews is to limit oneself to Judaism. But Jesus refuses to be contained in this way and so absents his body from the Galilean crowd through various travels and ruses. Eventually Jesus will absent himself completely from Galilee and travel to Jerusalem where his body will be taken away with the crucifixion. Even the resurrection fails to return the body of Jesus as the tomb is empty and all that is left is only a promise of meeting in Galilee. For Belo, that indicates a clear "road that is to be traveled (Galilee, Jerusalem, Galilee, pagan nations, the whole world)."[32]

Jesus's approach, then, as shown in what Belo calls the "messianic practice," subverted the dominant social codes and hierarchies. "The

---

30. Belo, *Materialist Reading*, 247.
31. Ibid., 245.
32. Ibid., 249.

strategy therefore challenged the relations of production (subasiatic mode of production; large-scale ownership of property), the political authorities, and the ideological relations (exclusion of property), the political authorities, and the ideological relations (exclusion of the rich, the masters, the scribes and the priests)."[33]

What Jesus presents instead is what Belo labels as a "radically communist strategy" which is at the same time a "nonrevolutionary strategy." Jesus sought to promote the classless kingdom of God which Belo labels a "communist ecclesiality."[34]

The shift from the language of the kingdom (which is political and universal and apocalyptic) to the language of church (which is communal), is an interesting feint on Belo's part. Belo argues against a further focusing on the personal, which he thinks most exegetes have done by making Jesus's message about the individual and interiority. From Belo's perspective, he offers a corrective to a bourgeois spirituality that neglects material needs.

Belo concedes, however, that he must leave Mark in order to retrieve the language of *ekklesia*; instead, he must turn to Paul or particularly Matthew ("upon this rock will I build my church") in order to find it. In contrast to this notion of open *ekklesia*, in the Petrine confession in Mark Jesus demands silence (8:30). Belo understands this command to silence, which he calls "clandistiny," as a strategy, the secret moves of a silent community. But Belo is confident that the implication of ecclesiality is to be found in Mark which corresponds enough to the other texts he pulls in that he can justify applying the term explicitly to Mark.[35]

But the use of *ekklesia* is important for Belo because it helps him dispense with the messy problem of apocalyptic in Mark. Belo equates the *ekklesia* with the "collective son of man;" the apocalyptic return of Jesus in the clouds now becomes a metaphor of the church's power on earth and no longer a mythological utopia. The goal is still utopian in one sense, the establishment of a classless society is a goal, utopian in itself; but by using the language of "Church" instead of "Kingdom," Belo can at least moor himself to political/social goals rather than the pie-in-the-sky approach of apocalyptic divine intervention.

33. Ibid., 261.
34. Ibid.
35. Ibid., 266–27.

Belo is very clear that he thinks the apocalyptic motif found in Mark is a "result of the lack of codes" that can envision successful revolution.[36] The Zealots proved definitively what the text of Mark suspects, that any attempt at revolution is doomed to failure. The apocalyptic in Mark then "functions as a kind of *textual suicide*" that is a product of its times. But, notes Belo, the situation is different now. The messianic narrative can now be read stripped of its apocalyptic despair because "for us revolution is the order of the day."[37]

In the end, then, Belo envisions a revolutionary church holding Mark in one hand and Marx in the other. Yet Belo cannot accept either all of Marx or all of Mark. The Marxist base/superstructure model along with the Marxist suspicion of religion is immediately dispensed with. At the same time, Belo's strategy of dividing the text into various "codes" and then pitting the codes against each other shows that he cannot accept Mark with its apocalyptic message. Such a message must be sanitized and while Belo's use of "codes" is clever, it functions for him as the opening to affirm only the portions of Jesus's message which speak to political and economic issues and simultaneously avoid those parts of the message which would subvert those ideas. The exclusion of the apocalyptic solution in Mark is the most significant of these maneuvers and shows the moment of peril for Belo. That the weight of French literary structuralism, Althusserian apparatuses and Nietzscheian philosophy are marshaled in order to effect this solution is impressive while at the same time illustrative of the problematic nature of trying to blend such conflicting systems.

Thus we must be reticent in letting Belo off the hook too quickly. As we have clearly seen, the logic of apocalyptic cannot be dispensed with so easily. Belo's attempt to separate the apocalyptic solution from the apocalyptic diagnosis betrays a recognition that there is simply no way that apocalypticism and Liberation Theology can co-exist. But what his quick move with base/superstructure at the beginning of his text likewise shows is that there is no facile way that Marxism and Liberation Theology can co-exist as well. Thus the struggles that we see Belo engaged in, the intellectual gymnastics that he is driven to, pointedly shows the untenability of combining these ideologies.

36. Ibid., 283.
37. Ibid.

Michel Clévnot: *Materialist Approaches to the Bible*

Michel Clévenot's book *Materialist Approaches to the Bible* is an interesting attempt to extend Belo's work interpreting Mark. Clévenot is a French Historian of Religion whose work is often cited as an example of Marxist exegesis. It has been called a popularization of Belo since it uses some of the same language and ideas as Belo. However, Clévenot is no parrot or abridger. His work represents an independent reading of the texts that, while dependent on Belo, still has its own vision.

Clévenot argues that the mythological elements of Mark, specifically the transfiguration, the passion predictions, and the little apocalypse of Mark 13 are in fact at variance with the majority of the text. "The foreknowledge that Mark suddenly bestows on Jesus negates the condition–Jesus's lack of foreknowledge–that determine all the narration of his practice."[38] The insertion of this material, Clévenot argues, is in fact a "remythologization" of the Markan text.

Clévenot is not particularly clear on what he is proposing here. Is this a literary argument which is suggesting a second redaction layer such that there was originally a version of Mark that was absent these mythological features or is it some ur-narrative of Jesus's life into which mythology has been inserted? Either hypothesis is congruent with Clévenot's position, but he is not that specific. What Clévenot focuses on instead is the social genesis of the "remythologization."

The source of Mark's move to myth is, of course, the fall of Jerusalem in 70 CE. However, Clévenot appends to this a concern at the time of the writing of Mark about the persecutions of Nero (64-69 CE). His argument is that Christians in Rome (where he supposes Mark to have been written) would be relatively unaffected by the fall of the Temple, particularly gentile Christians whose existence is testified to by Paul's letter to the Romans. However, couple the fall of Jerusalem with the persecutions of Nero and add in the delay of the *parousia*, and one has a true crisis in the making.

Mark, then, decides to go for broke. Rather than excusing the delayed *parousia* or placing it in the far distant future, Mark suggests that it is imminent. However, he is, of course, wrong, and later gospel writers will have much work to do to clean up this mistake.

---

38. Clévenot, *Materialist Approaches*, 111.

Clévenot, then, works to separate the apocalyptic from the Markan text through the mechanism of "remythologization." The real question is whether Mark is so easily sifted. Belo attempted to do this by establishing several different codes and sorted the texts accordingly. As a result, the mythological code could be easily dispensed with, and we could return to the true kernel of truth without the messy imposition of the undesirable side of apocalyptic.

Clévenot does not have such a neat system. His theory of "remythologization" only seems to include selected passages. The question then arises, can apocalyptic be so cleanly excised from the text? Our examination of the apocalyptic nature of Mark has shown that the logic of the apocalyptic system lies at the core of Mark's gospel. To avoid this, one must either ignore its ubiquitous presence or attempt to explain it away.

Clévenot decides to do both. On the one hand, he attributes the apocalyptic message to a rather misguided theological feint that Mark attempts in light of trying times. On the other, he suggests the mythology can be extracted, leaving us with a radical gospel sympathetic to liberationist aims. In making this move, he violates both the logic of the text and concomitant logic of apocalyptic upon which the text is dependent. Thus he once again brings into view the problem of the inherent contradiction between apocalyptic and the Marxist view.

Clévenot shows the basic problem of trying to blend the disparate systems of Marxism, Liberation Theology and apocalyptic. Clévenot must appeal to an Ur-Mark in order to remove the apocalyptic problems that come with Mark. The very fact that he must "invent" a literary ancestor to protect his analysis shows with crystalline clarity the basic problem of such a project of uniting these conflicting ideologies.

Ched Myers: *Binding The Strongman*

Ched Meyers was trained at the Graduate Theological Union in New Testament, but perhaps he is best known as the former director of the American Friends Service Committee, and more recently as co-founder of the Bartimaeus Cooperative Ministries and a forceful advocate of Sabbath Economics. Sabbath Economics calls for the redistribution of wealth and the voluntary abstention from the accumulation of wealth. Myers's book *Binding The Strongman* is an attempt to do an explicitly "political reading of Mark's story of Jesus." His approach is self-consciously Marxist "with regard to crucial elements of my approach."[39] Likewise he focuses on the apocalyptic nature of Mark to make his case. His emphasis on apocalyptic is curtailed only by the caution that Mark "felt apocalyptic was misunderstood by his contemporaries. His focus upon the cross set him against those who used apocalyptic symbolics to legitimate a militant practice of 'holy war' against their enemies."[40] Thus Myers is a prime example of the pattern of connection between Marxism and apocalypticism that we have been tracing.

Myers begins by theoretically positioning himself as a Marxist within the canons of biblical scholarship. Starting with the history of scholarship, Myers sees his work as rectifying what he perceives as an over-emphasis on sources that has caused the message of the Gospel of Mark to be lost. In response to this, he attempts to coordinate narrative/literary approaches with social-scientific/ideological approaches appropriating Marxist categories. The key is his demand for a political hermeneutic in reading the text.

Following English Marxist Fredric Jameson and others who have written on ideology, Myers establishes two different forms of ideology. On the one hand, there are ideologies that ultimately support the status quo either through direct advocacy or through presuming the presuppositions of the status quo in making their argument (reformism). On the other hand, there are "subversive ideologies." Subversive ideologies question those presuppositions through redefinition and are consequently challenging the legitimacy of the status quo. The determination of whether a given ideology (say Mark's) is supportive or challenging of the status quo can only be determined within the specific social and political context in which it functions.

The goal of theology in this vein, then, is to separate the wheat from the chaff, to identify the subversive and non-subversive ideologies in the text. But even more Myers aims to notice "when liberating ideologies, including Christian theologies, become oppressively hegemonic."[41] However, Myers has already stacked the deck, for he proclaims that the

---

39. Ibid., 37.
40. Ibid., 104.
41. Ibid., 21.

gospel "itself has an 'absolutely subversive' character."[42] We should not expect to find, then, that Myers's Mark will tell us a story that supports the hegemony of his day.

It is this pre-determination on Myers part that explains his preference for literary approaches as opposed to historical-critical approaches. For his part, he argues that historical-critical approaches have been hampered by idealism.[43] By this critique he intends to challenge the historical skepticism that historical-criticism has fostered. Using Kähler's categories[44] of *Geschichte* (the belief of the early church about Jesus) and *Historie* (the historical reality of Jesus) Myers argues that historical critics have attempted to access *Geschichte* not *Historie*.[45]

Be that as it may, Myers's answer is to appeal to literary/narrative criticism in his attempt to deconstruct Mark. However, literary/narrative criticism, as Myers understands it, is not really anti-historical criticism but more post-historical criticism. Literary critics choose not to concern themselves with the issues of the relationship between history and the text, instead focusing solely on the text as a discrete unit. Using the arsenal of literary-critical tools borrowed from literature departments, narrative criticism looks at the texts with an eye to plot, characterization, voice, sequence and other literary categories. However, Myers is not satisfied by this turn either, as he notes, "If historical criticism betrays the narrative integrity of the text, literary criticism betrays its historical integrity."[46]

Myers is unhappy because he wants to ground his reading in history (if historical-critical methods may be critiqued as idealist, narrative approaches also do not escape such a diagnosis). Seeing himself in the Marxist tradition, he is unwilling to divorce the text from its historical

---

42. Ibid.

43. Ibid., 23.

44. Kähler, *So-Called Historical Jesus*, 14–42.

45. This accusation however is probably not fair. Ernst Käsemann's lecture which inaugurated the new quest for the historical of Jesus states quite clearly, "The question of the historical Jesus is, in its legitimate form, the question of the continuity of the Gospel within the discontinuity of the times and within the variation of the kerygma ... For to his [God's] particularity there corresponds the particularity of faith, for which the real history of Jesus is always happening afresh; it is now the history of the exalted Lord, but it does not cease to be the earthly history it once was, in which the call and the claim of the Gospel are encountered" (*New Testament Questions*, 46–47).

46. Myers, *Binding the Strong Man*, 25.

underpinnings. To this end, he proposes "Literary Sociology." The aim of literary sociology is to look for the political dimension of the discourse that must, of course, be grounded in the historical reality of the time. Using an example from fairytale analysis, Myers notes that texts encode, often in indirect and symbolic ways, the social codes of their time and then proceed to interact with them. Thus in Hansel and Gretel "the witch" represents the aristocracy with glorious homes, ample food, and the "devouring" of the peasants. The death of the witch, then, is a symbolic attack on the status quo.

Yet the perceptive reader will already wonder whether Myers's method gets us back to Jesus or just to Mark. Has he really solved the *Geschichte/Historie* problem? The answer is: despite cobbling together various critical approaches, in the end he has, methodologically speaking, no more access to the events of history which lie behind Mark than any other critic. Myers seems to realize this and it is at this point, late in his introduction, that we get a series of faith statements. Mark (as well as the liberation theology pantheon of the prophets, the exodus, etc) "is a story Yahweh generated and continues to regenerate"[47]. Additionally, regarding the issue of Mark's historical veracity, Myers asserts, "I believe there is reliable continuity between Mark, his sources and Jesus."[48] And though he talks about "Mark's Jesus," he maintains that "this is for the purposes of modesty, not skepticism."[49] Thus Myers tries to wend his way through the forest of biblical criticism without succumbing to the temptation to abandon claims of historicity, even if "claims" are all he really has.

Such a demand to continue a link to history might be expected from someone committed to the Marxist tradition with its promotion of historical materialism. However as with biblical criticism, and here too with Marxism, Myers want to express some caveats. Myers accepts the label Marxist while eschewing the term "materialist." From his perspective, materialism adopts a transcendent position that sees class struggles as the eternal truth of humankind. Each moment of history is interpreted through that lens. Myers does not make the post-modern move of challenging the idea of the "transcendent," instead he appeals

47. Ibid., 37.
48. Ibid., 31.
49. Ibid.

to a different transcendent position: "the biblical narrative of liberation, from which Marxism is at most, derivative."[50] Thus Myers begins his work trying on the one hand to balance Marxism and belief, and, history and belief. The fact that ultimately Myers seems reduced to a series of faith statements shows how precarious such a balancing act is.

When Myers examines the text itself, it is interesting to note how he deals with the problem of apocalyptic. He readily admits the apocalyptic nature of Mark and notes the preponderance of citations and allusions from the book of Daniel found in Mark following the work of New Testament scholar Howard Clark Kee.[51] He argues that apocalyptic is in fact a motivator for change (citing Richard A. Horsley and John J. Collins). However, the place where he makes his most interesting move is a line that remains unexplained but is rife with possibility: "the most ideologically important characteristic [is] the Danielic conviction that the suffering of the just is somehow in itself efficacious in bringing down the old order and creating the new (Dn 7:21ff.)."[52] In making this claim Myers cites no sources or secondary texts to defend this reading of Daniel, and yet one easily sees the way this will play out in Mark with Jesus's crucifixion and return.

Still, the sticking point with apocalyptic is that it is ultimately unfulfilled. The eschaton has not come, the established order usually changes only slowly over time and through human action not divine. Yet Myers's focus gives us a further clue as to how he envisions the creation of change—the concept of radical discipleship. Myers uses this early on in his analysis of the Markan text. The calling of the first disciples involved "a fundamental reordering of socio-economic relationships."[53] This is shown in the abandonment of family and workplace for those called. This Myers quickly contrasts with the rich young ruler who will come later and be unable to leave his possessions behind. Thus radical discipleship will demand social action even if eschatology does not.

Along these same lines, another interesting point Myers makes is the insertion of John as a prophet at the very beginning of Mark. The baptism is preceded itself by the quotation of a combination of Malachi

---

50. Ibid., 37.
51. Kee, *Community of the New Age*.
52. Myers, *Binding the Strong Man*, 103.
53. Ibid., 133.

and Isaiah. John's attire is designed to remind the reader of Elijah. The point here, argues Myers, is that the prophetic voices that had previously been silent are now once again speaking—this time through John the Baptist. Of course, the prophets, as we have seen, are a favorite trope of liberationists since they speak to issues of social justice. That Mark begins his text with a reference to the prophets indicates how we are to understand both John and Jesus.[54]

All of this clearly sets Myers up for the radical Jesus that he has in mind. Certainly one is reluctant to argue the point. Jesus was radical enough to get himself killed (though this was common enough for prophets under Roman rule),[55] and yet we are still unclear where this radicality will lead the reader. For Myers it appears to be the cornerstone of a position on discipleship. Jesus as a proponent of radical discipleship plays the prophetic tradition against the apocalyptic tradition. On the one hand, the apocalyptic tradition envisions a different universal order which includes social and economic justice for all, while on the other hand invoking the prophetic tradition forecloses the option of pietism in the face of injustice. Thus this concept of radical discipleship is an idea that includes radical critique and social transformation that will have modern applicability for the reader as well.

When Myers turns to an interpretation of the text, then, he is eager to see both of the categories of apocalyptic and prophetic in the political ramifications of each of the various stories in Mark. He does this through a complicated process of sociological analysis and analogical reading. For instance, the demoniac at Garasene, when commanded to say his name, calls himself "Legion." For Myers, that name clearly is a reference to the Roman presence in Palestine.[56] His argument is strengthened by the fact that several terms relating to the herd of swine

---

54. It is, however, debatable whether prophetic voices really were silent. Many prophets arose in Palestine apart from Jesus, both before and after him. Horsley catalogs several prophets who appeared in the first century. It may be unclear how many of those episodes were common knowledge, but given that Myers wants to situate the gospel of Mark in Galilee rather than outside of Israel, these individuals were probably not unknown to the populace. An identification of Jesus and John as prophets may have been Mark's goal. However, it is not clear that this is a reinstatement of the prophetic office rather than merely the presentation of credentials for that office. Horsley and Hanson, *Bandits, Prophets, and Messiahs*, 160–87.

55. Ibid., 160–87.

56. Myers, *Binding the Strong Man*, 191.

(the words for "herd," "dismissal," and "charge") are all words with military connotations. Thus, the story becomes more than just a healing story; it works almost as a parable regarding the fate of Roman power in the hands of the "Son of the Most High God" (Mark 5:7).

In contrast to this story is the first account of an exorcism that occurs in the synagogue. Here the challenge is more direct and it comes from the scribes. Myers interprets the scribes as representatives of the Temple establishment.[57] "The demon in the synagogue becomes the representative of the scribal establishment, whose 'authority' undergirds the dominant Jewish social order."[58] When Jesus casts out the demon he challenges the authority of that order precisely in its local headquarters—the synagogue.

Healing, likewise, has a political content. Myers takes his cue from Mary Douglas and anthropology here.[59] Recognizing, of course, that ancient peoples did not have any conception of germs or viruses, Myers notes that the issue of illness takes on a decidedly social tone. There is a correlation between the body of the individual with an illness and the body politic. The social body is afflicted with the diseased person as the person him/herself is afflicted with the disease. Myers cautions us against trying to read this text biomedically. To see Jesus healing as equivalent to curing is to miss the point. What Jesus did was to reconcile the person with a disease to his/her society. "Mark's Jesus seeks always to restore the *social* wholeness denied to the sick/impure by this symbolic order."[60] In each of the healing stories Myers is not concerned with symptomology present or (afterwards) absent. Rather, Myers sees each healing miracle as "symbolic action." Each healing in Mark, then, represents a particular criticism directed against an institutional force in ancient Palestine such as purity codes, debt system, temple system, etc.

It is particularly interesting in light of this to look at Myers's take on the Pharisees. Recent work on the Pharisees has changed scholarship's

---

57. In terms of the narrative of Mark, this is undoubtedly correct, though historically the debate rages on as to whether scribes were not merely paid functionaries rather than representatives. Kloppenborg recaps this debate particularly as it relates to the issue of who wrote Q in Kloppenborg, *Excavating Q*, 200–201.

58. Myers, *Binding the Strong Man*, 143.

59. Douglas, *Purity and Danger*.

60. Myers, *Binding the Strong Man*, 146.

perspective on exactly how powerful the Pharisee party was during the time of Jesus.[61] That they became a force in Judaism after the fall of the temple and became the driving power in the formation of rabbinical Judaism is fairly well accepted.[62]

In some ways, then, the Pharisees could be considered a force for resistance in the face of Roman oppression as well. Since the temple establishment had aligned itself with the Romans, the Pharisees emphasis on personal piety rituals was opposed to the centralized power of the temple.[63] Myers, however, reads the pharisaic material in Mark straightforwardly as opposing Jesus. It is interesting that Myers is not more critical of Mark's use of the Pharisees. He notes that pharisaism "was a vigorous challenge to the elite clerical classes that made an attempt to be populist."[64] Unfortunately, from Myers's perspective, the Pharisees were more menshivist than bolshevist. He concludes that problematically, "theirs was a reformist strategy; they worked to extend the redemptive media of the dominant ideological order, not overturn them."[65] Thus, Mark's Jesus opposes the Pharisees because they are insufficiently revolutionary.

A similar conclusion is reached regarding the zealots, or "the Fourth Philosophy" as Josephus called them. Here too, while these were actively opposed to both the Roman project of colonization as well as their collaborators in the priestly caste, Myers finds them lacking. The zealots were clearly nationalist, but not truly revolutionary. "As far as I can see even the most radical Zealot faction never proposed more than supplanting the collaborationist priestly leadership . . . with a patriotic [one]. There is little indication of a rebel program for a systematic restructuring of wealth or power."[66]

---

61. Saldarini argues for the presence of Pharisees in Galilee but cautions against an over interpretation of that presence. "To affirm that the Pharisees were present in Galilee is not to affirm that they were in charge, or even a dominant force there" (*Pharisees*, 293).

62. Saldarini rightly cautions against seeing this as the immediate result of the fall of the temple in 70 CE. Instead it must be recognized that the rise of the "sages" to the prominence that they ultimately attained took many decades (ibid., 208).

63. Ibid., 213.

64. Myers, *Binding the Strong Man*, 83.

65. Ibid.

66. Ibid., 85.

Such a contrast casts into sharp relief how Myers interprets Mark. Myers's political reading of the text means that in each case Jesus was thrown into an apocalyptic battle with the powers and principalities that rule Israel. In contrast to other movements of the time, for Jesus, nothing but a radical prescription of a new order is sufficient to bring about change. Myers strives to show Jesus's solution in every action that he takes and every lesson that he teaches.

One of the longest lessons Jesus teaches in Mark is found in the thirteenth chapter, the so-called "Little Apocalypse." It is here that the problem of apocalyptic becomes acute. In the other texts Myers examines apocalyptic has been the backdrop in front of which Jesus's actions are played, but in Mark 13 we see the real breadth of Mark's access to the apocalyptic tradition. The invocation of the "abomination of desolation," the darkening of the sun, the falling of the stars and the return of the Son of Man in the clouds are all part of this passage and indicate the facility Mark has with apocalyptic tropes.[67] Myers embraces this language throughout his text leading up to Mark 13 precisely for its revolutionary connotation. But as we arrive at Mark 13, suddenly Myers's resolve beings to sway as the balance between the prophetic and apocalyptic tradition suddenly seems to shift decisively in the direction of apocalyptic.

Myers has an agenda for contemporary Christian discipleship. He wants to see Mark as a call to a new kind of Christian practice that the figure of Jesus authorizes. The text, then, rests on the legitimacy of Jesus to institute this new form of discipleship. Here, implicitly, Myers recognizes the analysis of apocalyptic that I have forwarded, namely the function of apocalyptic to ensure behavioral compliance. Submission to the demand of the apocalypticist is based on two factors: 1) the authority of the apocalypticist (who in this text is Jesus), 2) the believability of the message. If time elapses such that the message becomes seen as unreliable, the whole house of cards comes down.

Myers own use of apocalyptic in this case follows the same pattern as Mark. He also is dependent on the authority of the apocalypticist to forward his vision of "radical discipleship." Likewise his ability to enforce this sort of behavioral mandate is predicated on the believability of Myers interpretation of Jesus message. Thus, if Myers were to hold

---

67. Fiorenza, *Early Christian Apocalyptic*, 299–302.

that Jesus's predictions were either wrong or indefinitely deferred, Myers would lack the credibility to constitute such a new practice. Myers, then, has the same problem that the majority of Marxists using the apocalyptic texts of the Bible have—they must somehow save apocalypticism from itself–but with a twist. This time it is not just about excising the mythological, it is also about explaining away the delay of the *parousia*.

Myers thinks he is up to this task and clearly sees the choices facing him. He therefore sets forth a very nuanced argument. First, he argues we must understand that Mark has a slippery conception of time. In fact, the Greek word he uses for "time" is *kairos* not *chronos*. This is significant for Myers in that it indicates that Mark understands time archetypally or metaphorically—not in some linear manner. Thus, the fact that Mark talks about the destruction of the temple and *then* the coming of the son of man should not be understood as a clear sequence of events. How this sequence should be understood instead is not apparent. Myers does not elucidate the guiding principle of organization that is in effect instead of sequential order.

Myers has a second argument to make regarding this as well, and it is found in his interpretation of Mark 13:24–27. Here the passage reads, "But in those days, after that suffering, the sun will be darkened and the moon will not give its light, and the stars will be falling from heaven, and the powers in heavens will be shaken. Then they will see the son of man coming in clouds with great power and glory. Then he will send out the angels and gather his elect from the four winds, from the ends of the earth to the ends of heaven." Myers argues that all this is accomplished (except the gathering) within the narrative. At the cross, "representatives of both Roman and Jewish powers are assembled, spectating—and the light of the sun fails (15:31–33, 39). This is indeed the moment spoken of as 'the coming of the kingdom in power' (9:1)."[68]

This argument is slightly expanded when Myers takes up an analysis of the crucifixion text in Mark. Here he notes that in addition to the darkening of the sky for three hours, the curtain of the temple is also ripped. This Myers interprets as a final attack on the political powers. He concludes triumphantly, "The world order has been overthrown, the powers have fallen (13:24ff)."

---

68. Myers, *Binding the Strong Man*, 343.

The alert reader may not be so sure. Mark 13:24ff. has only been *partially* fulfilled at best. In the crucifixion text the moon is not mentioned (which is also supposed to be dark) and no stars fall from the sky (a clear indication of powers being thrown from heaven). Most importantly, however, the son of man does not descend from heaven in the clouds, but remains firmly affixed to the cross, hanging between heaven and earth. It is almost perverse to suggest that the character who has just cried "My God, My God, why have you forsaken me?" is somehow an expression of power and glory.

The strongest argument that Myers can muster for his theory of textual fulfillment is found in the concluding parable of the watchful servants, which concludes chapter 13. There Jesus commands his disciple to watch "for you do not know when the master of the house will come, in the evening, or at midnight, or at the cock crow or in the morning" (13:35). Myers, following Lightfoot, notes that each of these watches follow the passion narrative. The last supper is conducted at evening, Peter's denial at the cock crow, and the handing over of Jesus to Pilate by the Sanhedrin in the morning. While this is generally true, there is the glaring omission of a reference to midnight in the passion narrative. We pass from evening to the cock crow without a clear reference to any other time indications in the text.

Likewise, Jesus implores his disciples to "watch" in the garden (14:37–38), and the parable itself also commands the disciples to "watch" (13:34–35, 37). The correlation to the garden is fairly clear in that respect; for the exact thing Jesus warns his disciples about (the master comes and finds them sleeping) occurs in the garden when Jesus returns from his prayer to find his disciples asleep. But does this correlation between the parable and garden/passion scene argue for a complete fulfillment of the apocalyptic prophecies of Mark 13? Is it not also possible that what the garden does is illustrate the point of the parable without really addressing the rest of the passage? Certainly no one would argue that when Jesus returns from his praying in the garden he is the Son of Man coming in power, especially since he later predicts the scribes and priest will soon see the Son of Man coming in the clouds (14:62).

Moreover, while there is a partial connection between the watches in the parable and the trial of Jesus, certainly the point of the parable is lost in the passion. For the Son of Man does not appear unexpectedly, rather he is entirely expected thanks to the aid of Judas. In fact, if the point of the parable is the unexpectedness of the master's arrival, the scripted nature of the passion (it was predicted beforehand and foreshadowed throughout the text) seems to make exactly the opposite point. It therefore seems much more likely that Mark uses the parallels in this parable to engage in foreshadowing, but the extension that the apocalyptic predictions in chapter 13 are fulfilled is simply unmerited.

If Mark intended to make this point, it could have been done much more clearly, as Mark does elsewhere. Consider the prophecy Jesus makes in Mark 10:33–34. There Jesus predicts his own trial and death. The exactitude of the prediction is what is most interesting here. Jesus predicts that he will be "delivered to the chief priests and scribes," "condemned to death" and "deliver[ed] to the Gentiles" who will "mock him and spit upon him, and scourge him and kill him." Each of these predictions is fulfilled exactly without any omission or room for misinterpretation. It is Mark's ability to be so exact that causes one to wonder about trying to read in fulfillment to more ambiguous texts. Clearly if Mark wanted to show the Son of Man coming in the clouds, he could have constructed his narrative to show that. The fact that the narrative lacks crucial elements that Jesus predicts in Mark 13 should make us wary of Myers's conclusion. Mark has shown he is not prone to ambiguity in his predictions.

Additionally, Jesus's predictions in Mark 10 causes concern about Myers first point, the metaphorical nature of time. In Mark 10, the prediction which Jesus gives is quite linear and sequential. In the textual fulfillment of this prophecy the order is exactly the same as what was predicted. One therefore must have some reservations about whether Myers is right about Mark's "archetypal" use of time. When we compare Mark 13 with the clear prediction Jesus makes regarding his death in Mark 10, we do not see the circularity and ambiguity that Myers wishes to find in Mark 13.

It therefore seems quite unlikely that the predictions in Mark 13 are to be taken as anything but straightforward. Prophecies here are a sequence of events that Mark expects to happen in the order recounted, some of which may have already happened in Mark's time (as Mark's insertion of "let the reader understand" in 13:14 seems to indicate). The conclusion that one reaches, since clearly many of these predictions have to do with the Jewish War of 70 CE, is that Myers's theory of textual fulfillment cannot stand.

We can understand, of course, why Myers wishes to make this highly creative, if unsuccessful move. Myers fears the second edge of the apocalyptic sword. The goal of a new world that, for Myers, Jesus inaugurated and that his disciples, to this day, are compelled to work towards is one that inspires hope. This is a world that rejects hierarchy, class and patriarchy. Yet it is one that also has as its ultimate guarantor supernatural intervention. The *parousia* has been delayed far too long, with too much pointless bloodshed in the interim, to justify its postponement. In a post-Holocaust world the hope of divine intervention seems foolish or perhaps insane.

The text of Mark bears witness to this. The delay of the *parousia* for the forty years after Jesus's death seems more than enough for the gospel writer. As he sees the events of the Jewish War, he is clear that the end of time is at hand. Certainly he would be shocked that some 1900 years later time marches on. Thus the two edges of the apocalyptic sword, of justice and unfulfilled expectation, seem consistently to impale Marxist interpreters like Myers.

We have therefore seen another intriguing effort at mixing Marxism and the New Testament. Surely Myers political reading of Mark must be understood as a forthright attempt to do an uninhibited Marxist interpretation of the text. Meyers believes that Mark is the gospel best suited for such a reading as it highlights the radicalism of Jesus. In Mark, Jesus *is* engaged in cosmic battle with unjust forces. Yet the weapon of choice for Mark in this battle is the language of apocalypticism and as we have seen yet again, in order preserve the radicality that such language entails one must seek a way to switch its emphasis from future to present. Myers's attempts to do this prove ultimately unsuccessful, and yet he shows the problem clearly. His own reading of Mark is a type of modern apocalypticism; an example of the function of the system I have specified earlier. He, too, is focused on enforcing performative mandates. His reading also is problematized by the short-term nature of its authority particularly complicated by the passing of (a lot of) time. In the end, the logic of apocalypticism for both Myers and Mark proves to be an intractable problem with no clear resolution.

Conclusion

In this chapter we have been witness to a consistent, if disheartening pattern. Marxists reading the New Testament seem inexorably drawn to apocalyptic texts particularly the gospel of Mark. These are texts that speak of the kind of radical change most of these Marxists wish for. They envision a world in which injustice is vanquished and poverty is eliminated. They see in these texts a call for a new world, one in which class conflict is ultimately resolved. And so they look to these texts, and work with them hoping to find within them the impetus to world-changing action among believers.

Yet these texts bear their payload with an enormous cost. For as our analysis of apocalyptic initially showed, the revolution does not come from peasants with pitchforks storming the winter palace, but by the imposition of divine armies from on high mobilizing under a divine flag and destroying the earthly oppressors. Such a vision is not one that inspires political action but easily can inspire just the opposite—pietistic passivity. The believer may be equally inclined to endure their situation of oppression and wait for the promise of divine deliverance as take up arms and bring in the eschaton him/herself. Those attracted to Mark 13 must feel this sting most clearly as the only role given the believer is preaching.

The result is that Marxist New Testament interpreters have attempted to try to have it both ways. They have worked to cleave the world-changing language of a promised new world from the language that mythologizes its coming into a divine drama. This is done differently by the different authors: from the theoretical sophistication of an author like Belo and "remythologization" of Clévenot, to the revolutionary theological readings of Miranda, to the in-depth re-readings of Ched Meyers. All these thinkers share an attempt to sift the golden nuggets of revolution from the sand of apocalyptic mythology. As we have seen, all do so by making dubious leaps in both their theoretical and textual machinations.

In the end then, one is left wondering whether the problem is, as Meyers has argued, one of competing transcendents. Can class struggle share a bed with divine action? My earlier examination of the Marxist tradition would answer no. The Marxist tradition is always suspicious of religion. It has argued that religion is not a boon to political action but a form of distraction from it. The very fact of the mental/textual gymnastics required of the scholars surveyed in this chapter once more gives evidence of this very fact.

Additionally, based on my previous analysis of the apocalyptic system itself, coupled with the witness of the thinkers surveyed here, there is evidence that the problem lies in apocalyptic itself. The reason these scholars try vainly to extract revolution from apocalypticism is that the apocalyptic ideology is not about fomenting revolt, it is about stifling it. It is ultimately about securing forms of behavior in a temporary modality. It is based on the assurance of divine action in the near future. Of course that future is already past for us and failed to provide the promised new world. It is somewhat surprising then, that Marxist interpreters should attempt to rest their call for revolution on a ground that has already been found fallow.

5

Richard A. Horsley

THE INFLUENCE OF MARXISM HAS NOT BEEN RELEGATED TO THE PE-
riphery of New Testament studies; it has reached its center as well. In this chapter I will look at the way one particular New Testament scholar has appropriated Marxism in making his analyses: Richard A. Horsley. His work is often innovative and interesting precisely because of his implementation of Marxism.

In this chapter, however, as in the previous chapter, we find the same dilemma arising. Once again there is conflict between the liberation agenda, Marxism, and the interpretation of the (apocalyptic) text. Horsley, whose work on the historical Jesus is well-known, presents again the problem of apocalyptic for Marxist oriented scholars. Yet his later work shows an interesting attempt to still craft a liberationist message apart from a focus on apocalyptic, this time focusing on Jesus's message. I will demonstrate that the conflicts in the ideologies of Marxism, Liberation Theology, and apocalypticism caused Horsley to ultimately abandon an explicit dependence on apocalypticism and to veer away from Marxism, opting instead for the perspective of Liberation Theology. Following his work, we will enter into the scholarly discussions on the historical Jesus and the Q document. While the term apocalyptic ultimately takes a back seat, the search for a way to connect the message of Liberation Theology to the message of Jesus continues and is shown clearly in the debate over Q.[1]

---

1. The history of the Q debate in recent years has also focused precisely on this word "apocalyptic." Initially the term was used to describe a particular stratum of the Q document. Kloppenborg was actually somewhat careful in his usage by saying "The sayings most typical of the stratum are *prophetic judgment sayings and apocalyptic words*" (Kloppenborg, *Formation of Q*, 169). However, this was quickly glossed as the "apocalyptic layer" in scholarly dialogs. This then raised the question of whether the

Richard Horsley's work on the historical Jesus gained notoriety in the guild for many of its innovative readings of the gospel texts. In this section I will argue that Horsley's work can be shown to center on three fundamental precepts, each of which stems from a different ideology: 1) a Marxist-oriented social critique of systems of injustice found in ancient Palestine in both the Roman colonial rule and the Judean Temple System; 2) a Jesus who condemns in apocalyptic terms the exploitation of the poor as well as social/economic injustice and espouses a new egalitarian way of living found in the notion of the "Kingdom of God"; 3) Jesus as an exemplary and imitable revolutionary of Liberation Theology who has relevance for social activists today. In making his arguments based on these precepts Horsley moves through a series of positions from anchoring Jesus in apocalypticism, to a stake in the debate about Q, to a focus on orality. In each of these positions, which I will detail below, Horsley works to locate these three suppositions in the text. To that end, Horsley still sees the Biblical text as the final authority, yet the moves that he makes indicate the conflict of the ideological presuppositions inherent in his work often are exemplified in unique and interesting ways.

Horsley's best known text is *Jesus and the Spiral of Violence*.[2] In this work, he develops a vision of the historical Jesus that will lay the groundwork for his work for the next fifteen years. He begins with Marx. Marx said, "the history of the world is the history of class struggle." This point is seen clearly in *Spiral*. Horsley quotes Marx early[3] and then not again; but his book implicitly returns to Marx's statement over and over. Horsley argues that scholars have made a modernist division between religion and politics/economics. Such was not the case in first-century Palestine. Religion was both politics and economics. The rule of the religious hierarchy supported, and was supported by, the political structures of the Herodian kings and Rome, which integrated religion and politics. The support of these political institutions was conducted through the collection of religious tithes and taxes. Thus there was no division between church and state, between religious sentiment and political thought or economic analysis.

said layer of Q was "really apocalyptic." The semantic argument continues and I will examine it in more detail further on.

2. Horsley, *Spiral of Violence*.
3. Ibid., 33.

With this background in mind Horsley analyzes the Jesus movement. In his analysis the issue of apocalypticism comes to the forefront. Horsley's book, written in 1987, pre-dates the apocalyptic Jesus versus sapiential Jesus debate.[4] However, the issue shows up in an ancillary way when he rebuts Theissen's use of the cynics as models for the early Jesus movement.[5] Moreover, for the most part, the apocalyptic Jesus is a mainstay for Horsley and relatively undefended in his text. This is because Horsley wants to understand the Kingdom of God sayings as specifically apocalyptic. While other scholarship has challenged whether this is a necessary connection,[6] Horsley, in *Spiral,* is committed to it.

Part of the reason Horsley is dependent on apocalyptic is because it is in apocalyptic that Horsley sees a political/social/economic critique being made for him. To see the dissolution of the entire social order is to bring a judgment against it. It is to see the corruption that lies at its soul. Moreover, unlike prophetic critique that also may condemn the current order, apocalyptic envisions an entirely new order. Horsley claims apocalyptic engages two modes of thought: "creative envisioning" and "critical demystifying."[7] By employing the apocalyptic motif of a battle between light and dark, Satan and God, apocalyptic denaturalizes the current order and combats it.

Horsley argues that apocalyptic motivates resistance against the oppressive structures of society: "It is clear that apocalyptic visions of God's imminent action evoked hope and motivation for resistance among Palestinian Jews living in the Roman imperial situation . . . because God was about to effect a decisive 'revolution' (i.e., judging and removing the imperial regime and giving dominion to the people themselves)."[8] The Marxist language here is clear and class struggle gets a divine assist from the Almighty.

Horsley's argument is not completely convincing. As noted before, the kingdom of God language is not necessarily apocalyptic. Moreover, it is not entirely clear that apocalyptic does inspire action unless, as in Qumran, the end entails a battle that the faithful are to join. The

---

4. See discussion below.
5. Theissen, *Sociology*.
6. Borg, *Temperate Case*.
7. Horsley, *Spiral of Violence*, 144.
8. Ibid., 145.

Christian apocalyptic texts do not contain such a vision. In fact, the apocalyptic speech of Jesus (Mark 13) does not call for revolution but rather for flight (Mark 13:14). Additionally, Horsley himself gives an explanation for revolts from the time of Jesus that makes apocalyptic notions unnecessary by suggesting they were a reenactment of the Hebrew Epic, particularly the Exodus.[9] It is perhaps no accident that some of the stories of messianic pretenders that Josephus recounts occur in the desert, the site of God leading the Hebrews to freedom.

But even if we accept Horsley's argument that Jesus's proclamation was apocalyptic and that apocalypticism can motivate resistance, Horsley creates another problem related to the issue of the distinctiveness of the Jesus Movement. Early on Horsley cites Marx's famous "opiate of the people" statement. However, he emphasizes a portion of the statement not usually attended to.[10] Marx states about religion: "It is the fantastic realization of the human essence because the human essence has no reality . . ."[11] Here we find Horsley's operative category for other messianic movements—fantasy. He states, "Hence when the Jews celebrated the festival of Passover . . . the freedom celebrated was necessarily in *fantasy* form, there being no actual freedom."[12] A few paragraphs later he uses this same category again, ". . . prophetic movements were both expressions of and protests against real distress, and they sought liberation in fantasy form."[13]

Prophetic movements that Josephus recounts, then, are characterized by "fantasy." Horsley sees this as their downfall. "These movements, of course, are not protests in any ordinary sense. Their most distinctive feature is the lack of critical, *realistic* sense of the political situation."[14] It is not clear, however, why apocalyptic is exempt from this same critique since clearly apocalyptic movements while perhaps critical are by no means realistic. More interestingly, however, the very dichotomy of "fantasy" v. "reality" is itself a clear outgrowth of Horsley's Marxist perspective. The whole notion of "fantasy" relies on the same logic as

---

9. Ibid., 36.
10. Ibid., 33.
11. Marx, *Critique*, 54.
12. Horsley, *Spiral of Violence*, 34.
13. Ibid., 35.
14. Ibid., 36; emphasis mine.

Marx's conception of religion as "illusion." Here however, since Horsley is likewise indebted to Liberation Theology, it is only particular kinds of religion that constitute "fantasy," not religion as a whole.

But the problem for Horsley lies in how to understand Jesus. He does not want to paint the Jesus movement with the same brush as other "fantasy" oriented movements. The reader of *Spiral* may wonder, with this introduction, how the Jesus movement will differ? Will it perhaps advocate direct action instead of expecting God to intervene? It is with this question in mind that we reach Horsley's discussion of the cleansing of the Temple.

The reader may be excused if she suspects Jesus will turn out to be a revolutionary after all as Horsley makes much of the fact that Jesus was executed as a political criminal, that he prophesied the destruction of the temple by his own hand, and that the cleansing of the temple is an historical event. Likewise, Horsley's analysis of the "give unto Caesar" passage shows that Jesus is as critical of Rome as he is of the Jerusalem temple establishment.

So when Jesus marches into Jerusalem to the hail of the crowds and then enters the temple and begins turning over tables, one might think that this is the beginning of his revolution. Now we are not in the realm of fantasy any more, for we have direct action focused at the heart of an oppressive economic system. More evidence supports this revolutionary reading: hours later Jesus is picked up by the authorities and executed forthwith as a rebel. The argument for Jesus the revolutionary is complete.

Yet despite all this evidence, most of which is cited by Horsley,[15] he ultimately rejects this interpretation with an extremely telling comment: "It nevertheless seems unsatisfactory to reconstruct this as an attempted takeover of the Temple by Jesus and his followers despite the fact that it would fit well with the 'triumphal entry' and the subsequent arrest and execution of Jesus as a revolutionary leader. *It would mean that Jesus actions were naive and abortive.*"[16] This analysis is unsatisfactory because it would mean that Jesus *failed*.

Certainly, as Horsley admits, the evidence all fits. Moreover, Jesus, coming from Nazareth and avoiding the larger cities as far as we can

---

15. Ibid., 286–300.
16. Ibid., 298; emphasis mine.

tell, may have been in Jerusalem for the first time.[17] It is possible that he *was* näive and that his attempt at revolution *was* abortive as the text does not indicate that his actions drew the support of the crowds. Perhaps Jesus did bite off more than he could chew and had to retreat, ended up being identified as a troublemaker by the authorities, and was quickly dispatched.

Regardless of how well this conclusion flows from the evidence that Horsley has amassed, he will not follow it to the end. He will not repeat the mistake of Schweitzer who made Jesus incomprehensible to the modern world as a crazed apocalyptic who failed. Instead, Horsley reduces the cleansing of the temple from the start of the revolution to a "prophetic demonstration."[18] The result is that Jesus is a rather meek "social revolutionary" who "mediates God's liberation" to his people (and perhaps to us?) through word but not radical deed. Here, we clearly see Horsley's analysis is controlled by his theoretical commitment to Liberation Theology. Jesus, as an expression of God's liberating salvation on earth, must act as a paradigm to be emulated. He cannot, therefore, be a "failed revolutionary." Thus the logic of Liberation Theology forces Horsley to reject the clear outcome of his own evidence in service of his larger ideological end.

Instead, for Horsley, following the line of Liberation Theology, what Jesus offers is a new vision of social relations, one that establishes egalitarian relationships between villages, clans, and individuals. If we return to Horsley's category of "fantasy": has there been evidence amassed that would show Jesus operating outside that category? Horsley clearly thinks that Jesus's ethic, which seeks to build a non-hierarchical family structure, which encompasses the village, and which seeks to unite the peasantry and ultimately challenges the temple institution, moves him outside the realm of fantasy. But this must be weighed against the fact that while Jesus was setting up collectives in the villages, true liberation was expected to come from God who "was soon to judge the oppressive imperial regimes and give dominion to the people . . . God was effecting the revolution that would end the spiral of violence . . ."[19] Here Horsley cannot escape the logic of apocalyptic, and is this not fantasy?

17. Outside of Luke's legendary story of the young Jesus in the temple, we have no record of other visits in the synoptic gospels.

18. Horsley, *Spiral of Violence*, 299.

19. Ibid., 322.

Is this conviction any less fantastic than that of other messiahs like the Egyptian or Judas of Galilee who both equally expected divine intervention and ended up on the wrong side of a Roman sword? Here again we see the clash of Marxism, Liberation Theology, and apocalypticism as they come together in this analysis of Jesus.

Horsley, then, finds himself with the same problem that we have seen Marxists in previous chapters confront. He claims the apocalyptic mantle only to try to distance himself from it shortly thereafter. He turns to the category of "fantasy" in an attempt to distinguish the apocalyptic Jesus Movement from other prophetic movements following the logic of Marxism and yet, in the end, the same criticism that he aims at those other messianic movements is, by virtue of his commitment to an apocalyptic Jesus, applicable to his own analysis. This is only to be expected given the perspective of Marxism on religion as we saw earlier. The reading of Jesus as revolutionary in the temple surely corresponds to a Marxist reading of the text. However, rather than following his Marxist impulse through, his most prominent example of Jesus's revolutionary behavior he must ultimately undercut. Why does he engage in this problematic turn? To preserve a Jesus who can be followed, a Jesus who is a liberator to the oppressed, a Jesus who is relevant. To preserve the Jesus of Liberation Theology.

Ultimately, then, what is evident here is the same clash of ideologies that we saw in the previous chapter. Horsley has attempted to bring the three ideologies of Marxism, Liberation Theology, and apocalypticism into conjunction. He ends up confronting the same problems that those in the previous chapter did: apocalypticism is dependent on divine action, and apocalypticism is based on a false promise, both of which conflict fundamentally with the perspectives of Marxism and Liberation Theology. From the perspective of Marxism, Horsley must be critical of any attempts to resolve the fundamental economic oppression of society through "fantasy." It is somewhat ironic then to watch his turn to apocalyptic. His appeal to an apocalyptic Jesus attempts to provide a leader with a social critique that is applicable to today. And yet his commitment to Liberation Theology problematizes precisely this Jesus.

The issue of why Horsley makes this move, why Horsley turns away from a reading of the text which paints Jesus as a revolutionary has another aspect as well. I have already suggested Horsley's commitment to the imitable Jesus of Liberation Theology as one explanation. An expansion of that answer can be seen in his book *The Liberation of Christmas*.[20] The book is an interesting attempt to situate the infancy narratives, long dismissed as myths, in a social context. Horsley wants to bracket the history issues (he calls the texts "historical legends") and instead focuses on what social situations the texts may in fact be addressing. This leads him to suppose the texts are the result of Jewish Palestinian reflection. As a result, many of the features of the infancy narratives like the Herodian massacre, the census of Caesar, the magi and the shepherds are all interpreted within the political/social framework of the first century.

Horsley's reading of the infancy narratives, then, makes some fascinating connections between the historical situation of first century Palestine, which was largely colonial and oppressive, with an understanding of the elements in the birth narratives. Like in *Spiral*, Horsley's central point stems from his Marxist perspective. His is an understanding of the class dimensions of the situation described in the biblical texts. On top of the social ladder are the Romans and their Jewish vassals represented by the priestly aristocracy in Jerusalem and the Roman installed king: Herod. On the bottom are peasants who are buffeted by the taxes demanded by the Temple hierarchy on the one hand, and the Roman authorities on the other. Peasant lives were characterized by living hand to mouth and by often falling into debt which would strip them of their land.

The birth narratives, then, read in this perspective provide an interesting assessment of the situation. Herod's massacre of the infants, the problems caused by the holy family's trek to Bethlehem, the flight to Egypt all serve as a condemnation of these powers which afflict the peasants. Contrast the text's condemnation with the message of the angels who proclaim the coming of a savior who will free his people and the political ramifications are unmistakable. Jesus, from his very birth (and even before), is understood as a politically/socially redeeming figure who is a warrior of class struggle.

But returning to the question of Horsley's refusal to classify Jesus as a revolutionary, in the last section of *Liberation* Horsley completes the answer that is begun in *Spiral*. This section is Horsley's attempt to

20. Horsley, *Liberation of Christmas*.

draw an analogy between first century Palestine and today. He notes, quite rightly, that North American Christians identify with the lonely couple on a donkey seeking a place to stay. But such an identification is wrong, says Horsley. We are not the Jews; we are the Romans. The United States is the colonial power who oppresses other countries and lives off their wealth and blood just as the Romans did. It is third world nations, particularly Latin America, that are to be identified with Joseph and Mary, not us.

To that end, then, the birth narrative is not a message to rich north Americans, unless it is taken as a warning. The message of hope is for those whom we oppress. The rulers of this world will be brought down with the events inaugurated by the birth of the savior. This is the message of liberation theology, and it finds voice in the birth narrative.

The way Horsley shows this in the text is through the process of analogy. Using examples from Base Ecclesiastical Communities (BEC) Horsley shows how peasants read the text and identify with it. By seeing the text as precursor they are able to understand their own situation. "The people in the birth narratives thus become paradigms or prototypes for later readers or hearers: seeing that God helps earlier people, who venture to assert their freedom, they come to believe that God will help them as well and are able to take action in shaping their own lives."[21] In taking this position, Horsley in large part replicates the position of Liberation Theologians themselves. Horsley's commitment to the ideology of Liberation Theology is made manifest. Likewise, his need for a Jesus who is imitable is shown clearly to be an outgrowth of this allegiance.[22]

Herein lies the answer to the problem of Jesus as a revolutionary. Horsley cannot have a failed revolutionary because how can real revolutionaries identify with such a figure? A prophet proclaiming the coming redemption, *that* can be a prototype. A misguided apocalypticist has a much harder time inspiring emulation. Jesus, then, cannot be "naive" and "abortive" lest those who look to his example be the same. Thus for

---

21. Ibid., 156.

22. However, Horsley seems unaware that the critique of North America extends to him as well. My survey earlier of Latin American Liberation Theologians showed clearly that they are uninterested in theology from outside Latin America including such well intentioned thinkers as Horsley. Here again, Horsley is caught in a conflict between the presuppositions of the ideologies he employs.

Horsley, Jesus must be about real successful social revolution even if Horsley's own analysis gives cause for a very different reading.

Thus the basic problem of the conflict of ideologies reasserts itself. The logic of apocalyptic when applied to Jesus would make him problematic for modern day Christians. At the very worst Jesus as a failed revolutionary might be seen as delusional. Yet, herein lies the problem of ideologies: if Jesus is an apocalypticist then his perspective is both centered on divine, not human, action and ultimately wrong. Such a view cannot be sustained by either Liberation Theology, who refuse to see Jesus in this way, or Marxism which is skeptical of any notion of supernatural assistance. Moreover, a Marxist perspective would in fact embrace the notion of Jesus as a failed religionist as evidence of the ultimate failure of religion to effect real change—a view neither Liberation Theology nor Horsley would be willing to accept.

Horsley returns to the problem of Jesus and apocalypticism in his 1997 work *The Message and The Kingdom: How Jesus and Paul ignited a revolution and transformed the ancient world*. Here Horsley does a more popularized vision of his work on Galilee and archeology which we will discuss in detail later. Horsley makes the same argument he has made since *Spiral,* arguing that Jesus essentially taught a social ethic which envisioned a communal life focused around a call for Jewish renewal.

Horsley then returns again the issue of Jesus in the Temple. This time Horsley reinterprets the triumphant entrance into Jerusalem as parody rather than prophetic act. Horsley argues that Jesus riding on a donkey and the laying of palm branches symbols of Tiberias found on the Roman coins, were thus to be understood as "street theater."[23] His argument is founded on the notion that such an overt power grab as would be signified in a true messianic entry does not fit with Jesus: "It is inconceivable that Jesus—the tireless preacher against the evils of wealth and royal power—would have taken upon himself the mantel and trappings of the Davidic dynasty . . ."[24] Instead Jesus mocks such pretensions to power in his actions. These deeds, however, have been misinterpreted by the church and the gospel writers themselves.

It is intriguing to see how Horsley has struggled with the problem of Jesus in Jerusalem. His evidence led him in one direction while

---

23. Horsley and Silberman, *Message and the Kingdom*, 72.
24. Ibid., 73.

his analysis has led in another. His ideological commitments have prohibited him from carrying that logic through. Clearly he has been unsatisfied with his first answer with the result that one sees continued attempts at explanation. Each attempt has reinforced the central notion of the imitability of Jesus following the demands of Liberation Theology. Each reading moves Jesus farther from the picture of a failed revolutionary toward an understanding of Jesus as someone who can be followed and imitated. Thus we see Horsley being forced, by the logic of Liberation Theology which demands a Jesus who can be followed and has a revolutionary agenda, away from an interpretation that would compromise that reading.

Horsley's 1996 book *Archeology, History and Society in Galilee*[25] gives remarkable nuance to his theory articulated in *Spiral*. Early on he admits that there has been a very serious challenge to his reading of the Kingdom of God material as apocalyptic.[26] This leads Horsley to change his characterization of Jesus. While in reality Horsley spends very little time talking about the historical Jesus, when he does, he invokes the category of prophet.[27] One has to question the category of "prophet," however, for it seems somewhat undefined. For Horsley it seems that Jesus is a prophet because he called for a "renewal movement" in Galilee. While in *Spiral* Horsley criticized prophetic movements as "fantasy" based, it is interesting to note that, like the term "apocalyptic," the concept of "fantasy" is also abandoned in this text.

In this text, then, Horsley has abandoned his two key conceptual apparatuses. The ramifications of this are enormous. By abandoning "apocalyptic," Horsley must find a new place in which to ground the twin advantages he proclaimed apocalyptic provided: Critical vision and motivation for radical social change. Horsley wants to expand his notion of the "prophet" to take some of this weight. But he also wants to shift the locus of the discussion from large social revolution to localized reform. His reading of Base Ecclesial Communities (BEC) in Latin America that we saw in *Liberating* has given him a new model for envisioning the Jesus movement.

---

25. Horsley, *Archaeology*.
26. Ibid., 3.
27. Ibid., 189.

But beyond this, the movement away from these two categories also has ideological ramifications as well. Clearly, Horsley has now completely abandoned the apocalyptic system; its problems, as we have detailed, are too much to bear. But the elimination of the category of "fantasy" also has ideological import as well. The term "fantasy" for Horsley clearly was a signifier of his use of Marxist ideology, the notion that real change must be based on something other than an "illusion." By leaving this notion behind, one must wonder if in some way Horsley's use of Marxism has undergone some change as well.

The key question that yet remains is what sense to make of the Jesus movement? Regardless of the labels, the message is unchanged for Horsley. Jesus is still seen as opposing both the authorities in Rome and Jerusalem. The issue is now, without the convenient label of apocalypticism which envisions the destruction of all worldly powers (both Jewish and Roman), how does one justify an anti-Roman, anti-temple Jesus? Horsley turns to archeology for an answer.

Most of Horsley's work in *Archeology* is an attempt to read archeology in a way that supports the picture of the Jesus movement that he previously constructed in *Spiral*. Having moderated his position somewhat so that he is no longer saddled with the concept of "apocalyptic" Horsley still has several issues to address. In order to explore these issues some background is required. As Horsley is writing, in New Testament studies there were two competing visions of Galilee, both based on archeology: Those who saw Galilee as intensely Hellenized and those who saw it as very Judean. Archaeological evidence can be marshaled for both positions. Those who see Galilee as Hellenized point to the fact that major cities with tell-tale signs of Hellenization, such as the theaters and public baths, were constructed shortly before the time of Jesus. They posit that there is evidence of trade between the cities and the villages found in pottery and coins. The transaction of goods generally entails a commerce of ideas as well, and thus they argue that it likely that even a small Galilean village like Nazareth would be exposed to Hellenistic ideals and beliefs.[28]

This ties in well for those who hold that the some early Jesus movements may be understood on the model of the Greek Cynics.[29] The idea

---

28. Mack, *Who Wrote*, 38–40.
29. Ibid.

that Galilee was quite cosmopolitan and that ideas were floating around from different places would mean that Jesus quite likely could have been exposed to tales of the cynics or perhaps even the teachings of the cynics—the social gadflies of the Roman world. The wisdom teacher Jesus, then, can be read like the cynics, calling for simplicity and viewing the world with a knowing nod and a poke at its excesses.

On the other hand is the vision of Galilee that which makes it very Jewish and particularly influenced by Judea. The argument here hinges on the idea that the Galileans had blood ties with those in Judea as well as religious ties to the temple. The Galileans are understood as individuals who quite likely made regular trips to Jerusalem to participate in temple activities and Jerusalem festivals. These archaeologists point to the similarity in building construction between Judean and Galilean houses and other household utensils.[30]

The crux of the Judean-Galilean argument hinges on what happened after the Assyrian invasion of the northern kingdom. In the eighth century BCE Assyria conquered the northern kingdom of Israel which included Galilee and began a program of deportation. How extensive that program of deportation was is subject to debate. Second Kings tells us that Galilee was captured and taken to Assyria.[31] The real question, then, is how much of the population was deported. If only the elite and royal family were deported, as with the Babylonian captivity in the south, then there would remain an Israelite presence in the north. If, however, the Assyrians engaged in a wholesale deportation of the population, then a combination of gentiles from elsewhere and some Judeans from the south may well have moved to the unoccupied north and the Northern Israelite influence would mostly have evaporated. If the latter is the case, then Galilee would have a much more cosmopolitan feel, no longer being made up exclusively of Jews.

Not surprisingly Horsley makes this a primary issue of discussion. Horsley crafts a middle road between these two camps. On the one hand, he argues strongly that the Assyrian deportation included only "administrative towns" and that "they must have left most of the peasantry on the land"[32] in order to secure a tax base. Likewise he

---

30. See Reed, *Archaeology*.
31. 2 Kings 15.
32. Horsley, *Archaeology*. 23

rejects a Hellenistic Galilee. For him the Jesus movement remains a *Jewish* renewal movement not to be besmirched by gentile, Cynic or Greek ideals. On the other hand, the Jesus movement must not be a *Judean* renewal movement because that would connect it to the temple hierarchy in Jerusalem. Horsley hypothesizes an antagonism between the Galilean north and the Judean south. For Horsley, the Jesus movement opposes both Roman colonization/Hellenism and the Jerusalem power structure.

What Horsley envisions is a relatively isolated Galilean population. Left behind by the Assyrians, they were subsequently oppressed by both Judea and then also the Romans but those relationships were strictly based on taxes, tribute and tithes. As for issues of culture, Horsley envisions the Galileans holding on to the Israelite traditions of the northern kingdom. Thus the prominence of Moses, Elijah and Elisha in the earliest Christian texts bears witness for Horsley to an independent Israelite tradition employed by the Jesus movement.[33]

In *Archeology* Horsley maintains the outline of his picture of Jesus as the leader of this renewal movement as painted in *Spiral*. Jesus is still about a radical response to oppression. Jesus's constructive focal point, however, is remaking village life. Jesus envisions a new conception of the village as a non-hierarchical family which maintains solidarity in the face of economic oppression. The Roman powers, as well as the Temple Hierarchy, are in conflict with peasants. Jesus is engaged in a modified form of class warfare which on the one hand condemns the powerful exploitation by the elite and on the other envisions a new form of village life which addresses social/interpersonal relations.

Note what has happened here. Horsley is moving away from a sociological reading of the text to an appeal to archeology. Having lost his literary hook of apocalypticism he now endeavors to ground two of his fundamental precepts (critique and reform) in Archeology. In a sense this is the natural progression that his Marxist analysis has spawned. The shift to archeology represents a shift to materiality, a renewed focus on material reality as an indication of real life. But likewise it also is a macro approach to the topic, looking at society as a whole which is also a more classically Marxist approach. The result of this is Horsley's refocusing on the larger social environment that was the ground of the

---

33. Mack, *Myth*, 224–26.

Jesus movement. It is understandable that in the quest for a new understanding of these issues Horsley should turn to material artifacts.

However, Horsley's appeal to archeology also maintains Horsley's vision of an imitable Jesus, as well as attempting to reground his first fundamental precept of Jesus as a critic of an unjust social system. As a victim of Judean and Roman oppression Jesus responds as one who leads the way to radical social change. That change, of course, is no longer revolution on a societal level, it now occurs at the grassroots per his reading of Liberation Theology. The use of archeology allows Horsley to try to create an environment where such a reformist movement could be successful and at the same time become a model for modern liberation movements particularly the localized cells of the BECs.

We have seen, then, how Horsley is ultimately forced by the contradictions inherent between the ideologies of Liberation Theology, apocalypticism and Marxism to retreat from apocalypticism in his analysis. Here we also begin to see a move away from a more pronounced form of Marxism that envisions world revolution that is coupled with apocalypticism. Horsley now seems to be moving towards a form of thinking which is more focused on the local level. In the next section I will try to examine how this theoretical shift took place for Horsley.

It is interesting to watch Horsley struggle with the issues we have seen other scholars confront. Horsley begins with the same dilemma that others in the previous chapter have wrestled with. The two-edged sword of apocalypticism threatened to smite Horsley as it did others I have examined. But Horsley has another issue as well, which is imitability. Horsley wants a Jesus who is a model that can be followed. To this end apocalyptic is, in some ways, even more problematic for Horsley than for the other Marxists I have surveyed.

In the end, Horsley eventually does what the individuals in the previous chapter could not—he rejects apocalyptic. In *Message* he abandons completely this label "apocalyptic" noting "Theirs [the Jesus Movement] was not an other worldly or surrealistic apocalyptic vision …"[34] This departure was precipitated by two factors: Work on Q and the thought of Antonio Gramsci.

---

34. Horsley and Silberman, *Message and the Kingdom*, 113.

The Turn to Gramsci

It should come as no surprise, then, that Horsley ultimately jettisons apocalypticism. The price for it is too high. However the benefit of apocalypticism—its critique of the current power structure and its promise of a new just world is still important for Horsley. He is able to reconstitute this benefit through Q.

The final redaction of Q is ideally suited for Horsley. The judgmental sayings (which condemn those with power) express precisely the critique that Horsley wants (though he is inclined to interpret them as more specifically political than other interpreters). The sapiential (wisdom) material, then, functions to envision a new just world through the Kingdom of God.[35] The advantage of this, however, is that sayings that envision this kingdom assume that it is provided, not by divine act, but by local human action. In a sense, it is a different sort of social change—it does not envision changing the world but functions more as a micro-resistance to power.[36]

But the question that Horsley has yet to confront is whether the prophetic section of Q really surmounts the problems of apocalypticism. For the fire that "winnows the field" is the divine wrath of the "one who is coming," (Q 5) not the Q community. The cleansing of the old system is still dependent upon the action of the divine even if the new world is built by the believers. But Horsley seems untroubled by the fact that the text seems to require immediate divine intervention which leaves one to wonder, "why not?"

How does one explain Horsley's abandonment of apocalypticism with its revolutionary implications moving in the end to the more localized approach? Is there a way to theoretically account for Horsley's shift?

---

35. If the sapiential material can be divided from the judgmental material and seen as antecedent (as Kloppenborg and others do. Kloppenborg, *Formation of Q*, Kloppenborg, *Social History*, Mack, *Kingdom That Didn't Come*, Mack, *Lost Gospel*.), then the Jesus movement lacks the prophetic aspect in its earliest incarnation. The apocalyptic saying of Jesus thus become secondary and inauthentic. Horsley has been a strong critic of Kloppenborg's stratigraphy of Q (Horsley, *Questions*; Horsley, *Q and Jesus*; Horsley, *Archaeology*.) and Kloppenborg has equally been critical of Horsley's view of Q (Kloppenborg, *Formation of Q Revisited*; Kloppenborg, *Excavating Q*).

36. I am indebted to the able discussion of micro-resistance in a localized setting by Gottschal, *Deconstruction of Gender*, 279–99.

I think perhaps we may find a clue in his 1989 paper on Q.[37] In a section attempting to address the issue of the social context of Q, Horsley uses the term "organic intellectual"[38] in describing the leader of popular social movements. The phrase "organic intellectual" is a key concept in the work of Marxist Antonio Gramsci and a move to Gramsci may, in fact, explain much in terms of Horsley's own development.

We have already explored some of Gramsci previously; however, there are several concepts from Gramsci's writings which may prove extremely useful in understanding Horsley's analysis. Perhaps the most well known is the concept of "hegemony." The notion of hegemony is defined by Gramsci as "The 'spontaneous's consent given by the great masses of the population to the general direction imposed on social life by the dominant fundamental group; this consent is 'historically' caused by the prestige (and consequent confidence) which the dominant group enjoys because of its position and function in the world of production."[39] It is important to note that hegemony is contrasted with "coercion" which is associated with the state.[40] Hegemony itself is a function of civil society. Hegemony may be understood as the ideological glue which holds society together. Its failure represents the moment of crisis for a society in which the state must turn to coercion.[41]

The idea of hegemony is a cornerstone for Gramsci and appears throughout his work. The benefit of the notion of hegemony is that it postulates that society is not just about the power of the state but takes seriously the ideological component of society. Since society is controlled not just by force but also by the hegemony of a specific ideology, social change comes about through an elongated process. Much of this is predicated upon a statement by Marx in his *Preface to the Critique of Political Economy*. There Marx states, "No social order ever perishes before all the productive forces for which there are room in it have developed; and new, higher relations of production never appear before the material conditions of their existence have matured in the womb of the old society itself. Therefore mankind always sets itself

---

37. Horsley, *Questions*, 195.
38. Ibid.
39. Gramsci, *Selections*, 12.
40. Ibid.
41. Ibid., 275–76.

only such tasks as it can solve; since looking at the matter more closely, it will always be found that the task itself arises only when the material conditions for its solution already exist or at least in the process of formation."[42] The focus on this particular formulation by Marx actually gives Gramsci a long view in which to envision social change. Social change occurs when a time of crisis erupts on a macro scale. Such a crisis may be "sometimes lasting for decades"[43] which includes a long struggle by the forces currently in power to secure their position against the forces of opposition. The end is not foreordained as the rulers may still be able to consolidate their power and fend off these attacks. If, however, the "incurable structural contradictions have revealed themselves (reached maturity)"[44] then the opposition will win and social change can occur with the creation of a new social formation as a result. Such a change, however, requires that there be a concomitant alteration in the economic system.

The crisis of hegemony, then, is a crisis where established authority is questioned. Horsley's vision of the Jesus movement, with its critical approach to the current ruling classes (both Roman and Judean) and the establishment of a new ethic of living fits rather well into the Gramscian model. Horsley, then, allows for the deferral of the effect of the judgment sayings that are found in Q, in the same way that Gramsci seems to allow for a delay of the revolution of the proletariat which arises after the hegemonic crisis through his typology of "wars."

Gramsci postulates three distinct types of movements: The "war of movement," the "war of position" and "underground warfare."[45] The war of movement is the frontal assault on the current power structure, while the underground warfare appears to focus on secret preparations of troops and weapons. It is the middle category, the war of position, which is more ideologically oriented. Here Gramsci points to the actions of Ghandi against the English. The emphasis is on engaging in struggle through taking a stand for a different way of life, rather than overt warfare. The other categories are to be taken up when the situation

---

42. Marx, *Contribution*.
43. Gramsci, *Selections*, 178.
44. Ibid.
45. Ibid., 229–30.

warrants, the revolution is not avoided, but while one waits for the right time for the war of movement, one engages in the war of position.

The war of position is a battle for hearts and minds and becomes the preeminent battle which must be engaged. Gramsci argues, "in politics the 'war of position,' once won is decisive definitively."[46] Once this creates the "crisis of authority," Gramsci postulates, "the great masses have become detached from their traditional ideologies, and no longer believe what they used to believe previously."[47] The masses have moved beyond their rulers and now have a set of beliefs that no longer align with that of the dominators. In that moment, the rulers have lost consent and thus begins (possibly) their ultimate decline.

Certainly this war of position appears to fit well with Horsley's conclusion. He is no longer troubled by the words of judgment. He can appreciate their critique without having to work out their application. He can do this precisely in the way that Gramsci does, by bifurcating the war of movement and the war of position. There is now the war on poverty, oppression and injustice which is battled through the war of position—The Kingdom of God. And there is still the future world of the war of movement which is promised to come in "the fullness of time."

Gramsci's work shows us how to understand the turn in Horsley's position. It is not that he has just abandoned the eschatological language in the text, it is that there is now a new theoretical apparatus that allows for precisely the kind of bifurcation Horsley's own analysis needed. In the meantime he functions as an interesting example of one who has dodged the sword of apocalypticism.

We cannot leave it at that, however, because what remains unaddressed by this move to Gramsci is still the problem of religion. Horsley rather blithely assumes that these ideological moves towards more egalitarian communities will ultimately result in some sort of larger structural change. But, as we saw with the Birmingham schools' work, this assumes that the dominoes fall correctly. Instead, it is as probable that the same problem Comaroff found, which was that through their communities the South African Zionists ended up reinforcing the status quo, would occur in the situation of the Jesus people. The problem for

46. Ibid., 239.
47. Ibid., 276.

the Marxists is that the solution, linked to religion as it is, is still illusory, or to use Horsley's term "fantasy."

Additionally, it is no accident that Gramsci does not stop at the "war of position." The war of position is only a partial answer; it provides the opportunity when the moment of hegemonic crisis comes. But this is not all: Gramsci has not given up the notion of revolution; the war of position is not an end itself. The war of position must, Gramsci reminds us, be prepared for by underground warfare and followed by the war of movement. However, what is clear is that for these other two stages, Horsley is still bound to the logic of apocalypticism for structural social change, reduced to divine action rather than human revolution, even if that is indefinitely postponed.

Still, our earlier examination of Gramsci also shows that Gramsci's work is no more amenable to religion than other forms of Marxism. Gramsci sees Marxism as ultimately replacing religion. Such a position is clearly not part of Horsley's world view. Thus, while Horsley makes use of Gramsci, his abandonment of apocalypticism and uncritical perspective on religion makes it clear that his ultimate allegiance lies with Liberation Theology as the final arbiter of his positions.

The three fundamental precepts of class conflict, Jesus as social critic/reformer and Jesus as model for liberation, as they evolved in Horsley work, show that Horsley's adherence to them have illuminated the text in different ways and in different measures. What emerges as the guiding principal in the end is the ideology of Liberation Theology. The conjunction of the three ideologies and the problems they create show themselves as Horsley seems to, at points, rebel against the text itself. While ideally the text should reflect the various ideological claims what is exposed instead is the problematic nature of the text itself. The laudable goals of economic justice, human dignity and care for the poor and oppressed are undermined by the way the text makes its point. Yet, unlike a consistent Marxist position, Horsley does not engage in a critique of the texts themselves.

Still, Horsley's ultimate commitment to the ideology of Liberation Theology over the ideology of apocalypticism and Marxism leaves several issues unresolved, as we have seen. At the most basic level, there is a question of standing. Horsley as a white North American scholar is specifically barred from contributing to the work of Liberation Theology by the adherents of Liberation Theology. But bracketing that issue (since

Horsley is clearly free to participate whether invited or not) by aligning himself with Liberation Theology he takes on the same problems that we found in our earlier analysis. The Marxist critique of Liberation Theology is that its attempt to save religion, to find revolution in religion, is ultimately a form of engaging in an "imaginary" solution that in the end fails to address the real economic problems.

Additionally, as I have pointed out, the problem of apocalypticism is not resolved; it is merely deferred, subsumed for the moment by the sapiential sayings of Q which Horsley reads as a blueprint for an egalitarian world. Yet, the ultimate weight of enforcement behind these texts remains the threat of apocalyptic. As a whole, then, Q follows the logic of the apocalyptic ideology, and its function remains the enforcement of a set of behaviors that are secured by the coming divine action. And yet, as is the case with apocalypticism, the divine action does not occur, the axe never falls.

But more importantly, one must wonder whether a set of behaviors that are enforced by apocalyptic threat, even if the behaviors themselves are just and egalitarian, is really consistent with the principles of Liberation Theology. We have seen that the Liberation theologians themselves are quite circumspect, never appealing to apocalyptic texts. I have argued that the reason for this is that ultimately Liberation Theology is not comfortable with the notion that the revolution is dependent on divine action in the end as well as an implicit recognition of the coercive nature of apocalyptic generally. Horsley seems to believe that Q offers a way out to this dilemma, but in reality it is subject to the same apocalyptic logic and only postpones the problem.

Thus, we have seen after this extensive review of Horsley, the problematic nature of the texts. The struggle we have seen Horsley engage in as he tries to control the texts is an indication that the texts themselves are not free of ideology and that their ideology often conflicts with the ideology of the interpreter, be it Liberation Theology or Marxist. After all this, one may wonder, why show deference to the texts at all? I shall explore the individuals in New Testament studies who are asking just such a question in the next chapter.

6

Ideological Criticism

Horsley's move from a more classical Marxist approach to a Gramscian Marxism is an important bellwether of the change in New Testament studies in general. The problems that we have seen in the chapter on New Testament Marxist interpreters as well as the issues that arose in Horsley's early writings are indicative of conflicts that a Marxist analysis must surmount when trying to integrate the logic of Marxism, Liberation Theology, and apocalypticism. In recent years, the rise of a subdiscipline of biblical studies called "Ideological Criticism" has taken the same sort of tact as Horsley. These thinkers have made their investigations using the broader range of neo-Marxist thinkers like Gramsci and others. What I will show is that these scholars resolve the dilemma by opting here for Marxism as the controlling discourse; however, the result is the authority of the text continues to deteriorate. In the end, the question of the role of the text as a tool for the advocacy for real social change will come to the fore.

The Postmodern Bible

The Postmodern Bible is a scholarly attempt at outlining the methods of biblical studies in light of new disciplinary endeavors that have formed in the wake of postmodernism. The essay "ideological discourse" in *The Postmodern Bible* is very straightforward about the position and agenda of ideological criticism as a movement.

The authors of *The Postmodern Bible* trace the advent of ideological criticism to the work of Althusser and more recent Marxist literary critics. The work of Terry Eagleton and Fredric Jameson inform their position, but clearly Althusser's definition of ideology is pre-eminent.

Thus they state, "As an ethically grounded act, ideological reading intends to raise critical consciousness about what is just and unjust about those lived relations that Althusser describes, and to change those power relationships for the better. It challenges the readers to accept political responsibility for themselves and for the world in which they live."[1] Note the way Althusser is seen as a way to establish an ethical position to create social change. While Althusser's analysis of ideology is interesting, it is not clear that his structuralist position would really lay the groundwork for the kind of personal political action that the Collective would like.[2]

Still it is clear that the focus is on ethics. The authors assert, "Ideological criticism is to be seen as a resistant act, a positive, ethical response."[3] They concede that "not all ideological-critical reading[s] are transformative..."[4] and yet clearly the goal for these scholars is to engage in such transformative readings. The issue is clear here. There is no pretense to objectivity. Ideological criticism seeks to re-read the biblical text as a way of changing the "system of power that shape the lived relations not only of readers of the bible, but the vast majority of the world's people who in varying ways have suffered real poverty, oppression and violence."[5] Ideological criticism's method for creating this change is "exposure." There is something of the "intrepid reporter" in this analysis who changes things just by publishing the story about those who are abusing power. In this case, however, the abuse is not conducted by ruthless oil companies or monied big-tobacco; it is done through the pulpits of churches by the biblical text itself.

One may in fact be overawed by the immensity of the task that is laid out in the first section of their essay and also by the weakness of the methodological tools from which such awesome change is expected. In a sense, as Gershwin put it so well, the agenda of the biblical critic exemplified in "the things that you're liable to read in the bible, ain't

---

1. Collective, *Postmodern Bible*, 275.

2. Althusser's structuralist perspective becomes clear in his article "Contradiction and Overdetermination: Notes for an Investigation." Where it is the weight of the contradiction between labor and capital that ultimately brings the capitalist system down. In this way personal action seems somewhat irrelevant.

3. Collective, *Postmodern Bible*, 277.

4. Ibid.

5. Ibid.

necessarily so" has been in play since the origin of biblical studies. It is not anything new to attempt to expose the Biblical text, yet what is significant about ideological criticism is that it does so from a Marxist perspective. The focus on the text *as* ideology is thus a new layer, for it changes the locus of interrogation. The problem is no longer that the text through source manipulation or a history of tradition has had its message convoluted; the problem is the message of the text itself. The Biblical works have an intentional agenda that they are attempting to impress upon their readers which often is oppressive. Thus the problem is not that the "real" message is lost, rather it is the "real" message itself that is the problem.

Again, this might not seem particularly unique or new. The fact that the text has an agenda has been noted throughout the course of the history of biblical criticism.[6] Where ideological readings of the text become separated from traditional historical criticism is the agenda which ideological criticism has chosen. The focus on political/economic/social liberation as the point of reading (either in concert with the text or opposed to the text) puts a different emphasis on reading. The goal of ideological criticism is to engage the text in a dialog from an already existent perspective. "Hence, ideological criticism of the Bible entails the twin effort (1) to read the ancient biblical stories for their ideological content and mode of production and (2) to grasp the ideological character of contemporary reading strategies."[7] This is clearly mediated by an adherence to Marxism rooted in an understanding of ideology based in class conflict. Thus this agenda sets Marxism as the controlling discourse that is used to analyze the text.

But another important element about ideological criticism which is similar to what we have seen in Horsley is that there is a focus on the biblical text as paradigmatic call to action in the world. The text speaks to today. "A typical element of liberationist readings is the narrative identification of the context of ancient Israel with the contemporary context of the reader."[8] We saw this as one of the cornerstones of the twists and turns that Horsley makes as he attempts to construct his

---

6. Form criticism's focus on the liturgical use of the texts always assumed that the texts were shaped or formed by particular theological perspectives. Likewise redaction criticism focused on the larger agenda of the Gospel writers.

7. Collective, *The Postmodern Bible*, 277.

8. Ibid., 283.

portrait of the historical Jesus. We noted that Horsley is loathe to make Jesus a full-revolutionary precisely because it mitigates the issue of imitation. Thus here, as with Horsley, a demand to make the text relevant ultimately serves to undercut the Marxist analysis employed.

Still, the place where ideological criticism goes the next step beyond Horsley is in its examination of conflicting ideologies. The prime example given in the essay "Ideological Criticism" in the *Postmodern Bible* is the Exodus. The Exodus is a key operational metaphor for Liberation Theology as we have seen in Miranda and as is clear in liberationist movements from Latin America to Martin Luther King, Jr. Yet, as I have noted in my analysis of Miranda,[9] the Exodus narrative is not exclusively a liberationist text. For the march out of Egypt is followed by a march into Canaan and the subsequent destruction of its native peoples. The text proudly proclaims the utter destruction of an indigenous people and does so without apology.

Insofar as ideological criticism acknowledges and denounces the text in this instance as oppressive, it differentiates itself from both liberationist perspectives (which claim the liberatory message of the text) and historical critical perspectives (which focus on the historical genesis of the text). It also recovers a key idea that historical criticism noted but failed to appreciate – the political aspects of the text. Historical criticism held that the texts were constructed and preserved because they were relevant to a community or group. That said, the nature of a group is to focus precisely on issues of insider/outsider, exogamy/endogamy and to have those with power in the group praised and those without excoriated. Ideological criticism focuses on this exercise of power.

The final redaction of Q may be used to make this point. For as surely as Q pokes at the powerful, the proud and the rich, it likewise mercilessly attacks Bethsaida and Chorazin. While one may be enamored of Q's psuedo-hippie lifestyle, one must admit there were certainly those who were not and these two towns are representative of those who declined Q's invitation. Horsley notes that Tyre and Sidon with which Chorazin and Bethsaida are compared were examples of cities which exploited the resources of Galilee.[10] Thus we may be led to think that these cities attacked by Q also lived off of the oppression of others.

---

9. This argument is made forcefully in Warrior, *Canaanites, Cowboys and Indians*. see below

10. Horsley and Draper, *Whoever Hears You*, 248.

But can we so quickly conclude that all the Q adversaries were those who benefited from an unjust power system? Or could the rejectors of Q be those who advocated a different approach to oppression, perhaps a more direct attack on the powerful, who were repelled by Q's light prescriptions (perhaps the Sicarii)? On the other hand, the rejectors of Q may have been individuals who chose life: Those who had seen the fate of messianic pretenders in the past and what befell them and their followers (Josephus?). Does such an approach make those who reject Q weak or collaborators? It is not necessarily so, but *their* positions, *their* ideology is obliterated by the Q text. We do not know why the Q people were not welcomed; we only see the dust shaken off their feet as they walk on to the next village. An ideological critical approach has to question such a lacunae.

One of the more recent applications of Marxist theory to New Testament studies is thus found in ideological criticism. The genesis for this approach is undoubtedly found in the work of Norman Gottwald. Gottwald has truly taken seriously the issue of class and oppression in his reconstructions of Hebrew Bible texts. His most significant work deals with a reconstruction of the Israelite "conquest" found in Joshua and Judges.[11] Eschewing both conquest models[12] as well as the infiltration model,[13] Gottwald postulates a class revolt model. His model involves a combination of Canaanite peasants rebelling against their Canaanite/Egyptian overlords coupled with the collaboration of the Hebrew tribes. Gottwald, then, employs the primary Marxist concept of class conflict and uses it to examine the data regarding the conquest. While this theory has not received universal acceptance, it has earned a place among the other time-honored theories of Hebrew colonization of Palestine.

Gottwald's influence in the ideological discourse article is clear and he is referenced several times.[14] In fact the portion of the "twin effort" above which refers to determining the "mode of production" is a reference to Gottwald's article on sociological method.[15] However, while

---

11. Gottwald, *Tribes of Yahweh*.
12. Albright, *Biblical Period*.
13. Noth, *History of Israel*.
14. Collective, *Postmodern Bible*, 287–90.
15. Gottwald and Horsley, *Bible in Latin American Theology*, 142–53.

Gottwald may focus on more traditional Marxist analysis as well as ideological analysis, the Collective indicates it tends towards "a movement away from a concentration of the classic notion of class struggle and the negative identification of ideology with the mystification of truth"[16] to a more exclusive focus on ideological analysis which Gottwald has also pioneered in biblical studies.

Nonetheless, this move towards more ideological analysis to the detriment of issues like class struggle should give us pause. Ideological criticism shows a greater dependence upon Marxist analysis in that it takes a more critical approach to the text. It is willing to set the text against itself, "reading against the grain" and seeking to uncover the power dynamics that are in play. It therefore represents a move towards the critical approach to religion that is found in Marxism. Thus the Collective states, "Better ideological readings are those that support and encourage positive social change that affirms difference and inclusion."[17] The occlusion of class as the basis of the Marxist ethical stand ultimately contradicts the logic of the Marxist critique and indicates a move back towards a more theological bent. The very fact that the analysis is cast in solely ethical terms threatens to exchange Marxism for Populism and indicates that once again a theological agenda (that of Liberation Theology) is still exerting influence.

Yet the ideological critics are not all of one stripe. Certainly Norman Gottwald has been incredibly influential among Hebrew Bible scholars who are doing Marxist analysis. However, his influence has yet to spread to New Testament studies. In the ideological criticism bibliography in *The Postmodern Bible* there are actually very few New Testament scholars (currently publishing) who make the list. Of those that do, the most prominent is Tina Pippin

Tina Pippin

Tina Pippin's work is interesting as it is perhaps the most theoretically sophisticated of the New Testament ideological critics. Pippin's work shows engagement, not just with the text but also with the theoretical apparatuses that she employs. Her work also, interestingly enough,

---

16. Collective, *Postmodern Bible*, 276.
17. Ibid., 302.

focuses on apocalyptic and particularly the Apocalypse of John (commonly known as Revelation).

In her first book, *Death and Desire: The Rhetoric of Gender in the Apocalypse of John*,[18] Pippin approaches her work as a "feminist-materialist." She defines this approach as follows: "A Marxist-feminist reading stresses both women's experiences as readers and women's connection with the reproduction of power. The ideological structures of class oppression can be seen through both the presence of women in the text and the presence of women readers."[19] The focus of Marxist-feminist readings, then, are to pick-up on the gender aspect which is frequently given a backseat in traditional Marxist analyses which see class as primary. The Marxist-feminist approach, then, looks to incorporate "both class and gender reading."[20]

To this end the apocalypse proves rather dicey because of its multiple levels. On the one hand, from the perspective of class, the apocalypse certainly envisions the ultimate demise of the wealthy and the powerful. On the other hand, Pippin points out the continual misogynistic treatment of women in the text. The Marxist-feminist approach, then, allows her recognition of both these aspects.

Before engaging in a more detailed analysis of Pippin's work, it is worth surveying the work of her dialog partners on the apocalypse. Two feminist scholars have already contributed analyses of the apocalypse: Adela Yarbro Collins and Elizabeth Schüssler Fiorenza.

Adela Yarbro Collins, in her work, *Crisis and Catharsis* makes the argument that apocalyptic functions psychologically as a form of cathartic release. The situation of oppression (or perceived oppression, since Yarbro Collins cannot find evidence of real oppression occurring during the time of the writing of the apocalypse)[21] is characterized by tension. Individuals feel the strain of their situation. However, it is not so much a change in the attitude of the Roman government towards Christians which was the impetus of such tension; rather, argues Yarbro

---

18. Pippin, *Death and Desire*.
19. Ibid., 58.
20. Ibid., 59.
21. Collins, *Crisis*, 104–5.

Collins, it is the change in the mindset of the Christians which created the problem.[22]

Here, Yarbro Collins appeals to the idea of "relative deprivation" which she derives from John Gager's work.[23] Yarbro Collins focuses on the idea that it is not that the individuals attracted to apocalyptic are necessarily physically deprived, rather there is gap between what is expected and what is delivered. As Yarbro Collins puts it, there is "a marked disparity between expectations and their satisfaction."[24]

Yarbro Collins, then, argues that these early Christians are trapped in a cage of their own making. The proclamation of the Kingdom of God as present through Jesus entailed certain expectations. To live in the Kingdom of God as a favored son or daughter clearly should have significant and beneficial ramifications. Instead the community of the apocalypse found itself increasingly frustrated. "It was the tension between John's vision of the kingdom of God and his environment that moved him to write his Apocalypse."[25]

Yarbro Collins employs Leon Festinger's category of "cognitive dissonance" to explain sociologically how this may come about, which we have also examined.[26] Festinger's work certainly has its validity; however, I would question its applicability for New Testament studies.[27] Unlike early Christianity, the entire lifespan of the group Festinger studied cannot generously be put at anything longer than two years.[28] I would submit that Festinger's study shows, then, that while cognitive

22. Ibid., 106.

23. Gager, *Kingdom and Community*, 27. This notion is originally from Yonina Talmon's article, "Pursuit of Millennium."

24. Collins, *Crisis*, 106.

25. Ibid., 106

26. See above, ch. 3

27. There is a real question whether a twentieth-century U.F.O. cult might have anything in common with a first-century cult of the dead. Not to mention the rather problematic nature of the study where Festinger's students actually caused the group to balloon in size thereby creating a different dynamic than might have otherwise existed.

28. Another real problem occurs with the timeframe a careful reading of Festinger's study proposes. The first delay of the arrival of the U.F.O. was resolved with a postponement of the arrival date and a new emphasis on group recruitment. However, even after the second delay was effectively resolved, the group was not able to maintain cohesion. Festinger notes that only a year later the majority of members had drifted away from the group. Festinger, Riecken, and Schachter, *Prophecy Fails*, 130–33.

dissonance may explain spikes in evangelism, it is ultimately a recipe for group dissolution not long-term cohesion.

The theory of the cathartic nature of the apocalypse is focused on its violent imagery. While Yarbro Collins is quick to point out that no human-against-human violence is condoned (a point disputed by Pippin who notes the kings of the earth eat the flesh of the whore of Babylon), the text is riddled through and through with violent scenarios. Interestingly, Yarbro Collins explains this with an appeal to Theissen's work on aggressiveness.[29] Theissen's work on this topic is ultimately dependent upon a curious reading of Talcott Parson's work.[30] Thus, in this case, Yarbro Collins's analysis is dependent upon functionalism for her analysis.

In essence then, Yarbro Collins argues that the apocalypse functions as a release valve for the tension built up by a society that creates dissatisfaction in its membership. Yarbro Collins's appeal to functionalism, then, suffers from the problems that beset functionalism.[31] Yet Yarbro Collins's analysis of apocalyptic does ultimately concede the point that it does not lead to meaningful change. Yarbro Collins sees apocalyptic literature as a psychological salve that tempers the pain of real life. Eventually, of course as we have discussed earlier, the user

---

29. Collins, *Crisis*, 156.

30. Theissen discusses Christianity as a solution to aggression in *Sociology*, 52–87, which is an adaption of Talcott Parson's typology from Parsons, *Patterns of Aggression*, 316–17 (cf. Parsons, *Systematic Theory in Sociology*). A significant difference between Theissen's understanding of aggression and Parsons's is that Parsons sees it as something that is both necessary and beneficial to society. It is the engine that produces creativity. Theissen, on the other, hand sees aggression as a problem that Christianity is able to overcome through the concept of "grace." This is created through the haphazard merging of Weber notion of charisma with Parsons's ideas. Theissen's idiosyncratic reading of Parsons then ends up contradicting the basis of functionalism that sees the development of social attributes like aggression as functional for society. He does this ultimately, as he admits, to create relevancy in "the figure of Jesus—even down to our own time" (110).

31. There have been several critiques of functionalism from religion scholars. Hans Penner's work (*Impasse and Resolution*) focuses specifically upon the critique issues by philosopher Carl Hempel, (*Logic of Functional Analysis*), who argues that functionalism does not technically rise to the level of a scientific explanation. Likewise, Richard Horsley has noted that functionalism has an inherently conservative political agenda as well as an inability to account for change (Horsley, *Sociology*). Sociologists have likewise made similar arguments about the theoretical shortcomings of functionalism; see Gouldner, *Coming Crisis*; and Mills, *Sociological Imagination*.

becomes immune to the opiate effects of the text. We can see evidence of this in the early church's struggle with the delay of the *parousia*. Matthew and Luke both move to temper Mark's apocalypticism in the face of an increasing distance between Jesus and that time. Yarbro Collins concedes that one must question "the long-term effectiveness of the Apocalypse's means of reducing tension."[32] She worries that the dualistic approach to humanity—right believers versus non-believers/wrong believers ultimately leads to a devaluing of one's opponents humanity and "is a failure in love."[33]

In all this there is no hope of real social change. For, as Yarbro Collins notes, "the faithful are called upon to endure, not to take up arms."[34] Instead, Revelation functions as a protest. "The strength of the Apocalypse is the pointed and universal way in which it raises the questions of Justice, Wealth, and Power."[35] But Yarbro Collins is not content with what she labels "a partial and imperfect vision."[36] For while Revelation does not provide for human change, Yarbro Collins believes the role of the church is to "ally itself with those tendencies in society which hold promise of a movement forward toward the fulfillment of the eschatological promises of the Bible."[37]

Is Yarbro Collins, then, ultimately rejecting the "incomplete" message of Revelation? In the end, no. She ultimately still wants to sneak collective human change into apocalyptic. She argues: "The Apocalypse contains no specific program for meeting these challenges [of injustice]. It would seem, however, that collective forces must be dealt with collectively. Revelation thus supports the current trend in which the churches take public stands on social issues . . ."[38] Note the shift that Collins makes here. Rather than being a catalyst for real change, the most Collins can hope for is that Revelation will empower churches "to take a stand." Yet even this diminished expectation does not really follow from the catharsis theory, which is focused on the psychological well-

---

32. Collins, *Crisis*, 170–71.
33. Ibid., 170.
34. Ibid., 171.
35. Ibid.
36. Ibid., 172.
37. Ibid., 175.
38. Ibid., 174.

being of the church rather than social change. In the end, then, Yarbro Collins must be satisfied with putting forward a strictly psychological interpretation that focuses on the idea of "catharsis" for explaining the text of Revelation instead of direct action. Such a position, as we have seen before, is the unavoidable conclusion of the logic of apocalyptic.

The other scholar with whom Pippin is in dialog is Elisabeth Schüssler Fiorenza. Schüssler Fiorenza's work on Revelation has been quite influential, and argues less for the psychological efficacy of Revelation than as an example of "visionary rhetoric." A primary point of contention here is the question of whether there was actually a crisis in the Revelation community. Were the Christians of Asia Minor experiencing persecution both in terms of their lives and livelihoods? Clearly the implication of Revelation is "yes." However, as Yarbro Collins points out and Schüssler Fiorenza concedes, the historical evidence is lacking. There is evidence of persecutions under Nero; but the accounts of persecutions by Domitian appear to be motivated by a pro-Trajan agenda[39] and thus are historically suspect.

How, then, are we to account for the feeling of peril which surrounds Revelation? Schüssler Fiorenza argues that it is ultimately an issue of oppression. To define persecution or tribulation strictly in terms of bodies in the coliseum is to miss the institutionalized domination inherent in the Roman system. As she points out: "Many inhabitants of the cities of Asia Minor, staggering under the colonial injustices of oppressive taxation often combined with ruinous interest rates, were suffering from the widening gap between rich and poor. They were afraid of Roman repression of disturbances, paranoid prohibition of private associations and suspicious surveillance by neighbors and informants ... The fact is a majority of the population suffered from colonialist abuses of power, exploitation, slavery and famine ..."[40] From the perspective of "those on the ground" it may have indeed felt like persecution.

Additionally, Schüssler Fiorenza points out that while Christians may not have been systematically persecuted, they were often targets of denunciation and subsequently executed.[41] "The Christian cult was seen as troublesome, antisocial and as endangering the sociopolitical fabric

---

39. Schüssler Fiorenza, *Revelation*, 125. cf. Collins, *Crisis*, 104.
40. Schüssler Fiorenza, *Revelation*, 127.
41. Ibid.

of the empire. Apparently minor charges could be construed as treason . . ."[42] Schüssler Fiorenza also contends (though does not cite any evidence) that there was danger of economic repercussions for Christians as well.[43] Thus, while Yarbro Collins is content to talk about "relative deprivation," Schüssler Fiorenza is convinced that *real* deprivation and persecution were also on hand.

Schüssler Fiorenza, then, understands Revelation as a clear message in light of these hardships. Schüssler Fiorenza invokes the term "resistance" as a way of understanding Revelation's goal. "Revelation provides the vision of an alternative world in order to motivate the audience and to strengthen their resistance in the face of Babylon/Rome's overwhelming threat to destroy their life and livelihood."[44] What Schüssler Fiorenza argues then is that Revelation is a call for a "struggle" against oppression. The exact nature of this struggle is not clear in her writing. Perhaps it is merely being a part of this community and refusing the mark of the beast (as Schüssler Fiorenza indicates at one point)[45] that is sufficient for the battle. If so, then the more passive term of "resistance" rings truer than the more active notion of "struggle."

Tina Pippin has these two readings of apocalyptic (as somehow cathartic: Yarbro Collins and liberating: Schüssler Fiorenza) in mind, but chooses a different tact. She re-examines the text from the perspective of the horror genre. There is no doubt that Revelation is a bloody book. There is death, suffering and blood throughout the text. Bodies are piled high as the water is poisoned, plague breaks out and the armies of the beast attack. The suffering is immense and death is often lingering and terrible.

Such a vision is appropriate to the horror genre says Pippin. The same sort of blood splattering that is the hallmark of the slasher movie catches the reader in the apocalypse. "In the Apocalypse desire is linked with horror; there is a certain joyous response to the destruction and gory detail (e.g., Handel's *Messiah*)."[46] The blood ends in the New

---

42. Ibid.
43. Ibid., 127–28.
44. Ibid., 127
45. Schüssler Fiorenza, *Book of Revelation*, 193.
46. Pippin, *Death and Desire*, 86.

Jerusalem, a sparkling city descended from heaven in which the followers of the lamb are gathered together.

But the death is not completely indiscriminate, for its locus is the Whore of Babylon who lies with the kings of the earth but is ultimately devoured (in an act of cannibalism) before being destroyed. This seduction/mutilation scenario is, Pippin reminds us, a pornographic motif. Pippin suggests we should not fear to take the symbols literally, for the fact that it is a woman who is the seducer and then eventually is destroyed is significant. What Pippin does not note here (but does elsewhere) is that what follows hard upon this murder/banquet is the marriage of the Lamb to his bride, the New Jerusalem, who is virginal and dressed in white. Thus an analysis of gendered assumptions plays a major role in her reading of Revelation.

Pippin addresses Yarbro Collins's conclusion that apocalyptic provides catharsis. While not ultimately rejecting Yarbro Collins's assessment, Pippin suggests, "the cathartic explanation is limited."[47] This limitation is shown in two ways: First, it is not clear that the text ultimately removes all fear at the end. Indeed the text of Revelation concludes not with the happy ending of the New Jerusalem but with a solemn warning that the terrors contained are coming soon (Rev 22:18–20).

But second, the most troubling aspect of this text for Pippin is its image of God. For who is this deity who demands so much blood and destruction? In her essay on Mark 13[48] she states this position most clearly: "Is the only way to paradise through a bloody coup offering up heaps of bodies to a bloodthirsty god? What kind of covenant is 'apocalypse'? Is this an amoral deity poised to run amok on the world? A creator on a destructive, destroyer's binge? Is it 'legal' and ethical for the deity to destroy? Is God held to a different moral standard? ... Have we become co-conspirators with God, enabling global disasters and mass genocide?"[49] The God of the apocalypse is not the God of love, or the God of liberation; rather, he is the God of death, destruction and murder. In dramatic imagery Pippin connects the veil which lies over the symbolism of apocalyptic with the hood of the Klansman. She asks,

---

47. Ibid., 87.
48. Pippin, *Apocalyptic Bodies*.
49. Ibid., 23.

"Is God wearing a hood in Mark 13?"[50] With such a vision of God, is fear really released—catharsis achieved?

However, it is not so much that Pippin rejects the catharsis hypothesis (she actually seems to agree with it at one point)[51] as much as she questions whether the apocalypse provides an *appropriate* form of catharsis. "If hope is a moral action we must be moral about the way we hope."[52] The question that one is left with, for Pippin, is whether such a catharsis could not be accomplished differently.

The result, then, is a reading of the apocalypse that eschews the sort of liberationist reading that both Yarbro Collins and Schüssler Fiorenza attempt to give it. Pippin rebels directly against such a reading saying simply, "I do not find the Apocalypse to be a liberating story."[53] Pippin, then, unmasks the problem with an appeal to apocalyptic as a way of envisioning a new world, which makes no attempt to include human revolution as part of the apocalypse; rather, she reads the text straightforwardly as solely the act of the deity. Given that, however, she goes even further to ask what kind of deity it is that creates such mayhem and destruction, and she finds such a God wanting. For Pippin, this God is not a bold liberator; He is a mass murderer hulking around covered in blood. If we seek a narrative of liberation, we cannot look to the apocalyptic texts of the Bible; rather, we must create on our own, "a new and different creation, another text."[54]

What we see in Pippin's reading of Revelation, then, is a furtherance of the position we have seen previously. While the authors of the Postmodern Bible were playing texts against each other, Pippin has found that there is a basic antithesis between the text and the principal of human liberation itself (either as espoused by Liberation Theology or Marxism). It is important that her text is Revelation, because, as we have seen, Marxist-New Testament interpreters seem uniformly drawn to its promise of world re-creation. Yet, as Pippin has shown, the price for such an image is a series of connected images that do not correspond

50. Ibid., 28.
51. Ibid., 17.
52. Ibid., 8.
53. Ibid., 117.
54. Ibid., 77.

with an agenda of social/economic equality. For Pippin, the text is to be rejected in light of the principles of the liberation of humanity.

Pippin and Ideology

But even if the texts are to be rejected, there remains the next step in the ideological critical journey which seeks to understand how the texts work as forms of ideology. To this end Pippin is once again very useful. While Tina Pippin is an innovative Biblical Scholar whose radical readings of the text are fascinating, it is her employment of the notion of ideology which bears particular examination. Pippin derives her vision of ideology from the work of Slavoj Žižek. Žižek's perspective now requires a closer examination.

Pippin is particularly interested in Žižek's use of fantasy which is an important part of his ideological analysis. Beginning with a reading of Lacan, Žižek argues that there are two steps to the process of Lacanian psychoanalysis. The first is interpreting the symptom. The second is "transversing" the fantasy structure. The fantasy structure cannot be interpreted on its own; in fact, Žižek would argue, it is not interpreted at all. Interpretation is reserved for the symptom. The symptom is a coded message which the unconscious uses to attempt to convey to "the big Other" (the symbolic social-system) a message, a traumatic kernel which is not integrated into the symbolic system. Psychology as the talking cure, then, is intended to bring that message into the light, to integrate that traumatic kernel within the linguistic/symbolic system, to make the inexpressible explicable.

However, the later Lacan found that this was not the end of the story, for patients often would persist in their symptoms long after they had properly verbalized the message which it contained. The reason for this, argued Lacan, was enjoyment. The patient (as the title of one of Žižek's work states so succinctly) enjoyed his/her symptom.[55] Žižek cites the example of the individual who makes a so-called "Freudian slip." The individual is quick to engage in self-analysis, in determining the meaning of this unintended piece of speech, even though the actual slip may have caused embarrassment; nevertheless, there is pleasure in the process of explicating this moment.

---

55. Žižek, *Enjoy Your Symptom*.

Fantasy, on the other hand, is pleasurable in the experience and painful in the analysis. Žižek's concept of fantasy is not a simple one. The category is one with much flexibility, and Žižek uses it to address a number of different issues. On the one hand, fantasy is that which creates desire. I do not fantasize about eating a steak because I desire a steak, rather my fantasy focuses my desire upon a steak. As Žižek states, "a fantasy constitutes our desire, provides its co-ordinates, that is, it literally 'teaches us how to desire.'"[56] On the other hand, fantasy indicates my place in the world. It is within fantasy that I position myself in relation to others. "At its most fundamental, fantasy tells me what I am to my others."[57] Fantasy is not just about my desire, but others' desire of me. Returning to the steak example, my fantasy of eating steak is also a fantasy about myself as one who eats steak. A series of homologous correlatives align with that. Eating steak means that I am perceived as perhaps manly, bold, aggressive and virile. The exact set of correlatives differs from situation to situation but the fantasy includes a social context even if the fantasy in itself is solitary.

The best example of this is, of course, the sexual fantasy. If one fantasizes about sex with an attractive partner, part of the fantasy is the individual's own desirability. While the focus may be on the partner, the fantasy fails if the fantasizer's role in it is negated. Thus, the desire of the other is a significant part of the fantasy. To this end, Žižek labels fantasy as intersubjective.[58]

Perhaps the most significant point Žižek makes is that fantasy "is the primordial form of *narrative*, which serves to occult some original deadlock."[59] In the fantasy construction, the individual overcomes some essential problem, some point of basic discord with which the individual struggles. Žižek's example is anti-Semitism. The stereotype of the Jew in anti-Semitism is portrayed as the reason the system does not work; he is the corrupter who constantly stops the perfect grinding of the gears of society. This caricature of the Jew actually functions as an important ideological part of the system. It ensures that the failure of the system is explained, and the course of action necessary to perfect the system

56. Žižek, *Plague of Fantasies*, 7.
57. Ibid., 9.
58. Ibid., 8.
59. Ibid., 10.

is clear and ultimately will not seriously challenge the system. Thus, if the Jew is the obstacle to the perfect functioning of society, the obvious answer is his/her removal. Of course, such a solution would obviously fail as the whole point is to misdirect action away from the real systemic problem.

Clearly in our modern capitalist society we see the same sort of ideological rhetoric. For modern capitalism the "problem" is two-fold: on the one hand is government intervention in the form of taxation and regulation. This intervention constrains innovation and the efficient functioning of the self-regulating marketplace. On the other hand is the laziness of the citizens. Individuals who lack a concern for appropriate industriousness are actually the reason that there is a poor underclass. Were government to be restrained and all people properly motivated the social/economic system would work perfectly and benefit all. The solutions which stem from this logically (and have seen codification in law over the past decades) have been a drawing down of the social welfare system. The poor now are expected to be motivated by their need for survival and therefore will become productive. Governmental withdrawal from the arena of social welfare ultimately is the first step to implementing the "solution" of capitalism.

Of course, from the Marxist perspective of Žižek, the elimination of government regulation or the lazy poor, just like the elimination of the Jew, will not overcome the basic antagonism between labor and capital. Moreover, the elimination of the poor, like the elimination of evil, is a goal that is ultimately unattainable. However, in the short term, it functions to provide the rationalization for the failure of the system. The idea that if we eliminated these two obstacles capitalism would function for the benefit of everyone is the ideological fantasy which conceals the real reason for the failure of the capitalist system.

Fantasy, then, works as a sort of misdirection. It functions to hide a central kernel of traumatic reality which the system cannot resolve. Of course, the system also cannot exist without it. It is precisely this central conflict that creates the need for fantasy and at the same time ensures the continuance of the conflict. Žižek puts it this way, "fantasy is a means for an ideology to take its own failure into account in advance."[60] Society

---

60. Žižek, *Sublime*, 126.

cannot do without fantasy, yet at the same time the existence of fantasy indicates that something is ultimately wrong.

But has Žižek really advanced the conversation? After all, is not this basically what Marx said when he described religion as the "fantastic realization of the human being...the illusory happiness of men..."[61] in his *Contribution To The Critique of Hegel's Philosophy of Right*? Žižek would say no. For it is precisely the fact that fantasy is not "illusory" that distinguishes Žižek from Marx. Marx believes the problem is simply wrong thinking. Marx opined that "the criticism of religion disillusions man so that he will think, act and fashion his reality as a man who has lost his illusions and regained his reason..."[62] Žižek believes that fantasy is part of the fabric of reality.

Of course, one may argue that this idealist perspective is symptomatic of the early Marx. Certainly the notion of "commodity-fetishism" so important to scholars of the later Marx is not to be ignored. However, it is precisely here that Žižek feels his real contribution is to be made. The notion of the commodity fetish is that there is an illusion which conceals the real source of the value within a commodity. However it is the language which Marx uses to describe this process which is most significant for Žižek. The simplest definition of ideology, argues Žižek, is found in Marx's maxim, "we are aware of this, nevertheless we do it anyway."[63] It is the "doing" which is most essential for Žižek. It is not that reality is one way and ideology blinds us to its true nature. It is rather that ideology has "always-already" structured reality. Žižek tries to make this clear by noting, "This formula [Marx's] can be read in quite another way: 'they know that, in their activity, they are following an illusion, but still, they are doing it.' For example, they know that their idea of Freedom is masking a particular form of exploitation, but they still continue to follow this idea of Freedom."[64] The concept of commodity fetishism, then, allows us to get to a vision of ideology which is dependent upon action not just knowledge. But Marx also talks about "the secret" that commodity fetishism conceals and it is this secret that can be seen as equivalent to the "symptom," that thing which the system cannot symbolically accommodate.

61. Marx, *Critique*, 54.
62. Ibid.
63. Marx, *Capital*, 322.
64. Žižek, *Sublime*, 33.

For Pippin, Žižek's construction of ideology is important. In a flurry of citations Pippin follows Žižek stating that "the 'ideological fantasy' is not a false illusion hiding the real but is an (unconscious) fantasy structuring our social reality itself."[65] Fantasy actually supports reality rather than masks it.[66] "Ideological fantasy is a spectre that haunts because it raises unconscious desires."[67]

What we are left to wonder, however, is how Žižek's analysis helps us make sense of Revelation. Pippin's work gives us a start. The question then is what is the central contradiction, that obscene antagonism that the fantasy of Revelation seeks to mask? Here, Pippin gives us our best clue by pointing to the misogyny of the text. The text, as we have seen, is suffused with images of women who are powerful and then are destroyed. These women are promiscuous and idolatrous and are contrasted with two sets of oppositions: 1) the 144,000 virginal men who bear the mark of God and 2) the new Jerusalem, the Bride of Christ who is virginal and adorned to meet her husband. "The virginal 144,000 male followers of the lamb are allowed to enter the Bride. The scene is disturbing because the imagery is that of mass intercourse. After the holy war all the blessed (men) partake in a double ecstasy: killing the enemy woman and sharing in the victors spoils of war."[68] The continued contrast of whore vs. virgin makes the point clear, John continually uses sexualized language to equate power with promiscuity, and therefore indicates these women are worthy of destruction.

More evidence is given from the letter section of Revelation. Here the author rages against the woman he calls "Jezebel" whom he claims has led the church into committing fornication (*porneusai*). The sexual implication is clear as the resolution is to throw the woman and her disciples into "a bed of great tribulation" (*eis klinan . . . eis thlipsin megalan*). Whether or not sexual immorality was actually involved, the use of sexualized language here is revealing. It is interesting that the phrase "great tribulation" appears only in two places in Revelation: once in chapter 2, and again in chapter 7 where the 144,000 virgin males are those who have "come out of the great tribulation" (*erchomenoi ek tes thlipseos tes*

---

65. Žižek, *Invent the Symptom*, 313. cf. Pippin, *Apocalyptic Bodies*, 9.
66. Žižek, *Invent the Symptom*, 325–27. cf. Pippin, *Apocalyptic Bodies*, 9.
67. Pippin, *Apocalyptic Bodies*, 9.
68. Pippin, *Death and Desire*, 80.

megales). Again it is striking the contrast between "chaste" men and sexually immoral women.

Clearly, then, in the text of Revelation, the sexuality of women present a symptom in the Lacanian sense. The fantasy of Revelation shows sexualized women as being killed and worse, while contrasting them with de-sexualized men. The fantasy of Revelation, then, attempts to erase the trauma that women with power have (be it sexual, theological or other). Pippin's work shows us precisely the nexus of the traumatic lack that exhibits itself in the text.

The power of fantasy in Žižek's Lacanian schema is located in enjoyment. It is a pleasurable activity like my fantasy of eating steak. In Revelation, that enjoyment has been recast by Yarbro Collins in terms of "catharsis," a relieving of tension. Pippin is right in suggesting that the fantasy of Revelation does not so much relieve anxiety as it gives a pleasurable place for horrific acts to occur. Today we can see a parallel phenomenon with the fundamentalist translation of the horrors of Revelation into the horrors of modern technology set upon the world. The "Left Behind" series with its dramatic and detailed look at life within the "great tribulation" shows precisely the sort of obscene enjoyment which is characteristic of fantasy for Žižek.

Conclusion

Pippin, then, extends the pattern that we saw begun with the other members of the ideological discourse movement. There is a strong desire for the assertion of human liberation as the goal. On the other hand, there is a growing recognition that the Biblical text cannot fully provide the avenue to accomplishing that goal. One person's freedom fighter is another person's terrorist. The story of liberation from Egypt is a paradigm for one group but not another. The sacrifice of Jesus is an example to be followed, unless you are a battered woman. And Revelation is a story about the destruction of the kings of this world but through the metaphor of the death, mutilation and cannibalization of women.

What we see here, then, is the collision of ideologies. This time it is apocalypticism that helps expose the problem between Marxism and Liberation Theology and religion in general. The ideological critics seem to implicitly recognize that the religious text is actually part of the problem, rather than the solution. The basic Marxist analysis of religion is starting to be seen as working its way into the scholarly discourse of New Testament studies.

There is, then, a shift that we can see from the move to reinterpret texts to make them liberating (Marxist-New Testament interpreters and Horsley), to separating liberating texts from non-liberating texts (ideological criticism), to a general question about whether the text is an appropriate foundation for liberation at all (Pippin). The ideological criticism movement is slowly coming to the conclusion that there is an inherent problem using the text. Yet as we have seen, even in the work of Ideological Critics, the theological agenda of Liberation Theology still seems to exert some pull. Thus, while the alternative has so far not been clearly articulated, the evidence of this chapter shows that it is apparently moving, if haltingly, in the direction of the Marxist critique of religion. Hence, when Pippin says she is not interested in getting through the "no" to the text in order to get to a "yes,"[69] it is not clear where there is a "yes" to be found for her and such would align with the Marxist view of the text.

---

69. Pippin, *Apocalyptic Bodies*, 117.

7

The Critique of Biblical Studies

THE KIND OF CRITICISM OF THE BIBLE THAT WE HAVE EXAMINED IN the last chapters of this book has expanded in several different ways. Three movements have continued the kind of criticism we saw in the work of the ideological criticism scholars: Postcolonial Criticism, New Secularism, and New Atheism. Each of these has continued the debate inaugurated by the ideological critics and yet moved the discussion in a variety of different directions. Importantly, however, these new movements represent a pivotal cultural moment. What I will show here is that these new movements have moved the dialog along in two ways: They have continued the critique of the text as inadequate to the cause of human liberation; secondly, they have also trained their critical eye on biblical scholarship itself and have challenged whether biblical critics themselves have done a disservice to the text by attempting to make it relevant theologically, politically, and socially to the modern world. There is a call then for a new kind of biblical criticism, one which is not focused on meeting the needs of the faithful in the end but addressing the text through a variety of methods that preclude, much as we saw with Marxist scholars, the appeal to the text for modern morality. Thus while Marxism may not be at the center of these different approaches (an indeed some may be openly hostile to Marxist economics) we still see the flowering of the seed that was planted by Marxist criticism of the New Testament.

Postcolonialism and the Bible

A fairly recent movement in cultural studies in general and in biblical studies as well is Postcolonialism. Postcolonialism finds its origination in the work of three seminal thinkers: Edward Said, Homi Bhahba, and Gayatri Spivak. Yet, to limit Postcolonialism to these three authors is to diminish the field because, as multiple readers in Postcolonial Theory make clear, Postcolonialism has been constructed from the work of many different thinkers.[1] Given the breadth and diversity of Postcolonial Theory my comments here will be only a beginning.[2] However, a basic definition by R. S. Sugirtharajah, one of the most prolific postcolonial biblical critics, is helpful in getting a sense of what Postcolonialism is: "Postcolonialism is essentially a style of enquiry, an insight or a perspective, a catalyst, a new way of life. As an enquiry, it instigates and creates possibilities, and provides a platform for the widest possible convergence of critical forces, of multi-ethnic, multi-religious and multicultural voices, to assert their denied rights and to rattle the centre . . . As Postcolonialism is not a theory in the strict sense of the term, but a collection of critical and conceptual attitudes, and apt description would be to term it a criticism."[3] Thus Postcolonialism is theoretically informed but not a theory per se; it perhaps has too much freedom within the work of its practiners to qualify as a theory. Yet there is no doubt that it stems from the line of postmodern thinkers like Jacques Derrida, Michel Foucault, and Jacques Lacan.[4] Thus, Postcolonialism is continually engaged in the process of deconstructing sites of authority, particularly as they relate to the Bible and politics.

Postcolonialism then often reflects the same sort of critical stance towards the Bible that we saw in the Ideological Critics. Tat-siong Benny Liew's 1999 article on "Colonial Mimicry" in Mark might serve as an example. Starting with the recognition that the Gospels are in fact products of a colonial world, Liew carefully examines the way Mark portrays Jesus's authority in his gospel. What he finds is that the kinds of authority that Jesus exercises are not so different than that which the Roman Empire engages in. The notions of "kingdom" and "family" that show up throughout the book of Mark are not a new vision of these

---

1. Williams and Chrisman, *Colonial Discourse*; Mongia, *Contemporary Postcolonial Theory*; Loomba, *Postcolonial Studies*; Desai and Nair, *Postcolonialisms*; Ashcroft, Griffiths, and Tiffin, *Empire Writes Back*; and Nordquist, *Postcolonial Theory*.

2. For interested readers, a wonderful "cartography" is found in Moore, *Empire and Apocalypse: Postcolonialism and the New Testament*, 3–23.

3. Sugirtharajah, *Postcolonial Criticism*, 14.

4. Ibid., 21.

concepts that remove their hierarchical nature, but rather re-implementations of the same basic hierarchies, only this time with Jesus on top. The criterion that determines who is in and who is out is different for Mark than for the Romans, but ultimately the structure is the same. The best example is the apocalypticism of the text that threatens the Roman social structures with destruction thereby exhibiting the same coercive approach that the Romans themselves used. Liew notes: "Presenting an all-authoritative Jesus who will eventually annihilate all opponents and all other authorities, Mark's utopian, or dystopian, vision, in effect, duplicates the colonial (non)choice of 'serve-or-be-destroyed' (Said 1993: 168; see also p. 80)."[5] Liew describes this as "colonial mimicry" which serves to "reinscribe colonial domination . . . what we have in the Gospel are recurring themes of 'empire' such as tyranny, boundary and might."[6]

The Bible then is looked upon with a certain amount of suspicion by many Postcolonial critics. R. S. Sugirtharajah emphasizes this biblical skepticism in his critique of Liberation Theology, which he characterizes as too Bible-focused in its attempt to speak to third-world people.[7] Postcolonialism on the other hand takes a different approach. "What is important is to be mindful that the Bible contains elements of bondage and disenfranchisement. What postcolonial biblical criticism tries to do is make this ambivalence visible and clear and to demonstrate that the Bible is part of the conundrum rather than a panacea for all the ills of a postmodern world."[8] Similar to what we saw with ideological criticism, Postcolonialism is unafraid to be critical of the Bible when it deems it necessary.

And yet postcolonial biblical criticism may also find moments in the text when in fact it sees something redemptive in the text. For instance Musa W. Dube cites Mosti Torontle who rereads the Samaritan Woman at the Well (John 4) in such a way that it can speak to the postcolonial questions of identity. First, Dube explicates the clear colonizing command of the preface to the story, the call to go to other lands

5. Liew, *Tyranny, Boundary and Might*, 23.

6. Ibid., 26–27.

7. "There is an inherent Biblicism in its [Liberation Theology] approach. The texts which speak of dehumanizing aspects are conveniently passed over," Sugirtharajah, *Postcolonial Criticism*, 114.

8. Ibid., 119.

and "harvest." Yet in the end while acknowledging the imperialist call of the text she notes that there is yet something beneficial to found in the text: "Torontle's decolonizing reading of John 4 challenges biblical readers, hearers, believers and writers to acknowledge and embrace their Samaritan social spaces of heretics and half-breeds. Similarly, Biblical critical practice must be dedicated to an ethical task of promoting, decolonizing, fostering diversity, and imagining liberating ways of interdependence."[9] What is perhaps most telling is that Dube does not call for the dismissal of the text (contra Pippin), despite its clear sanction of colonialism. Rather she seeks a way to reconstruct the text such that it still can serve some emancipatory purpose.

Some Postcolonialists then, while clearly seeing the problematic nature of the text can, at times, find ways to still preserve the text. Yet the field is clearly divided on this; Sugirtharajah states plainly: "However much Dalits, feminists and other crusaders against oppression may tantalizingly recuperate the emancipatory potential of the text, the Bible continues to be an unsafe and problematic text. For every redeeming aspect of the narrative there is an unredeeming feature linked to it."[10] Such a position is likewise taken by David Jobling who in his review of *The Postcolonial Bible* questions whether the Bible has any relevance at all since it was written in a completely different historical mode of production than our time.[11] As Jobling notes, "Simple links between the Bible and current situations, whether they leave the Bible looking good or bad, convey no lasting benefit."[12]

On the other hand, Fernando F. Segovia, who Jobling specifically points out as making precisely the kind of illegitimate comparative move that Jobling denounces, responded quite forcefully. Segovia retorts that the notion of a "mode of production" is the product of a historical moment itself and is "neither conveyed nor demanded by the 'data' for proper interpretation."[13] Hence, Segovia exempts his work from the Marxist critique by suggesting that Marxist tools of analysis (like "modes of production") are themselves arbitrary human constructs cre-

9. Dube, *Decolonization*, 37.
10. Sugirtharajah, *Postcolonial Criticism*, 100.,
11. Broadbent, *Four Reviews*, 117.
12. Ibid., 118.
13. Segovia, *Decolonizing Biblical Studies*, 138.

ated at a particular time and therefore not viable for transhistorical use.[14] Instead Segovia, with some historical qualifications, believes that the conjunction of Postcolonialism and biblical studies can be legitimately accomplished.[15] The reason for this is simple, "The proposed postcolonial optic in Biblical Studies is obviously a discourse of resistance and emancipation."[16] What Segovia calls for then is "a re-reading and re-interpretation of the Biblical texts from outside the Western context ..."[17] with particular attention to the texts' construction of its desired world, "a world in which peace and justice prevail."[18]

Thus while postcolonial biblical studies is divided on the issue of the validity of the Bible for the struggle for human liberation, one area where there does seem to be agreement is the use of the Bible by Western imperial powers as a way of colonizing indigenous peoples. For postcolonial scholars, biblical studies hands are clearly dirty in this endeavor, and much work in postcolonial biblical studies has focused on how biblical criticism has often acted as a supporting agent for the efforts of colonialism. For instance in the biblical story of Ruth, Ruth chose assimilation and conversion. Such a perspective, Sugirtharajah argues (citing Laura Donaldson's analysis), essentially vindicates the colonialist perspective. Instead Donaldson denounces Ruth and looks to her sister Orpah, who remains in her father's house, as a model for preserving cultural identity.[19] This kind of reading points out the flawed and complicit nature of western exegesis and Postcolonialism seeks to uncover such acts.

---

14. I think it pretty clear that a Marxist would object that this is comparing apples and oranges. To suggest that Marxist tools of analysis are the product of a particular time does not ultimately invalidate the criticism which is the larger question of cross-cultural/transhistorical comparison. Jobling's use of "mode of production" merely is a shorthand way of asking this question. Segovia critique of Jobling fails to shed light on the question at hand (though he then does go on to straightforwardly address the question).

15. Segovia, *Decolonizing Biblical Studies*, 139.

16. Ibid., 140.

17. Ibid., 176.

18. Ibid.

19. Donaldson, *Sign of Orpah*. cited in Sugirtharajah, *Third World*, 261. While Sugirtharajah is actually making a critique of Liberation Theology, there is no doubt that his perspective extends to biblical studies in the West in general.

Thus in the tradition of ideological criticism, postcolonialist criticism conveys a similar suspicion of the text as it often recognizes the "unsafe" nature of the text itself. Yet Postcolonialist Criticism goes a step farther in that it is even more critical of Biblical Studies that has too often imported colonialist conceptions into its analysis. Such a position is clearly consonant with the position of Ideological critics who likewise express suspicion of biblical criticism that has been motivated by theological interests (either conservative or liberating). While Postcolonialist can be hostile to Marxist analysis (like the debate between Jobling and Segovia), Postcolonialism and Marxism actually have much in common in their criticisms of both the text and the discipline.

Criticism of Biblical Criticism—The New Secularism

The preceding discussion of Postcolonialism's suspicion of biblical studies provides an opening to discuss what is appearing more frequently in books and journals of the discipline—a thoughtful questioning about the goal and results of biblical studies. The Postcolonial critique suggests that there may in fact be external reasons (often political and in the service of imperialism) that explain why biblical studies has produced the readings it has. Yet there are several thinkers who would agree that Biblical Studies has produced results that are slanted, but for a different reason—a desire to protect the Bible itself.

I have discussed at length above Burton Mack's work on Mark, but Mack makes another contribution in calling New Testament studies to come to a new understanding of Christian origins. His iconoclastic work, beginning in *Myth of Innocence* and continuing into his latest work *Myth and the Christian Imagination*,[20] have all functioned to challenge the reticence with which scholars have attempted to explain the origins of Christianity using historical, non-supernatural categories. Mack's work is without doubt the starting point for anyone interested in moving towards a social/theoretical understanding of earliest Christianity.

Taking up the challenge however that Mack has lain down, there are several scholars of religion who are thinking very carefully about the motivations that apparently underlie much of what is done in biblical studies. James G. Crossley in particular has done some provoca-

20. Mack, *Christian Nation*.

tive work on this question in his book *Why Christianity Happened: A Sociohistorical Account of Christian Origins*. Crossley begins his work with an interesting discussion about the history of the field. In a fascinating chapter titled, "Toward a Secular Approach to Christian Origins," Crossley engages in a history of the use of sociological methods in New Testament Studies. He argues that there is a historical gap in New Testament Studies from the work of the Chicago School in the 1920s and the beginning of a renaissance of the methodological use of sociology in the 1970s. He asks an important question: Why the gap? The answer interestingly enough is Marxism. McCarthyism in the U.S. and the Cold War in general made Marxism an off-limits topic. Crossley argues that changed to some degree because of the work of the Annales School. The Annales School focused on structural institutions as a way of reading history over a long period (the *longue durée*) and thus had a social/economic focus to their work. Great leaders would come and go, but social structures outlasted them all. Crossley argues that the Annales School thus broke the chains previously holding historical study and allowed historians to start thinking in terms of long-lasting institutions.

At the same time, in the 1960s in England Marxist historians were reaching the height of their influence with the full flowering of the Communist Party Historian's Group. Marxism thus dominated the landscape in the field of History. Yet New Testament Scholars would have none of it and were suspicious that an atheist approach could illuminate the New Testament. Thus Crossley uncovers a Marxophobia that persists into the 1970s (undoubtedly fueled by the heightening of the Cold War because of Vietnam). Citing Gerd Theissen's (a German scholar) defense that he is not a Marxist even if some of his conclusions have some Marxist tendencies, Crossley states, "the fact that Theissen even has to defend Marxist influence and stress that it does not equate to being a Marxist speaks volumes about the interests and fears of NT scholarship."[21] Of course Stalin figures into this fear as well as the fact that Germany, split into west and east, was simultaneously the central theater of cold war drama as well as the dominant locus of New Testament studies through the 1960s.

Crossley argues that the redemption of sociological methods for New Testament studies comes with the translation of the work of Max

---

21. Crossley, *Why Christianity Happened*, 13.

Weber into English in the 1960s and 1970s. With Weber we had a sociologist who was not a Marxist and whose notion of charisma seemed to dovetail nicely with pre-existing assumptions of New Testament scholars. In a sense, Weber saved sociology for Christianity. This opened up an avenue for scholars of Christian origins to safely engage social theoretical models in their work without fear of Cold War politics overshadowing their analyses.

But Crossley bemoans the fact that it has taken so long for social-scientific approaches to be applied to New Testament studies. "The above history of social sciences and NT studies shows that the neglect of such approaches has proven to be profoundly detrimental."[22] As such there has been a paucity of what he terms "non-theological" approaches and he sees his own work as an attempt to approach Christian origins from the perspective of a non-theological social-scientific perspective that is really about New Testament Studies entering the mainstream of the academy. Comparing N. T. Wright's skepticism of Gamliel II's daughter's meeting with the emperor with Wright's defense of the Matthean story of the rising of the saints during the crucifixion he argues,

> It would be fair to say that for many nonbelievers and for many mainstream historians outside biblical studies and theology, some lass talking to an emperor[23] is far more historically plausible than dead people rising from tombs [Matthew 27]. Notwithstanding the unethical feel to these arguments, it should be clear that Christian stories can be treated differently because of Christian dominance, which allows the more literalistic advocates to make such claims.[24]

There is then a different standard for New Testament scholarship that allows scholars to make the argument for the plausibility of events that would not be accepted in other disciplines of the academy, particularly history. Crossley then calls for the inclusion[25] of non-theologically

---

22. Ibid., 21.

23. This is a references to the clearly fictional discussion between the Roman emperor and Gamaliel II's daughter found in rabbinic literature (b. *Sanhedrin* 90–91a).

24. Crossley, *Why Christianity Happened*, 25.

25. It is interesting how tepid Crossley's argument is in the end. Unlike other scholars who take a similar perspective he is not calling for repentance, but merely the inclusion of non-theological voices in the conversation suggesting they may offer a new perspective much like Jewish scholars have. He concludes, "The dominance of Christian scholarship really does need to be challenged, but its insights must not be

oriented scholarship, those streams that stem from social-scientific approaches and (though this point is implicit) would be considered appropriate from the perspective of the rest of the academy.

An opinion making the same point but with a more radical prescription is found in Hector Avalos's book *The End of Biblical Studies*. Avalos's work might be considered a Jeremiad against the theological bent of biblical studies. Unlike Crossley, who calls merely for more openness, Avalos wants to burn the discipline to the ground. Avalos's work speaks truth to power in its revelation that in biblical studies the emperor has no clothes. First, he argues that people are not as piously interested in the Bible as we think they are. While the majority of Americans' pledge allegiance to its importance, they are not actually reading it. Somewhere between one-fifth and one-third of Christians say they "never" read the Bible, [26] and given a Biblical literacy test, the majority of Christians cannot identify the basic chronology and events of the Bible. What then are those of us who study and teach biblical studies doing? Avalos's diagnosis is stark, "Biblical scholars, for example, are almost solely devoted to maintaining the cultural significance of the Bible not because any knowledge it provides is relevant to our world but because of the self-serving drive to protect the power position of the biblical studies profession."[27] Biblical studies is an iatrogenic disease, a self-perpetuating malady that professes to speak to the world but in the end is speaking only to itself, because the world does not care. But beyond that, it is engaged in a pattern of obfuscation and intentional deception to hide the fact that the Bible has no real relevance or reliability.

Avalos's claim is breathtaking and his subsequent survey of a series of topics in Biblical studies is pursued at breakneck speed. His attacks are quick and unfaltering. He engages topics like a knight in battle, slashing his enemies (mortally?) and then moving on.

Avalos attacks with the basics: rock, paper, scissors—archaeology, text criticism, and the historical Jesus. Starting with text criticism, he shows how the notion of the Bible is problematic in two ways. First, the manuscript tradition is such a mess that the text that lies on nightstands

---

ignored," ibid., 33.

26. Avalos, *End of Biblical Studies*, 19.

27. Ibid., 23.

and in pews is a scholarly "best guess" lacking any of the kind of surety Christians take for granted. Second, the process of translation is just as problematic as modern interpreters fill the multiple gaps of the text with theology. Archaeology is no cleaner. Archaeology is sometimes heralded as lacking the subjectivity of text studies. Yet while pottery may not lie, Avalos argues that archaeologists with theological agendas have acted as ventriloquists, lying for their pottery. Ultimately siding with the archaeological movement called "minimalism," Avalos puts the conclusion rather starkly, "David's existence is still more akin to that of [King] Arthur, and the Tel Dan Inscriptions tells us no more about David than the Modena Inscription tells us about Arthur. There is no independent evidence for a kingdom headed by Solomon, so that is where we have to leave the claim—inconclusive . . . We can now affirm . . . that there is not much history to be found in the era of the kings . . ."[28] Archeology then can give no certainty to the most important stories of the Bible. From Abraham to Moses to David to Solomon archeology has found an empty hole.

Thirdly, Avalos takes a skeptical view of the quest for the historical Jesus. Ironically, the quest for the Historical Jesus is usually attacked from the right as being too skeptical. Here, Avalos turns the tables and argues it has not been skeptical enough. Pointing at the Jesus Seminar, Avalos notes that the methods that the Seminar used to identify authentic sayings of Jesus amounted to handful of sayings printed in red. Yet even these few sayings, when the reasoning is critically examined, are the result of a tautology that presumes to know things that are not in evidence. We cannot know what the early church actually thought (that is one of the things we allegedly find out in this process), so we cannot decide what the early church could or could not conceive of Jesus doing or saying, thus the category of dissimilarity fails as a helpful method. Even the more popular method of multiple attestation only allows us to show the existence and persistence of a particular tradition about Jesus but tells us nothing about Jesus himself. Finally, our data is skewed as we privilege canonical texts (since they are in the most abundance) yet when we see the testimony of the non-canonical texts we realize that Jesus is merely a cipher in which communities could freely project all kinds of theological and ethical ideals. "What these 'Christianities'

---

28. Ibid., 163.

have in common is their claimed connection with a 'Christ,' who is portrayed in astoundingly variegated fashion."[29] Like Albert Schweitzer before him, Avalos pronounces this latest quest for the historical Jesus as "failed," and proclaims "Jesus cannot be found and any notion of following actual words or deeds of Jesus is vacuous."[30]

The combination of these three things strikes at the heart of biblical studies. Were he to rest his case here, Avalos's contribution would have been secure. Yet he goes on to make several more interesting arguments. He unmasks literary studies of the Bible for their attempts to avoid the hard historical questions and sneak theology in through the guise of "beauty" or "story." He attacks biblical theology as a form of "Bibolatry" that attempts to reconceptualize the Bible in some way that imports relevance to it so that it still has meaning today. The price of this he claims is too high; it requires a selective exclusion of texts replete with violence and intolerance. Even American Liberation theologians are criticized for ignoring the anti-liberationist themes in the Bible in a quest to authorize their image of "liberation." Yet Avalos remarks, "And just as liberation theologians are prepared to repudiate Nazi literature completely for its genocidal and imperialist thoughts, liberation theologians should be willing to repudiate completely a prophetic literature that endorses genocide and Yahwistic imperialism."[31] Reconceptualization of the biblical narrative and texts ultimately espouses a set of non-biblical perspectives and tries to force the Bible to fit this new mold. But, as I once heard Christopher Hitchens (who would have certainly benefited from reading Avalos's work) penetratingly ask, what other domain of knowledge do we work so hard to transport from the Bronze Age so completely? Why should we travail so mightily to import this one?

Finally, Avalos's attacks the institutions of biblical studies, the professional meetings, the publishers and the journals that are all bent on self-perpetuation through the fostering of the illusion that the Bible still has relevance in our time and otherwise seeks to secret themselves away. In the end Avalos demands we must admit the Biblical Studies is not relevant for today. It fails its audience by not telling the truth and

---

29. Ibid., 211.
30. Ibid., 212.
31. Ibid., 208.

allowing them to selectively choose what they want to find relevant to today.

Avalos's attack is scathing; and unlike Crossley, he does not suggest that a new approach to the texts might bear more fruit. In fact he states, "The sole purpose of biblical studies ... would be to help people move toward a postscriptural society."[32] Yet Crossley and Avalos are in agreement that the interest the Bible has is strictly historical without relevancy for the modern world. A non-theological approach is the only one that thus can actually acknowledge the Bible for what it is—a remnant text of antiquity.

The kind of critique that Avalos is making is not just the case in biblical studies; in the larger field of religious studies a similar argument is being made by the scholar Russell McCutcheon. McCutcheon is perhaps most well known for his book *Manufacturing Religion*. McCutcheon launches an assault in that work against the unacknowledged presupposition of religious studies—that religion is *sui generis*.[33] Such a claim is particularly problematic as it eliminates religion from a socio-political form of analysis. If nothing is like religion, if nothing causes religion, then there can be no explanation of religion, only description and perhaps adherence.

McCutcheon calls for the implementation of naturalist theories of explanation that challenge the *sui generis* supposition of religious studies and instead seeks to find an explanation for religion in the realm of human action seen as historical, political, social, psychological, etc. He makes this point from a variety of different perspectives in the course of his book. He summarizes his solution when he states: "one important step toward the functional and secure self-identity within the modern teaching and research university will be the development of a number of cross-disciplinary, clearly articulated and rationally defensible theories of religion that are recognized from the outset as theories, models rather than perfect representations of what is or ought to be, that ground definition and develop methodologies and explanations ... As such description and interpretation do not provide the entire basis for a naturalistic study of religion."[34] McCutcheon, like Crossley and Avalos,

32. Ibid., 341.

33. McCutcheon defines this term as "the claim that religious data are ... distinct, unique, self-caused," *Manufacturing Religion*, 18.

34. Ibid., 208–9.

suggests that much of the current product of scholarship, including biblical studies, is outside the realm of the academy. McCutcheon's point is even more theoretically pointed, there has been a concerted effort to section-off religion from the academic study of human practices that have been conducted in every other field. His call is to end this theoretical ghettoization and to make a concerted effort to enter into the larger realm of the academy. The first step then is to unmask and abandon what he calls the theological and cryptotheological work in religious studies that finds its ultimate bulwark in the classification of religion as *sui generis*.

McCutcheon extends the work just surveyed in his book *Critics Not Caretakers*. This text is a powerful defense of a secularist approach to doing religious studies. McCutcheon's agenda is without pretense; it is the attempt to clearly identify the discipline of religious studies with a series of methods that take a critical stance towards religion. The result of this is a new emphasis on a pivotal term that functions to re-orient the discipline: "explanation." The notion of explanation is one that is somewhat out of fashion in certain quarters of the academy. Such a notion bespeaks a reductionist colonialism, "we" tell "them" what they are really doing. Yet while recognizing such a critique, McCutcheon does not shy away from invoking the notion of explanation anyway: "our goal should not be for experiences to overlap with those of the other, but rather, to explain from our admittedly entrenched point of view, what we perceive to be going on out there and, given our own theoretical interests, why it is going on."[35] The call to explanation then involves an understanding and acknowledgment of our own positionality and the concomitant power, privileged, and implicit oppression that goes along with it. It requires what Pierre Bourdieu called reflexivity.[36] Yet it does not mean that the territory of explanation is thereby surrendered. Rather explanation must be grounded in what McCutcheon labels as "clearly articulated and defensible theories of human culture and belief systems."[37] In the end, what is important for McCutcheon is to bring religious studies in to the light of human practices that have their

---

35. McCutcheon, *Critics Not Caretakers*, 82.
36. Boudieu and Wacquant, *Invitation*.
37. McCutcheon, *Critics Not Caretakers*, 82.

origin in human social contexts and can thereby be studied as human products.

What I believe that we see here is a trend within a certain segment of religious studies and particularly biblical studies. It is the culmination of a line that we have traced in biblical studies, starting with ideological criticism moving to Postcolonialism and then to a new current of secularist approaches to the Bible represented by Mack, Crossley, and Avalos, and expanded to religious studies in general by McCutcheon. These biblical scholars have argued that the text is problematic when examined from a confessional perspective. The orientation differs between them, yet what has become clear is that there is an increasing number of scholars unwilling to (as Pippin was quoted above) "go through the 'no' to get to the 'yes'" in regards to the text. The status of the text is decreasing and the scholarship that has supported that status is under attack.

What we see in its place is a call by these scholars, whom I am calling the New Secularists, for a new way of viewing the text apart from theological concerns. McCutcheon helps us to understand that it is not simply the controlling interest of theology that has gotten us to this position but a form of privileging religion that makes it immune to explanation. What all these scholars have advocated in response to this is to turn to non-theological and more often social-scientific methods that understand religion in general and the bible in particular as an artifact of human creativity and construction. The way to examine such an artifact is precisely to analyze it like any other human artifact with the tools of the academy repositioned to explain religious practices and texts, but without the constraints that the discipline has heretofore placed on its practitioners. What we see is a bold and critical movement arising that is intent on the deconstruction of the past and the launching of a new bold and critical approach to the texts. One that will no longer be happy to insulate Religion from social-scientific scalpel of the biblical critic, now dressed in the white lab coat instead of the pastoral frock.[38]

This New Secularist movement in biblical studies is one that is still in its infancy. More and more scholars are joining its ranks. Yet, I wish to argue that this is a part of a pivotal moment in American Culture, because even as biblical scholars are taking a more secularist

---

38. I borrow this image from Steven Moore (*God's Gym*), who compares the biblical critic to the forensic scientist conducting an autopsy.

approach to text, there is also a more popular movement that seems to have a hunger for just this type of analysis. Heretofore relatively ignored by serious religion scholars it may provide a new and excited lay audience that has "ears to hear" this new approach to the text and to religion in general.

The New Atheism as a Cultural Moment

The so-called "New Atheism" movement has appeared in the last few years as an impressive and public approach by a set of individuals to challenge theism in a forceful and straightforward way. A core group of writers stands at its core: Scientists Richard Dawkins, Michael Shermer, philosopher Daniel Dennet, journalist Christopher Hitchens, and writer Sam Harris are the most well known of the New Atheists. Their collective works make entertaining reading and their success represents a new attempt to challenge religion in general and Christianity in particular.

While the New Atheists often seemed to be attacking religion in general (observe the subtitle of Christopher Hitchen's *God is Not Great: How Religion Poisons Everything*), we might note that it is really monotheism that gets the bulk of the New Atheists ire. Very little time, comparatively, is spent attacking religions of the East;[39] instead it is, by and large, Christianity, Judaism, and Islam that get the lion's share of their attention.

Importantly, the works of these authors have not disappeared into obscurity resurrected only in fundamentalist apologetics as has happened in the past. The majority of the authors above have been on the New York Times' Bestsellers list. Several of them have sold over 250,000 copies. At this writing, on Amazon.com Richard Dawkins's *The God Delusion* has been in the top 100 religion best sellers for 541 days and RichardDawkins.net boasts over 1.5 million copies have been sold. There is no doubt that the New Atheists are making an impact in the publishing world.

But it also appears that something is happening in the world of the believer. The American Religious Identification Survey showed an

---

39. One might note that Sam Harris even seems sympathetic toward the more mystical tradition of Eastern Religions like Buddhism (Harris, *End of Faith*, 215–21) to the point he must defend in his afterword that he is not just trying to substitute one irrational religion for another (ibid., 234–35).

increase in people who claim "no religion" to 15 percent of the population. Those whose beliefs actually reflect either a disbelief in God, and agnosticism towards the existence of God, or a belief in a deistic nonpersonal God, astonishingly comprise almost a quarter of the population (24%). The number of self-proclaimed atheists has almost doubled since 2001. While there have been no clear studies explaining these changes, there can be no doubt that the burgeoning New Atheist movement is supported by the popularity of these demographic shifts.

Yet even though there is an increasingly vocal atheist movement one of the ironies of this movement is its complete divorce from modern biblical scholarship. One might expect that the kinds of scholarly discourse that I have traced in this book would be fastened upon by New Atheists as at least fodder for their argument, yet one looks in vain for such citation. Even the critical tradition of biblical scholarship is largely ignored by these writers. In their often long recitation of biblical citations, there is rarely any contextualization through reference to scholarship. Not to say that the command in Numbers 31 that commands the death of all male children would be made less horrific to modern sensibilities by appropriate contextualization; on the other hand it may certainly be the case that a clear understanding of the agendas of the sources that are in play in our texts would make the establishment of the Bible as a human document more palatable and plausible to a general public. This is precisely the goal that most New Atheists have in mind, and yet they have steadfastly ignored this resource.

A good example of this is found in Christopher Hitchens, *God is Not Great: How Religion Poisons Everything*. Hitchens is somewhat unique among the New Atheists in that he devotes a chapter to the New Testament and certainly gives the impression that he is versed in scholarship. And yet one must only read a few pages to see that Hitchens's erudite veneer is gossamer thin. His first scholarly reference is to H. L. Mencken from his *Treatise on the Gods*.[40] Biblical scholars may be forgiven if the name Mencken is unfamiliar. Mencken was not a biblical scholar but a journalist from the first half of the twentieth century. Mencken states, "The simple fact is that the New Testament, as we know it, is a helter-skelter accumulation of more or less discordant documents, some of them probably of respectable origin but others palpably apoc-

---

40. Mencken, *Treatise*.

ryphal, and most of them, the good along with the bad show unmistakable signs of having been tampered with."[41] And while Hitchens's quote from Mencken is generally correct—given a particular understanding of words like "tampered with," "respectable," and "apocryphal"—the very fact that he does not turn to a biblical scholar seems to reflect an ignorance of the scholarship (one notes a quote from Bultmann might very well have conveyed a similar notion if not in quite the same casual manner).[42]

The second scholar Hitchens's brings to the table is C. S. Lewis, where he pits himself against the argument in *Mere Christianity*, undoubtedly Lewis's most popular nonfiction work. Here Hitchens's brings out the well-worn "liar, lunatic, or Lord" argument and finds it flawed but on the right path since Hitchens concludes: "Either the Gospels are in some sense literal truth or the whole thing is essentially a fraud and perhaps an immoral one at that."[43] And thus Lewis was on to something, but his conclusion that this is evidence of Jesus divinity was the wrong conclusion. Hitchens then descends into a brief discussion of oral tradition that is generally accurate but problematic since it mixes apples and oranges. Lewis was a scholar of English literature and a popular theologian, not a Biblical scholar, and, despite Hitchens's protestations to the contrary, not appropriately authoritative for a chapter allegedly dealing with the New Testament. That Hitchens is unaware of this distinction is precisely the problem.

The last scholar that Hitchens cites (for a total of three supposed New Testament scholars in his chapter) is Bart Ehrman. Here Hitchens has finally employed a bona fide biblical scholar in his argument at last. But it is clear that Hitchens has not done his homework. He has apparently read some of Ehrman's *Misquoting Jesus*, as he focuses on the text-critical problem of John 7:53—8:11.[44] Yet he shows himself to be a

---

41. Ibid., cited in Hitchens, *God Is Not Great*, 39.

42. One is reminded of this quote, not nearly as sweeping, but certainly conveying a similar message, "What the sources offer us is first of all the message of the early Christian community, which for the most part the church freely attributed to Jesus. This naturally gives no proof that all the words which are put into his mouth were actually spoken by him. As can be easily proved, many sayings originated in the church itself; others were modified by the church," Bultmann, *Jesus and the Word*, 12.

43. Hitchens, *God Is Not Great*, 42

44. Ehrman points out that John 7:53—8:11 (the story of the woman saved from stoning) is not found in our earliest manuscripts. The story appears in John and in some

poor reader, for even though he notes earlier that Ehrman "could not quite reconcile his faith with his scholarship,"[45] he seems to think that Ehrman is still inclined toward an Evangelical perspective. He shows this by first asserting that Ehrman "concedes" the John text is not found in the earliest manuscripts.[46] Hitchens next proclaims he has been thoroughly objective since he has "selected my source on the basis of 'evidence against interest': in other words from someone whose original scholarly and intellectual journey was not at all intended to challenge holy writ."[47] Such statements seem to imply an orthodox perspective on Ehrman's part that anyone familiar with the scope of his work knows is absent. On the contrary, it seems clear that Ehrman's scholarship has been designed precisely to "challenge holy writ" in a number of ways.

Yet despite these flaws, when it comes to the major New Atheist authors, somewhat dishearteningly, Hitchens is the closest to someone who actually addresses New Testament scholarship, and it is clear that his understanding of it is cursory.[48] We might take a moment to ponder why this is the case. Why have the New Atheists, who certainly could benefit from the results of 200+ years of historical critical scholarship failed to engage it? There are perhaps two immediate reasons that come to mind, though at this point I have no evidence that either is correct. First, as we have seen in the critique of the New Secularists, perhaps it is because for so long Biblical Criticism has been the handmaiden of Theology. For many years Biblical Studies has been populated by believers who, as we have seen in this study as well, have been loathe to follow their criticism to its logical conclusion. Second, it is evident that biblical scholarship has been successful in flying under the radar. Only in the past decades has it started to raise itself to public awareness through the works of people like John Dominic Crossan, Burton Mack,

---

manuscripts in Luke but not in the earliest manuscripts of either. Thus the famous line, "Let anyone among you who is without sin be the first to throw a stone" is something that, textually speaking, is quite doubtful (Ehrman, *Misquoting Jesus*, 64–65).

45. Hitchens, *God Is Not Great*, 42
46. Ibid., 43.
47. Ibid.
48. I should note that John W. Loftus (*Athiest*), a lesser known but rising star in the New Atheism movement actually does a much better job than the major players I have surveyed here. Loftus does appear to have an outsider's grasp of New Testament studies, though even he tends to rely overly much on reference works like *The Harper's Bible Dictionary* and *The Anchor Bible Dictionary*.

Bart Ehrman, and most notably Robert Funk and the Westar Institute, which was founded to educate the public about the results of biblical criticism.[49]

Despite the New Atheists' ignorance of biblical studies, the advent of the New Atheism movement represents a cultural moment that biblical scholars would be remiss to ignore. For it is here that we see a cultural movement that is interested and open to a critical discussion of the text. In particular, scholars who have attempted to employ Marxist methods in order to understand the text may now find intellectuals companions in the New Atheists. Not simply because they share the atheistic presuppositions of Marxism, but because they too have stumbled upon the very realization that increasingly the Ideological critics and Postcolonialist critics have come to, namely that the text itself is often a hindrance to liberation and needs to be judged by an external set of criteria.

This is the message the New Atheists have increasingly focused upon, often in a ham-fisted way. Sam Harris, in his *The End of Faith: Religion Terror and The Future of Reason*, introduces his reader to Deuteronomy 13, a commandment to stone family members who suggest idolatry. Harris rightly notes that such a passage is indeed problematic for those who might argue for a moderate approach to the text.[50] Additionally in his *Letter to a Christian Nation* Harris points out the clear approval of slavery in the Hebrew Bible and New Testament with multiple passages. He argues that that the abolitionist argument in the end was made in spite of the Bible rather than because of it. He quotes Reverend Richard Fuller, who stated in 1845: "What God sanctioned in the Old Testament, and permitted in the New, cannot be a sin."[51] In many places, as people like Tina Pippin have also shown above, the text is anything but moderate.

Harris's insights are not limited to the more gruesome quotes of the Bible. Indeed he argues later on that politics in the United States, particularly under the Bush administration, is still dominated by a reverence for a text that is highly problematic. A lengthy quote by Supreme Court Justice Antonin Scalia indicates that the justification for the death penalty is in fact found in the Bible and is therefore appropriate as the

---

49. It is regrettable that, despite the best efforts of Robert Funk and the Jesus Seminar to gain some notoriety, none of the New Atheists seem aware of their work.

50. Harris, *End of Faith*, 16.

51. Harris, *Letter*, 8.

law of the land.⁵² Harris's approach then replicates much of what we have seen above, the text itself is challenged and is seen as the problem for appropriate moral action, rather than what motivates it.

Thus the popularity of New Atheism provides a new opportunity for legitimate Biblical Studies to make its arguments to a new audience. There is clearly a receptive group of people who wish to engage in the kind of strong-minded rationalism that is the hallmark of biblical criticism at its best and to which the New Secularist demand return. Biblical studies, perhaps keeping their heads low in light of the rise of the Moral Majority of the 1980s and the Christian Coalition of 1990s, might now re-emerge into the sunlight with its own story to tell. We see this already beginning to happen in the work of one scholar we have earlier touched on but now return to: Bart Ehrman.

Bart Ehrman has become a popular giant in the public understanding of biblical studies. Starting with his book *Misquoting Jesus*, Ehrman has brought biblical studies (in this case the very obscure methods of textual criticism) into the public realm. Ehrman is straightforward about his particular position. Formerly an enthusiastic Evangelical, his faith was ultimately shaken by his discoveries studying the New Testament.⁵³ In the book I want to examine in more detail here, *God's Problem: How the Bible Fails to Answer Our Most Important Question—Why We Suffer*, he proclaims himself an agnostic.⁵⁴ Yet he takes a far more moderate position than the New Atheists, stating, "I am not interested in destroying anyone's faith or deconverting people from their religion. I am not about to urge anyone to become an agnostic. Unlike other recent agnostic or atheist authors, I do not think that every reasonable and reasonably intelligent person will in the end come to see things my way when it comes to the most important issues of life."⁵⁵ Such a statement is notable for its personal humility. And yet as Ehrman goes through the various biblical explanations of suffering, it becomes clear that in fact

---

52. Harris, *End of Faith*, 156–57.

53. To be clear, Ehrman states that while many of his theological concepts from his days as an Evangelical were ultimately dispensed with because of historical criticism, he became an agnostic because of the problem of suffering. Ehrman, *Jesus, Interrupted: Revealing the Hidden Contradictions in the Bible (and Why We Don't Know About Them)*, 275–78.

54. Ehrman, *God's Problem*, 4.

55. Ibid., 17–18.

explanations that are dependent upon presumption of the existence of God ultimately fail.

The problem is of course clear and reverts to some of the oldest formulations of theodicy, as Ehrman points out. If God is good and all-powerful, and suffering still exists, then one of the propositions of the argument are flawed. Theologians have attempted to reformulate either the notion of God's goodness (appeals to God's otherness) or God's power (Process Theology), but neither remains comfortably within traditional norms of American Christianity. As Ehrman argues God's goodness cannot be some inexplicable kind that includes what we would characterize as evil or the notion of goodness is ultimately meaningless.[56] And how worthy of worship is a God who cannot intervene in his own creation?[57] In the end, Ehrman concludes "In this book I've looked at a range of the biblical answers, and most of them, in my opinion, are simply not satisfying intellectually or morally..."[58] What Ehrman fastens on in the end is a position he takes from Ecclesiastes in which we must live life to the fullest and take responsibility for our fellow human beings and our planet. But, we should note, at this point all language of God disappears (just as in much of Ecclesiastes), and we are left with humanity alone.

Ehrman's work represents precisely the kind of crossover with the New Atheists that I see as being especially relevant for this cultural moment. It is clear that Ehrman himself does not see himself as a New Atheist, in fact he distinguishes himself from them in the paragraph quoted above. But the argument he makes is in fact the same sort of argument the New Atheists have made.

Sam Harris, in his *Letter to a Christian Nation*, reiterates the larger view of Ehrman in a poignant phrase, "An atheist is a person who believes that the murder of a single little girl— even once in a million years—casts doubt upon the idea of a benevolent God."[59] Harris then goes on to list a particularly significant occasion where God has "failed" to protect humanity: Hurricane Katrina. His argument from theodicy sounds astonishingly like Ehrman: "Of course, people of all faiths regu-

---

56. Ibid., 275.
57. Ibid., 272.
58. Ibid., 274.
59. Harris, *Letter*, 18.

larly assure one another that God is not responsible for human suffering. But how else can we understand the claim that God is both omniscient and omnipotent? This is the age-old problem of theodicy, of course, and we should consider it solved. If God exists, either He can do nothing to stop the most egregious calamities, or He does not care to. God, therefore, is either impotent or evil. You may now be tempted to execute the following pirouette: God cannot be judged by human standards of morality. But we have seen that human standards of morality are precisely what you use to establish God's goodness in the first place."[60]

The similarity of the argument here with Ehrman's cannot be denied, the point is the same even if the rhetoric is slightly different. The problem of suffering is a blow against any theistic conception of God.

What makes Ehrman different from the New Atheists is not his conclusion but rather his method. While the New Atheists are content to wildly throw around biblical verses in service of their argument with only the slightest concern for the body of critical scholarship that has accrued over the past 200+ years, Ehrman shows precisely how the same point can be made using the canons of biblical scholarship.

Conclusion

In approaching the Biblical text, there are two different kinds of criticism that we see in ideological criticism, Postcolonial Criticism, New Secularist Criticism, and New Atheism. One is a moral criticism of the text. This approach is found in ideological criticism, Postcolonial Criticism and the New Atheism. This kind of critique says that the biblical texts are more often morally deficient in contrast to our enlightenment humanist values. The Biblical texts are instead a product of their historical time, place and culture that held very different priorities and values. On the other hand there is second kind of criticism that is methodological in nature. This critique suggests that Biblical Studies has had its areas of inquiry, data and results skewed by theological, political and philosophical constraints that have prevented a free and academically responsible inquiry into the text. This sort of critique is forwarded by the New Secularists, the Ideological Critics and the Postcolonial Critics. These are two different and yet compatible criticisms.

60. Ibid.

Both these lines of criticism were pioneered by Marxist criticism. The Marxist critique has always been one that passionately denounced injustice and called for a secularist analysis of human activity. Marxism has refined its tools for analysis, its principles for historical explanation and its integration of other insights like postmodernism. Yet for all that, it is built upon a core moral evaluation that the system of class is one dependent upon oppression. Likewise, as we have seen, it has steadfastly engaged in a type of analysis that is incompatible with notions of *sui generis* and theological interpretation.

Going in a different direction than Marxism then, ultimately all these different strains of biblical criticism (and Marxism as well) come together on the issue of relevancy. They all concur explicitly or implicitly on the notion that the Biblical text either through its moral inadequacy or its cultural/temporal otherness is simply not applicable to modern social needs.

The kind of analysis that the New Atheists are doing of the text can indeed be buttressed by careful interaction with biblical scholarship. For all their denunciations of those who fear to confront the work of scholarship in the sciences, it is clear that the New Atheists have not followed their prescriptions by looking at the scholarship on the biblical literature.[61] And yet they need not fear the scholarship, for while biblical scholars have different perspectives, the critical examination of the text is the foremost rule and an essential part of our disciplinary history. The work of exploring the text from an explicitly secular orientation, as I have shown above, continues to grow. The New Atheists would reap many benefits by interacting with that literature.

While New Atheism has largely staked its territory on the metaphysical question of the existence of God, it recognizes as well that part of its argument must rest upon the question of the relevancy of the

---

61. Daniel Dennet provides an example of this when he demands that creationist "educate yourself in evolution theory and its critics and see for yourself whether what I say is true," and then noting that he need not defend himself "because I have directed everyone to the literature"; but in terms of the opposite position "I haven't yet been directed to any such literature ... but if it exists, it would indeed warrant consideration as a topic for another day and another project." Ultimately Dennet's appeal is to the scholarly literature, yet his own brief foray into the New Testament seems devoid of having taken the same sort of admonition to heart and certainly has not been adopted by writers like Hitchens, Dawkins or Harris who address the Bible in greater detail (Dennet, *Breaking the Spell*, 61–62).

biblical text. Even apart from the question of whether God's existence (or nonexistence) can be definitively proven; there remains the question of whether the Bible might still not be the "best" guide for human happiness and morality. To that end, the New Atheists must confront the text and argue its merits. Biblical scholarship, particularly as envisioned by the movements surveyed here, can contribute to that debate as they provide substantive evidence of both the moral danger of the text, and its distinctly human and culturally/temporally specific origin and significance. The New Secularism more particularly shows, through its application of social-scientific methods, the Bible as the product of human creativity and a record of the (often oppressive) exercise of human power.

On the other hand, perhaps even more importantly, this represents an important opportunity for New Testament Scholarship. The success of Bart Ehrman's work represents only the most graphic example of someone whose critical scholarship has reached a broader populace.[62] While clearly not matching the popularity of Dawkins's work, the reception of Ehrman's books indicates that there is an audience for biblical scholarship in a popular format that can take a critical perspective toward the texts and provoke the kind of thinking that the New Atheists are also engaged in.

My argument then is that this represents a cultural moment in which the forces that we have seen slowly building through the bulk of this survey are coming to a possible time of fruition. The advent of New Atheism has opened up a space that needs Biblical Scholarship to fill it. It is precisely the kind of approach that we have seen emerging that is ideally suited for this audience, one that has a no-holds-barred approach to understanding religion and the biblical text as a human construction. The scholarly work of the Ideological Critics, the Postcolonial Critics, and the New Secularist biblical scholars all have an approach that has a point of connection with the New Atheism. While clearly the goals are very different, what this conjunction of intellectual movements points to is the possibility of a cultural confluence where biblical scholarship can come into the larger public light (as is starting to happen with the work of Bart Ehrman, as we have seen) and participate in the larger public discourse about the value and role of the biblical text in political

---

62. *God's Problem* ultimately reached #9 on the New York Bestseller list of books.

and cultural life. It is unclear whether Ehrman, who seems the first to step across this divide, will be the start of something or whether he will remain an outlier, yet if he is the beginning of a trend we may yet see an exciting and critical new chapter in the public understanding of religion.

Conclusion

THE QUESTION THIS BOOK HAS RAISED IS: HOW DOES ONE COMBINE the three disparate systems of Marxism, Liberation Theology and apocalypticism? In the case of the Marxist New Testament interpreters there was an attempt to avoid the problem, to de-fang apocalyptic while still attempting to hold Marxism and Liberation Theology together. The result was the ultimate inability to be consistent with either ideology and a violation of their presuppositional logic.

Whether it was the highly structured and complicated system of Fernando Belo, the passionate approach of Jose Porofino Miranda, the search for an Ur-Mark in Michel Clévenot, or the close reading of Ched Meyers, in the case of each of the Marxist New Testament interpreters we saw incredible effort expended to subvert the doxa of the apocalyptic texts: that massive social change will only arrive with God's intervention at the end of time. These thinkers, in the end, ostensibly achieved their goals but only through a process that foiled the presuppositions of the very systems they sought to employ.

Richard Horsley began in the same vein as these Marxist New Testament interpreters, and yet ultimately the conflicts between the three ideologies became part of the reason he jettisoned apocalyptic. For Horsley, apocalyptic was burdened by being too synthetic a category for analysis. The notion of an apocalyptic Jesus in general likewise suffered from criticism that was also part of Horsley's decision to abandon it. But perhaps more importantly Horsley found he did not need the problems of the apocalypticism system as he hewed more closely to the Liberation Theology agenda. Horsley attempts to bypass the problem through the use of Q that involves both prophetic and what he calls "covenantal" sayings. What we see, then, is a shift away from apocalyptic to other types of texts that can be used to validate the same sort of liberationist perspective without the logical problems or mythological baggage.

I have argued, however, there is still some mythological baggage even with Horsley's shift that he seems content to ignore for the time being. He is able to do this because one of the significant benefits of his shift to Q is that the responsibility for creating the new world is no longer based on God establishing a new order (which apocalyptic mandated), but through the gradual mustard seed growth of the kingdom (which the sapiential sayings envisioned). Thus the threatened apocalypse that requires divine action (and still exists in Q) can function only as judgment passed but not executed and be safely ignored except for rhetorical purposes. Thus, while Q still contains the logic of apocalyptic, Horsley simply ignores it.

Horsley's shift did not occur in a theoretical vacuum. I have argued that in his later work we can see the influence of Antonio Gramsci's ideas. Gramsci is used to create precisely the type of bifurcation that Horsley seeks. The "war of position" can then roughly equate to the sapiential material of Q, while the "war of movement" is designated by the apocalyptic sayings and thus is postponed.

The logic of apocalyptic, however, cannot be ignored. By reading Q as a whole, the text becomes dependent upon the promise of divine intervention for its legitimacy and to validate its program. Its critique and prescription are based again on the logic of apocalyptic. Horsley's bifurcation violates both the clear logic of the system of apocalyptic and the logic of Gramsci's Marxism. His selective blending indicates that another logic is in control.

Thus it has become clear that the real reason for Horsley's move is that Liberation Theology becomes for him the master discourse, and in so doing he moves away from the text acting as the ultimate arbiter of authority. Horsley is guided by two important concepts: liberation and imitability. Both of these take priority over the text and they are the lens through which Horsley views the text. Horsley still looks to ground his position in the text but, as I showed (and the same is true with the Liberation theologians themselves), the overriding concerns of Liberation Theology has mandated the types of texts that are of interest and the ways in which those texts are read. Horsley's trajectory in this direction, then, correlates definitively with a move towards Liberation Theology and away from Marxism and the system of apocalypticism. Thus Horsley inherently shows my basic thesis, that the presuppositions of the three ideologies ultimately conflict to the extent that they cannot co-exist with integrity. Attempts to force such a union will require a series of logical and textual incongruencies.

In the work of ideological critics, there is also a shift vis-à-vis the texts, but this time it is a shift towards Marxism and a conscious challenge to the authority of the text themselves. The ideological critics, by disputing the liberating effect of some texts, are in essence moving the locus of authority to the principles of Marxism, which has a more critical view of the texts and religion than Liberation Theology. The more humanistic principles of justice, freedom and economic/social equality now become the guiding principles that govern the interpretation, or more importantly, the acceptance of the texts themselves. While these ideological critics may ultimately argue these ideas stem from parts of the text, it is the principles that sit in judgment on the text rather than the other way around.[1] There is thus an implicit recognition, and the beginning of an adoption, of the Marxist view of religion. While we have yet to see in the ideological critics we examined its full-flowering into a complete critique of religion, we can see a line developing towards that end.

An important example of this new path has been shown in the work of Tina Pippin. Here we see not just a denigration of the authority of the text but rather an unabashed *rejection* of its authority. With Pippin the notion of ideology as a means of hiding a traumatic kernel that expresses itself through the fantasy of the text becomes the point where the text is now completely subject to the principles of Marxist-Feminist critique. The text is ultimately rejected precisely because it cannot embrace the ideals of Marxism. Thus the conflict of the logical systems of Marxism, Liberation Theology and apocalypticism here resolves in favor of Marxism over the others. As more and more of the Bible is studied in this way, it becomes clear that there is growing concern among ideological critics like Pippin that the biblical text itself is an opponent of revolution not an ally.

Which brings us back to the question of whether Marxism and the Bible can live together. In past chapters we have looked at attempt after attempt to make these two things blend with the aid of apocalypticism.

---

1. It certainly could be argued that Liberation Theology functions in the same way. Its principles dictate the reading of the texts. Yet for Liberation Theology this is manifested in the selection of the texts for study or the interpretation of the texts (as we saw in chapter on Marxist New Testament interpreters). For Marxists the validity of the text itself is what is at issue. Based on the principles of Marxism texts may be criticized and consciously rejected with a freedom that we do not see with Liberation Theology.

But there is within Marxism a central core that, as I have pointed out earlier, requires the disillusioning of religious ideals. This is what we have seen here. Biblical scholars have embraced the Marxist ideal of liberation and the dignity and freedom it promises. They have tried to blend it with the religious texts of the Bible and the notions of Liberation Theology. Yet, in the end, Marxism is skeptical of any theological answer. For Marxism, the biblical texts are not the avenue to liberation; rather, Marxist liberation principles are an avenue to freedom from the texts themselves.

Like the spark from the hearth that proceeds to destroy the house that contained it, Marxism, whatever its original debt to Christianity, now sits in judgment on Christianity. It critiques any appeal to divine actions in the world to right the scales of justice. Whether structuralist or individualist, Marxism sees the end of capitalism and the beginning of the new socialist utopia as an eminently human creation. The Bible in its apocalyptic texts expresses, as Marx said, "the sigh of the oppressed creature."[2] But the resolution for Marxism of that oppression is not found in the text's hope of a divine salvation (even if some texts allows for a human assist); rather, that resolution is found in a revolution that is explicitly not divine.

This is thus the logical result of trying to blend three very different, and contradictory ideologies. The logic of each of the ideologies of Marxism, Liberation Theology, and apocalypticism ultimately entails the exclusion of the others. The real question that results from the situation has been, in New Testament studies, how would those contradictions be mediated, or which of these ideologies would prevail in the end?

The answer, of course, is not uniform. I have shown a wide range of responses, from the confused (and sometimes arcane) attempts of the Marxist New Testament interpreters to the triumph of Liberation Theology in Horsley to the move towards Marxism in Pippin and ideological criticism. Still, it is interesting that starting with ideological criticism we can see the formation of a line of criticism the hews more closely to perspective of post-modernist Marxism.

Perhaps then, as Pippin (with the help of Žižek) and the ideological critics exemplify, the trend in the discipline is to see the text not as the solution but rather as the problem. Perhaps resistance against the forces

2. Marx, *Critique*, 54.

of oppression so clearly defined by our Marxists scholars is accompanied by a growing suspicion that such is not aided by the text, but rather should be focused *on* the text. Ideological critics' gradual unmooring of liberation from the text may represent a way of breaking dependence on the texts as the impetus towards liberating action.

It appears that this is the conviction that a number of movements in contemporary biblical studies have reached. Many Postcolonialist scholars have expressed a similar need to expose the texts as precisely tools of imperialism and biblical studies as its willing accomplice. Likewise the New Atheist movement has, from an outsider perspective reiterated the same message—the texts are not the avenue to liberation but a hindrance to liberation. The New Secularists have reinforced this by ruling theological considerations out of bounds and emphasizing the ancient and human nature of the texts; thereby challenging any notion of their relevancy for modern life. Thus the tradition of skepticism towards the usefulness of the Bible for true liberating change has now expanded both inside and outside the academy.

I want to follow this up with a brief examination of José Míguez Bonino's essay "Marxist Critical Tools: Are they Helpful in Breaking the Stranglehold of Idealist Hermeneutics,"[3] which I believe states the problem correctly. Bonino begins his article with an admission that religion is part of the arena of ideology and therefore viewed negatively by Marxism. "Marxism presents itself, whether as scientific analysis or a revolutionary theory and ideology, as a blunt negation (or overcoming) of religion in general and of the Christian religion in particular."[4] Any attempt at a Christian Marxist hermeneutic must immediately run up against this core opposition from Marxism.

Of course Bonino is not content to let it sit there. He goes on to argue, based on the concept of "God's Word," for renewed Christian action in the world that leads to liberation.[5] Still, Bonino, to his credit, does in fact recognize the essential incongruity of this reading with the clear message of the texts. Additionally he concedes at the end, "An interpretation that would limit itself to a Marxist analysis could not, certainly, make sense of what we have been saying . . . There is no

---

3. Bonino, *Marxist Critical Tools*.
4. Ibid., 108.
5. Ibid., 112.

'wherefrom' and no 'power' in such interpretation except in people's own action. Anything else is a human projection, the reification of relationships which man has not yet understood or wants to mystify."[6] Ultimately, then, Bonino suggests that Christians and Marxism have to part company at this point. Bonino argues that a Christian hermeneutic must ground itself in power that is supernatural. Bonino then puts a fine point on the principal that the doxa of Marxism and Christian hermeneutics ultimately are in conflict.

The question is why is such a union between Christianity and Marxism doomed to failure? It is here that we must return to the Marxist critique of religion. For Marx (and later Marxists have followed in his footsteps), religion constitutes a form of ideological control. Marx says, "This state, this society, produces religion that is an inverted world consciousness, because they are an *inverted world consciousness*. Religion is the general theory of this world, its encyclopedic compendium, its logic in popular form, its spiritual *point neurones*, its enthusiasm, its moral sanction, its solemn complement, its general basis of consolation and justification."[7] Such a statement makes clear his view of religion as a secondary means of control. As David McClelland states so well in his study of religion in Marxism, the Marxist perspective is one that "is committed to the view that all religion . . . is an alienation, a symptom of social malformation."[8]

In the end, the message of Marxism is to endorse an expectation of change that is human and not supernatural. Whether the revolution comes through the rise of the proletariat as in Marx's *Communist Manifesto* or through the collapse of the capitalist system by virtue of its inherent contradictions as in *Critique*, the revolution is a distinctly human affair. The position of the divine in the biblical text is seen as one that at best is irrelevant to this occurrence and at worst is an ideological hindrance.

Such an understanding, I think, does reveal in a straightforward way what we have seen repeatedly in Marxist analyses of New Testament texts. Ultimately, the theological and social concerns of Liberation Theology have dictated the limits of Marxist readings as the presup-

---

6. Ibid., 114.
7. Marx, *Critique*, 53–54.
8. McLellan, *Marxism and Religion*, 168.

positional conflicts between the two have become manifest. Likewise, apocalyptic is roundly condemned by Marxism and Liberation Theology alike as mystification and an obstacle to real change.

The problem left is the one that I think is accurately asked by Bonino and then avoided by him: Is there a place for the union of Christianity and Marxism? The answer from our examination of the logic of these three systems is clear in the negative, and increasingly the results of those doing a Marxist analysis of the New Testament seems to be "no" as well. There may be points of connection between the two, but ultimately the oppressive legacy of the texts along with its mythological baggage become too much for the Marxist interpreter of the New Testament to bear. The path that we have traced sees a greater and greater attempt to locate the center and motivation for radical social change outside the biblical texts.

The line of critique is also followed by many Postcolonialists and the New Atheists. They too, often speak of the inappropriate nature of the texts to the goal of human liberation. In fact both the Postcolonialists and New Atheists argue, in different ways, that the text has in fact been a vehicle to prevent human liberation. They make the equation that liberation from oppression necessarily includes liberation from the biblical texts.

While the New Secularists are often more circumspect than the overt denunciation one finds in the New Atheists and many Postcolonialists, what one does find is an aversion to the kind of application of the biblical texts to modern problems and situations, which is in fact the impetus for the critique of both the Postcolonialists and the New Atheists. Where all three can agree is that the study of the Bible can no longer serve the public interest if its intent is to find answers to modern questions in antiquity. Rather the search must be the study of social/historical moments for their own sake, and if, as with the study of any historical moment, we can learn something about the course of human civilization that instructs a contemporary moment, all the better; but the Bible can claim no superior vantage point to reveal such insights than any other human text. The advocacy of a strictly secular approach to the text that the New Secularists call for, requires that biblical studies and religious studies in general re-examine its motivations and its purposes.

Generally then, the New Secularists promote social-scientific methods in order to study the Bible. These methods, including Marxism, presuppose a secularist starting point. Currently there is dispute among New Secularist whether descriptivist social-scientific methods might actually in some ways implicitly smuggle back in the *sui generis* presuppositions that give rise to theological and cryptotheological explanations of religion and the biblical text.[9] Yet the main traditions of social-scientific study, Marx, Weber, and Durkheim as well as postmodern studies (when not themselves a fig-leaf for theological readings[10]) all take a secularist starting point and attempt to explain religion as a human product without reference to anything outside the natural world.

To conclude then, we might broaden the question and ask what instead might be an appropriate use of social science approaches to New Testament texts? How might we learn from the mistakes that have been uncovered in this study? Clearly there is much that can be learned by applying sociological theory being mindful of the boundaries and limits of its doxa. I now will try to show how such theories may be used.

There is much that sociological approaches can still reveal about New Testament texts. Burton Mack has shown some promising work in his application of Althusser to the question of "social formation" in early Christianity.[11] Yet what the discipline has yet to see is a thorough application of someone like Althusser or Gramsci to a text in New Testament studies.[12] For instance, how might Althusser's theory of ideology, or the function of appellation within ISA's, reveal interesting insights in the work of Paul (certainly someone very concerned with ideology!)?

Taken seriously and rigorously applied, Althusser or Gramsci's work (to name only two) might generate many new insights. However, we must also note that these Marxists would view Paul critically, as they do most ideologies, thus we cannot expect that such analysis would produce theological benefit, certainly we cannot presuppose such an

9. Some of this debate is seen in McCutcheon's steadfast defense of explanation over description.

10. See McCutcheon's exploration of this phenomena in his chapter "'My Theory of the Brontosaurus . . .': Postmodernism and 'Theory' of Religion" in *Critics Not Caretakers*, 103–21.

11. Mack, *Social Formation*.

12. Roland Boer has done some exception work along these lines for the Hebrew Bible in *Marxist Criticism*.

expectation as so many of the authors surveyed here have done. An important point is the absolute necessity of separating sociological/historical concerns from theological ones. But by doing this what would be gleaned are new understandings of the way the text affected its readers/hearers.

Such a process clearly has much promise. As an example of where this new approach might lead, let me return to apocalyptic for a moment. Perhaps now Žižek can be reinvoked to understand apocalyptic, as seen in Revelation, in another way. Let us begin by recalling that fantasy for Žižek is differentiated from a symptom. A fantasy is not meant to be interpreted, rather it is experienced. Moreover, what underlies fantasy is ideology. Fantasy is the expression of the ideology, in some sense, it is a working out of that ideology; forming desire around ideology. To this end, for Žižek ideology is structural. It is always-already structuring reality and therefore exemplifies post-Althusserian ideological analysis.

An application of Žižek's work, then, encourages us to look for the "lack" that fantasy conceals. The fantasy of apocalyptic points to some portion of "the real" that is improperly signified. Besides the misogynistic bent of the texts that Pippin alerts us to, there is yet another larger "traumatic kernel" that the apocalyptic text hides. This other contradiction lies in the problem of an inactive God. The fantasy of the apocalyptic hides the fact of a God who fails to act in the present by projecting that action into the future, as though God were saving his strength for the "Big Game." From a Marxist perspective, what apocalyptic may be is not as much hope for the future as embarrassment about the present.[13]

Žižek also holds that the function of ideology is to account for systemic failure. The apocalyptic fantasy does this as well. The time before the arrival of the divine retribution and the armies of heaven wrecking vengeance upon those who have wronged the believers, is a period of suffering and tribulation. In fact in Revelation there is more effort in the description of the trials that will confront the believers and the terrors unleashed upon the earth than in describing the future bliss after God

---

13. Žižek makes a similar argument in regards to the crucifixion and Christ's lament "Father, why have you forsaken me!" He states the lament is not, "a complaint to the *omnipotent* capricious God-Father whose ways are indecipherable to us, mortal humans, but a complaint that hints at an *impotent* God: it is rather like a child who, having believed in his father's powerfulness, discovers with horror that his father cannot help him." Žižek, *Puppet and the Dwarf*, 127. Apocalyptic likewise "hints" at the same discovery though this time through its bravado.

has righted the world. Thus the failure of the movement, the negative experiences, from the loss of social status to direct persecution, are marshaled, not as a sign of failure, but as a precursor of ultimate success. Apocalyptic then acts to anticipate failure and explain it ideologically. The solution it presents however is as doomed anti-Semitism's quest to eliminate the Jew or Capitalism's quest to reverse government regulation and eradicate the unmotivated.

Additionally, contrary to those scholars who highlight the resistant nature of such subcultural fantasies, we must look at the clear social effect of this ideology. Does the apocalypse motivate social change? Clearly not. As I have repeatedly pointed out, apocalyptic is dependent upon divine action—not human—for massive global change. By excusing the failure of the movement's ability to make change, the apocalyptic ideology also gives the larger social inequity a pass by deferring any real push for change to the divinely-ordained future.

In the short term, however, the ideology also functions to constrain and control the behavior of the believers as was pointed out before. Thus, as Žižek points out, the fantasy constructs desire and in so doing controls action. Not just through divine threat, but also embedded within the apocalyptic is a vision of the "saved" and of the concomitant conduct that is commensurate with that status. The propping up, through divine mandate, of the leadership of the group then has a secondary, yet equally important, effect of propping up the larger social status quo as well.

Note what must be absent from such an analysis is any idea that the result will forward the agenda of Theology. Such an analysis shows that the text itself is attempting to conceal the current problem, to misdirect attention from God's current inaction to some future action and the social consequences that result. Perhaps it might not be inappropriate to suggest that there is an inversion at play here. The level of God's predicted future involvement is inversely related to His current absence in light of trying times. Thus the hole that the apocalypticist is covering is very (cosmically) large.

The result of such an analysis is to give us a new insight to the way apocalyptic works and its ideological role both within the group and within society. The use of Žižek offers up a way of viewing apocalyptic that does not however provide material for theology or inspiration to the oppressed except insofar as it shows clearly more subtle modes of oppression. But it is not incumbent upon New Testament studies to provide fodder for our brethren in Theology. The use of Marxist social theory is most effective when such a goal is abandoned as such a Liberationist agenda is ultimately unachievable without logical or textual inconsistency.

There is a price to be paid in using a social theory. Every social theory has its limits and its constraints. In applying a social theory to the New Testament, the biblical interpreter must consider whether he/she is willing to pay that price. In this study we have seen multiple examples of individuals who are unwilling to "pony up" in the face of theoretical presuppositions that subvert, or are antagonistic toward, their goals. Yet this is truly an important moment in history that is rife with possibilities for a new consideration of these issues. The work of the New Secularists has begun to show us this new vista of possibility.

I have argued in the previous chapter that the time is now right for such an exploration. The different movements within biblical studies and without indicate that there is, perhaps as never before, an audience for precisely this type of work. The knowledge gained from such experiments need no longer be constrained solely to the academy. While the secular exploration of the Bible does lend itself to a critical view of the text, it functions to highlight the creativity of human beings in the pursuit of meaning and power. It is precisely the creativity of the human spirit that may still have relevance in today's world.

Bibliography

Albright, William Foxwell. *The Biblical Period from Abraham to Ezra*. New York Harper and Row, 1963.
Althusser, Louis. "Contradiction and Overdetermination: Notes for an Investigation." In *For Marx*, 87–128. New York: Verso, 1990.
———. "Ideology and Ideological State Apparatuses (Notes Towards an Investigation)." In *Lenin and Philosophy and Other Essays*, 127–88. New York: Monthly Review Press, 1971.
———. "Marxism and Humanism." In *For Marx*, 219–48. New York: Verso, 1990.
Althusser, Louis, and Etienne Balibar. *Reading Capital*. London: Verso, 1968, 1970.
Ashcroft, Bill, Gareth Griffiths, and Helen Tiffin, editors. *The Empire Writes Back: Theory and Practice in Post-Colonial Literatures*. 2nd ed. London: Routledge, 2003.
Assmann, Hugo. "Theology for a Nomad Church." In *Practical Theology of Liberation*. Maryknoll, NY: Orbis, 1976.
Aune, David. "The Apocalypse of John and the Genre of Apocalypse." *Semeia* 36 (1986) 65–99.
Avalos, Hector. *The End of Biblical Studies*. Amherst, NY: Prometheus, 2007.
Beasley-Murray, George R. *Jesus and the Last Days: The Interpretation of the Olivet Discourse*. Peabody, MA: Hendrickson, 1993.
Bell, Daniel M. *Liberation Theology after the End of History: The Refusal to Cease Suffering*. London: Routledge, 2001.
Belo, Fernando. *A Materialist Reading of the Gospel of Mark*. Translated by Matthew J. O'Connell. Maryknoll, NY: Orbis, 1981.
Betz, Hans Dieter. "The Problem of Apocalyptic Genre in Greek and Hellenistic Literature: The Case of the Oracle of Trophonius." In *Apocalypticism in the Mediterranean World and the near East*, edited by David Hellholm, 577–97. Tübingen: Mohr/Siebeck, 1983.
Boer, Roland. *Marxist Criticism of the Bible*. London: T. & T. Clark International, 2003.
Boff, Leonardo. *Introducing Liberation Theology*. Translated by Paul Burns. Edited by Clodovis Boff. Maryknoll, NY: Orbis, 1987.
———. *When Theology Listens to the Poor*. Translated by Robert R. Barr. San Francisco: Harper & Row, 1988.
Bonino, José Míguez. "Marxist Critical Tools: Are They Helpful in Breaking the Stranglehold of Idealist Hermeneutics." In *The Bible and Liberation: Political and Social Hermeneutics*, 107–15. Maryknoll, NY: Orbis, 1993.
Borg, Marcus. "Portraits of Jesus in Contemporary North American Scholarship." In *Jesus in Contemporary Scholarship*, 18–43. Valley Forge, PA: Trinity, 1994.

———. "A Temperate Case for the Non-Eschatological Jesus." *Foundation and Facets* 2.3 (1986) 81–102.
Bourdieu, Pierre. *Outline of a Theory of Practice*. Translated by Richard Nice. Edited by Jack Goody. Cambridge Studies in Social Anthropology. Cambridge: Cambridge University Press, 1977.
———. "The Scholastic Point of View." In *Practical Reason*, 127–40. Stanford: Stanford University Press, 1998.
Boudieu, Pierre, and Loic J. D. Wacquant. *An Invitation to Reflexive Sociology*. Chicago: University of Chicago Press, 1992.
Brandon, S.G.F. *Jesus and the Zealots: A Study of the Political Factors in Primitive Christianity*. New York: Scribner, 1967.
Broadbent, Ralph, Ivy George, David Jobbling, and Luise Schottroff. "The Postcolonial Bible: Four Reviews." *Journal for the Study of the New Testament* 74 (1999) 113–21.
Bultmann, Rudolf. *Jesus and the Word*. New York: Scribner, 1958.
———. "What Does It Mean to Speak of God?" In *Faith and Understanding*. Philadelphia: Fortress, 1969, 1987.
———. *The World and the Beyond*. Translated by Harold Knight. New York: Scribner, 1960.
Burridge, Kenelem. *New Heaven, New Earth: A Study of Millenarian Activities*. Oxford: Blackwell, 1969.
(CELAM), Latin American Episcopal Council. "Medellin Document on Peace." In *Third World Liberation Theologies: A Reader*, edited by Deane Willam Ferm, 3–11. Maryknoll, NY: Orbis, 1968.
Clark, John, Stuart Hall, Tony Jefferson, and Brian Roberts. "Subcultures, Cultures and Class." In *Resistance through Rituals*, edited by Stuart Hall and Tony Jefferson, 9–74. Cambridge: Cambridge University Press, 1975.
Clévenot, Michele. *Materialist Approaches to the Bible*. Translated by William J. Nottingham. Maryknoll: Orbis, 1975.
Collective, The Bible and Culture. *The Postmodern Bible*. Edited by George Aichele and Bible and Culture Collective. New Haven: Yale University Press, 1995.
Collins, Adela Yarbro. *The Beginning of the Gospel: Probings of Mark in Context*. Minneapolis: Fortress, 1992.
———. "The Book of Revelation: Apocalypse and Empire." *Journal of Biblical Literature* 110 (1991) 748–50.
———. *Crisis and Catharsis: The Power of the Apocalypse*. Philadelphia: Westminster, 1984.
———. "The Early Christian Apocalypses." *Semeia* 14 (1979) 61–121.
———. "Introduction." *Semeia* 36 (1986) 2–10.
———. "Persecution and Vengeance in the Book of Revelation." In *Apocalypticism in the Mediterranean World and the near East*, edited by David Hellholm, 729–49. Tübingen: Mohr/Siebeck, 1983.
Collins, John J. "The Apocalyptic Imagination: An Introduction to Jewish Apocalyptic Literature." In *Introduction to the Jewish Matrix of Christianity*. Grand Rapids: Eerdmans, 1998.

———. "From Prophecy to Apocalypticism: The Expectation of the End." In *The Origins of Apocalypticism in Judaism and Christianity*, edited by John. J. Collins, 129–61. New York: Continuum, 1998.

———. "Introduction: Toward the Morphology of a Genre." *Semeia* 14 (1979) 1–20.

Comaroff, Jean. *Body of Power, Spirit of Resistance: The Culture and History of a South African People*. Chicago: University of Chicago Press, 1985.

Crossan, John Dominic. *In Parables: The Challenge of the Historical Jesus*. New York: Harper & Row, 1973.

Crossley, James G. *Why Christianity Happened: A Sociohistorical Account of Christian Origins (26–50 CE)*. Louisville: Westminster John Knox, 2006.

Cullmann, Oscar. *Christ and Time: The Primitive Christian Conception of Time and History*. Translated by Floyd V. Wilson. Rev. ed. Philadelphia: Westminster, 1964.

———. *Jesus and the Revolutionaries*. Translated by Gareth Putnam. New York: Harper & Row, 1970.

Dennet, Daniel C. *Breaking the Spell: Religion as a Natural Phenomenon*. New York: Penguin, 2006.

Desai, Gaurav, and Supriya Nair, editors. *Postcolonialisms: An Anthology of Cultural Theory and Criticism*. New Brunswick, NJ: Rutgers University Press, 2005.

Donaldson, Laura E. "The Sign of Orpah: Reading Ruth through Native Eye." In *Vernacular Hermeneutics*, edited by R. S. Sugirtharajah, 20–36. Sheffield: Sheffield Academic, 1999.

Douglas, Mary. *Purity and Danger: An Analysis of the Concepts of Pollution and Taboo*. London: Ark, 1984.

Dube, Musa W. "Reading for Decolonization (John 4:1–42)." *Semeia* 76 (1996) 37–60.

Eagleton, Terry. *Ideology: An Introduction*. London: Verso, 1991.

Ehrman, Bart D. *God's Problem: How the Bible Fails to Answer Our Most Important Question—Why We Suffer*. San Francisco: HarperOne, 2008.

———. *Jesus, Interrupted: Revealing the Hidden Contradictions in the Bible (and Why We Don't Know About Them)*. San Francisco: HarperCollins, 2009.

———. *Misquoting Jesus: The Story Behind Who Changed the Bible and Why*. San Francisco: HarperOne, 2007.

Engels, Friedrich. *Anti-Duhring*. Karl Marx Friedrich Engels Collected Works 25. New York: International Publishers, 1877, 1987.

———. "Letter to Joseph Bloch." In *Marx–Engels Reader*, edited by Robert C. Tucker, 760–65. New York: Norton, 1890.

———. "Ludwig Feuerbach and the End of Classical Philosophy." (1886).

———. "On the History of Early Christianity." *Die Neue Ziet* (1894–95, 1957).

Festinger, Leon, Henry W. Riecken, and Stanley Schachter. *When Prophecy Fails*. Minneapolis: University of Minnesota Press, 1956.

Gager, John G. *Kingdom and Community: The Social World of Early Christianity*. Englewood Cliffs, NJ: Prentice-Hall, 1975.

Gottschal, Marilyn. "The Ethical Implications of the Deconstruction of Gender." *Journal of the American Academy of Religion* 70 (2002) 279–99.

Gottwald, Norman K. *The Tribes of Yahweh: A Sociology of the Religion of Liberated Israel, 1250–1050 B.C.E.* Maryknoll, NY: Orbis, 1979.

Gottwald, Norman K., and Richard A. Horsley. *The Bible and Liberation: Political and Social Hermeneutics*. Bible and Liberation Series. Maryknoll, NY: Orbis, 1993.

Gouldner, Alvin Ward. *The Coming Crisis of Western Sociology*. New York: Basic Books, 1970.

Gramsci, Antonio. "The Modern Prince." In *Selections from the Prison Notebooks*, edited by Quintin Hoare and Geoffrey Nowell Smith, 123-205. New York: International Publishers, 1971.

———. *Selections from the Prison Notebooks of Antonio Gramsci*. Edited by Quintin Hoare and Geoffrey Nowell-Smith. London: Lawrence & Wishart, 1971.

———. "State and Civil Society." In *Selections from the Prison Notebooks*, edited by Quintin Hoare and Geoffrey Nowell Smith, 206-76. New York: International Publishers, 1971.

———. "The Study of Philosophy." In *Selections from the Prison Notebooks*, edited by Quintin Hoare and Geoffrey Nowell Smith, 321-77. New York: International Publishers, 1971.

Gutierrez, Gustavo. *A Theology of Liberation: History, Politics and Salvation*. Translated by Sister Caridad Inda and John Eagleson. Maryknoll, NY: Orbis, 1971.

———. *The Truth Shall Make You Free: Confrontations*. Translated by Matthew J. O'Connell. Maryknoll, NY: Orbis, 1990.

Harris, Sam. *The End of Faith: Religion, Terror and the Future of Reason*. New York: Norton, 2004.

———. *Letter to a Christian Nation*. New York: Random House, 2008.

Hellholm, David. "The Problem of Apocalyptic Genre and the Apocalypse of John." *Semeia* 14 (1986) 13-64.

Hemple, Carl. "The Logic of Functional Analysis." In *Symposium on Sociological Theory*, edited by Llewellyn Gross. New York: Harper & Row, 1959.

Hitchens, Christopher. *God Is Not Great: How Religion Poisons Everything*. New York: Twelve, 2007.

Horsley, Richard A. *Archaeology, History, and Society in Galilee: The Social Context of Jesus and the Rabbis*. Valley Forge, PA: Trinity, 1996.

———. *Jesus and the Spiral of Violence: Popular Jewish Resistance in Roman Palestine*, 1987. Reprinted, Minneapolis: Fortress, 1993.

———. *The Liberation of Christmas: The Infancy Narratives in Social Context*. New York: Crossroads, 1989.

———. "Q and Jesus: Assumptions, Approaches and Analyses." *Semeia* 55 (1991) 175-209.

———. "Questions About Redactional Strata and the Social Relations Reflected in Q." In *Society of Biblical Literature 1989 Seminar Papers*, edited by David J. Lull, 186-203. Atlanta: Scholars, 1989.

———. *Sociology and the Jesus Movement*. New York: Crossroads, 1989.

Horsley, Richard A., and Jonathan A. Draper. *Whoever Hears You Hears Me: Prophets, Performance, and Tradition in Q*. Harrisburg, PA: Trinity, 1999.

Horsley, Richard A, and John S. Hanson. *Bandits, Prophets, and Messiahs: Popular Movements in the Time of Jesus*. San Francisco: Harper & Row, 1988, 1985.

Horsley, Richard A, and Niel Asher Silberman. *The Message and the Kingdom: How Jesus and Paul Ignited a Revolution and Transformed the Ancient World*. 1997. Reprinted, Minneapolis: Fortress, 2002.

Kähler, Martin. *The So-Called Historical Jesus and the Historic, Biblical Christ.* Translated and edited by Carl E. Braaten. Philadelphia: Fortress, 1964.
Käsemann, Ernst. "The Beginnings of Christian Theology." *Journal of Theology and the Church* 6 (1969) 17–46.
———. *New Testament Questions of Today.* Translated by W. I. Montague. Philadelphia: Fortress, 1969.
Kautsky, Karl. *The Foundation of Christianity: A Study in Christian Origins.* New York: International Publishers, 1908, 1925.
Kee, Howard Clark. *Community of the New Age: Studies in Mark's Gospel.* Philadelphia: Westminster, 1977.
Kloppenborg, John S. *Excavating Q: The History and Setting of the Sayings Gospel.* Minneapolis: Fortress, 2000.
———. "The Formation of Q Revisited: A Response to Richard Horsley." In *Society of Biblical Literature 1989 Annual Meeting Seminar Papers*, edited by David J. Lull, 204–15. Atlanta: Scholars, 1989.
———. *The Formation of Q: Trajectories in Ancient Wisdom Collections.* Philadelphia: Fortress, 1987.
———. "Literary Convention, Self-Evidence and the Social History of the Q People." *Semeia* 55 (1991) 77–102.
LaHaye, Tim, and Jerry B. Jenkins. *Left Behind: A Novel of the Earth's Last Days (No.1).* Carol Stream, IL: Tyndale, 1996.
Lenin, V. I. "The Attitude of Workers' Party to Religion." In *Lenin Collect Works*, 402–23. Moscow: Progress Publishers, 1900, 1973.
———. "Classes and Parties in Their Attitude to Religion and the Church." In *Lenin Collected Works*, 414–24. Moscow: Progress Publishers, 1909, 1973.
———. "Socialism and Religion." In *Lenin Collected Works*, 83–87. Moscow: Progress Publishers, 1905, 1965.
———. "The State and Revolution." In *The Essential Left: Four Classic Texts on the Principles of Socialism*, 147–255. New York: Barnes & Noble, 1919, 1961.
Liew, Tat-Siong Benny. "Tyranny, Boundary and Might: Colonial Mimicry in Mark's Gospel." *Journal for the Study of the New Testament* 73 (1999) 7–31.
Linton, Gregory L. "Reading the Apocalypse as Apocalypse: The Limits of Genre." In *The Reality of Apocalypse: Rhetoric and Politics in the Book of Revelation*, edited by David Barr, 9–41. Atlanta: Society of Biblical Literature, 2006.
Loftus, John W. *Why I Became an Atheist: A Former Preacher Rejects Christianity.* Amherst, NY: Prometheus, 2008.
Loomba, Ania, editor. *Postcolonial Studies and Beyond.* Durham: Duke University Press, 2005.
Mack, Burton L. "The Kingdom That Didn't Come: A Social History of the Q Tradents." In *Society of Biblical Literature 1988 Seminar Papers*, edited by David J. Lull, 608–35. Atlanta: Scholars, 1988.
———. *The Lost Gospel: The Book of Q & Christian Origins.* San Francisco: HarperSanFrancisco, 1993.
———. *Myth and the Christian Nation: A Social Theory of Religion.* Edited by Russell T. McCutcheon, Religion in Culture. Oakville, CT: Equinox, 2008.
———. *A Myth of Innocence: Mark and Christian Origins.* Philadelphia: Fortress, 1988.

―――. "Social Formation." In *Guide to the Study of Religion*, edited by Willi Braun and Russell T. McCutcheon, 291–96. London: Cassell, 2000.

―――. *Who Wrote the New Testament? The Making of the Christian Myth*. San Francisco: HarperSanFrancisco, 1995.

Marx, Karl. "Capital, Vol. 1." In *Marx-Engels Reader*, edited by Robert C. Tucker, 294–438. New York: Norton, 1978.

―――. "Contribution to the Critique of Hegel's Philosophy of Right: Introduction." In *The Marx-Engels Reader*, edited by Robert C Tucker, 16–25. New York: Norton, 1978.

―――. "A Contribution to the Critique of Political Economy." In *The Marx-Engels Reader*, edited by Robert C. Tucket, 3–8. New York: Norton, 1959.

―――. "The German Ideology." In *The Marx-Engels Reader*, edited by Robert C. Tucker, 146–200. New York: Norton, 1845.

―――. "On the Jewish Question." In *The Marx-Engels Reader*, edited by Robert C. Tucker, 26–52. New York: Norton, 1843.

―――. "Supplement." *Rheinische Zeitung* 195 (1842).

Marx, Karl, and Friedrich Engels. *Marx and Engels on Religion*. Moscow: Progress Publishers, 1966.

―――. *Selected Works*. Moscow: Foreign Language Publishing House, 1962.

McCutcheon, Russell T. *Critics Not Caretakers: Redescribing the Public Study of Religion*. Issues in the Study of Religion. Albany: State University of New York Press, 2001.

―――. *Manufacturing Religion: The Discourse on Sui Generis Religion and the Politics of Nostalgia*. New York: Oxford University Press, 1997.

McLellan, David. *Marxism and Religion: A Description and Assessment of the Marxist Critique of Christianity*. Basingstoke, UK: Macmillan, 1987.

Meeks, Wayne A. "Social Functions of Apocalyptic Language in Pauline Christianity." In *Apocalypticism in the Mediterranean World and the near East*, edited by David Hellholm, 687–705. Tübingen: Mohr/Siebeck, 1983.

Mencken, H. L. *Treatise on the Gods*. New York: Random House, 1963.

Mills, Charles W. *The Sociological Imagination*. Oxford: Oxford University Press, 1959.

Miranda, Jose Porfino. *Marx and the Bible: A Critique of the Philosophy of Oppression*. Translated by John Eagleson. 1974. Reprinted, Eugene, OR: Wipf & Stock, 2004.

Mongia, Padmini, ed. *Contemporary Postcolonial Theory: A Reader*. New York: St. Martin's, 1996.

Moore, Stephen D. *Empire and Apocalypse: Postcolonialism and the New Testament*. The Bible in the Modern World 12. Sheffield: Sheffield Pheonix, 2006.

―――. *God's Gym: Divine Male Bodies of the Bible*. New York: Routledge, 1996.

Myers, Ched. *Binding the Strong Man: A Political Reading of Mark's Story of Jesus*. Maryknoll, NY: Orbis, 1988.

Nordquist, Joan. *Postcolonial Theory: A Bibliography*. Santa Cruz, CA: Reference and Research Services, 2000.

Noth, Martin. *The History of Israel*. Translated by P. R. Ackroyd. 2nd ed. New York: Harper & Row, 1960.

Otto, Rudolf. *The Idea of the Holy: An Inquiry into the Non-Rational Factor in the Idea of the Divine and Its Relation to the Rational.* Translated by John W Harvey. London: Oxford University Press, 1958.

Parsons, Talcott. "Certain Primary Sources and Patterns of Aggression in the Social Structure of the Western World." In *Essays in Sociological Theory.* Glencoe, IL: Free Press, 1954.

———. "The Present Position and Prospects of Systematic Theory in Sociology." In *Essays in Sociological Theory.* New York: Free Press, 1945.

Penner, Hans H. *Impasse and Resolution: A Critique of the Study of Religion.* New York: Lang, 1989.

Perrin, Norman. *The New Testament: An Introduction; Proclamation and Parenesis, Myth and History.* New York: Harcourt Brace Jovanovich, 1974.

Pippin, Tina. *Apocalyptic Bodies: The Biblical End of the World in Text and Image.* London: Routledge, 1999.

———. *Death and Desire: The Rhetoric of Gender in the Apocalypse of John.* Louisville: Westminster John Knox, 1992.

Reed, Jonathan L. *Archaeology and the Galilean Jesus: A Re-Examination of the Evidence.* Harrisburg, PA: Trinity, 2000.

Robinson, James M. *The Problem of History in Mark and Other Marcan Studies.* Philadelphia: Fortress, 1982.

Saldarini, Anthony J. *Pharisees, Scribes and Sadducees in Palestinian Society: A Sociological Approach.* Wilmington, DE: Glazier, 1988.

Schottroff, Luise. "Die Gegenwart in Der Apockalyptik Der Synoptischen Evangelien." In *Apocalypticism in the Mediterranean World and the Near East: Proceedings of the International Colloquium on Apocalypticism, Uppsala, August 12–17, 1979,* edited by David Hellholm, 707–28. Tübingen: Mohr/Siebeck, 1983.

Schüssler Fiorenza, Elisabeth. *The Book of Revelation—Justice and Judgment.* Philadelphia: Fortress, 1985.

———. "The Phenomenon of Early Christian Apocalyptic." In *Apocalypticism in the Mediterranean World and the Near East: Proceedings of the International Colloquium on Apocalypticism, Uppsala, August 12–17, 1979,* edited by David Hellholm. Tübingen: Mohr/Siebeck, 1983.

———. *Revelation: Vision of a Just World.* Proclamation Commentaries. Minneapolis: Fortress, 1991.

Scott, Bernard Brandon. *Hear Then the Parable: A Commentary on the Parables of Jesus.* Minneapolis: Fortress, 1989.

Segovia, Fernando F. *Decolonizing Biblical Studies: A View from the Margins.* Maryknoll, NY: Orbis, 2000.

Segundo, Juan Luis. *Liberation of Theology.* Translated by John Drury. Maryknoll, NY: Orbis, 1976.

Smith, Jonathan Z. "A Pearl of Great Price and a Cargo of Yams." In *Imagining Religion: From Babylon to Jonestown,* 90–101. Chicago: University of Chicago Press, 1982.

———. "Wisdom and Apocalyptic." In *Map Is Not Territory: Studies in the History of Religions,* 67–87. Studies in Judaism in Late Antiquity 23. Leiden: Brill, 1978.

Stone, Jon R., editor. *Expecting Armageddon: Essential Readings in Failed Prophecy.* New York: Routledge, 2000.

Sugirtharajah, R. S. *The Bible and the Third World*. Cambridge: Cambridge University Press, 2001.

———. *Postcolonial Criticism and Biblical Interpretation*. Oxford: Oxford University Press, 2002.

Talmon, Yonina. "Pursuit of Millennium: The Relation between Religious and Social Change." In *Reader in Comparative Religion: An Anthropological Approach*, edited by W. Lessa and E. Vogt. New York: Harper & Row, 1964.

Theissen, Gerd. *Sociology of Early Palestinian Christianity*. Translated by John Bowden. Philadelphia: Fortress, 1978.

Thompson, Leonard. *The Book of Revelation: Apocalypse and Empire*. Oxford: Oxford University Press, 1990.

———. "A Sociological Analysis of Tribulation in the Apocalypse of John." *Semeia* 36 (1986) 147–74.

Warrior, Robert. "Canaanites, Cowboys and Indians: Deliverance, Conquest and Liberation Theology Today." *Christianity and Crisis* 29 (1989) 261–65.

Williams, Patrick, and Laura Chrisman, editors. *Colonial Discourse and Post-Colonial Theory: A Reader*. New York: Columbia University Press, 1994.

Worsley, Peter. *The Trumpet Shall Sound: A Study of Cargo Cults in Melanesia*. 2nd ed. New York: Schocken, 1969.

Yoder, John Howard. *The Politics of Jesus*. Grand Rapids: Eerdmans, 1972.

Žižek, Slavoj, editor. *The Dwarf and the Puppet: The Perverse Core of Christianity*. Short Circuits. Cambridge, MA: MIT Press, 2003.

———. *Enjoy Your Symptom! Jacques Lacan in Hollywood and Out*. New York: Routledge, 1992.

———. "How Did Marx Invent the Symptom?" In *Mapping Ideology*, edited by Slavoj Žižek, 296–331. London: Verso, 1994.

———. *The Plague of Fantasies*. London: Verso, 1997.

———. *The Sublime Object of Ideology*. London: Verso, 1989.

www.ingramcontent.com/pod-product-compliance
Lightning Source LLC
Chambersburg PA
CBHW062044220426
43662CB00010B/1642